DOOR COUNTY ALMANAK

No. 2

The Dragonsbreath Press
Sister Bay, WI

Publisher:
Lon Kopitzke
Fred Johnson

Editor:
Fred Johnson

Contributors:
Richard Carter
John Cease
Toni Christenson
Ruth Cook
Tom Davis
Jeanne Dorschel
Kate Dorschel
Conan Bryant Eaton
Lon Emerick
John Enigl
Harold Grutzmacher
Jan Jablonski
Delphine Johnson
Gary Jones
Liz Maltman
Amy McKenzie
Evelyn McNamara
Mike Nelson
Shirley Nelson
Bev Njaa
Jim Perry
Maggie Perry
Charles Peterson
Susan Peterson
Henry Shea
Linda Silvasi-Kelly
Mary Ellen Sisulak
Karen Stillman
Duncan Thorp
Mary Jo Van Lanen
Gregory Vidas
Judy van der Nuell
Richard Weidmans
J.K. Woitesek

DOOR COUNTY ALMANAK

Artists/Photographers:
Julia Bresnahan
Joe Cook
Martha Coventry
Tom Davis
John Enigl
Jave Hughes
Jan Jablonski
Fred Johnson
Mike Judy
Jane McNamara
Shirley Nelson
Bev Njaa
Charles Peterson
John Sieger
Linda Silvasi-Kelly
Mary Ellen Sisulak
Bryon Smith
Greg Steffen
Stern
Rosemary Utzinger
Ken Zilisch

Cover: Drawing by Mary Ellen Sisulak - after graduation from U.W.-Milwaukee in 1974 - moved to Door County. She set up a mail-order and custom leather workshop. Has illustrated a number of books and does free-lance artwork. She teaches Drawing at the Peninsula Art School. Her leatherwork may be seen at Edgewood Orchard Gallery and Clay Bay Pottery. Leatherwork and Artwork may be commissioned at her home and studio - Turtle Ridge on Mink River Road - Ellison Bay.

DOOR COUNTY ALMANAK

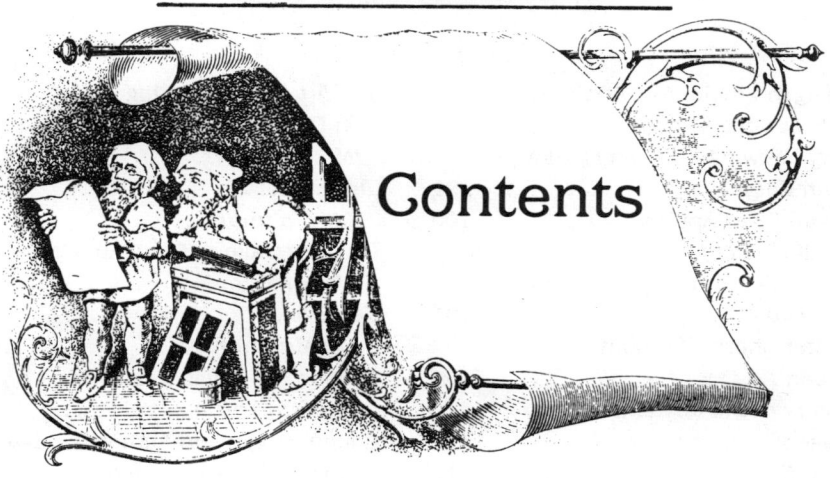

Contents

Preface 5

The Search for Perfection
  Ruth Cook 7

World's Finest Fruit — "The Apple"
  Kate Dorschel 10

How to Preserve the Fragrance
  of Door County
  Jeanne Dorschel 12

Carole Williams' Apple Dolls
  Gary Jones 16

Grow What You Eat, Naturally
  Toni Christenson & Jim Perry 20

Horseradish
  Scientific American 24

Recipes
  Delphine Johnson 25

Orchards
  Duncan Thorp 32

Aslag's Orchard
  Charles L. Peterson 34

The Names in the Orchard
  Tom Davis 37

Door County's First Cherry Cannery
  John Enigl 41

Pickers Camps
  John Enigl 48

Reflections of an Apple Baron
  Anonymous 56

The California of the North
  *Excerpts from a book
  published in 1914* 59

Wink Larson:
  Orchard in His Blood
  Gary Jones 63

"You've Got to Work It":
  The Krowas Orchard
  Tom Davis 73

A Family Background in the
  Cherry Industry
  John Enigl 79

The Door County Almanak is published annually in May by the Dragonsbreath Press, 10905 Bay Shore Drive, Sister Bay, Wis. 54234. Additional copies of this issue may be ordered from the publisher for $5.95 plus $1.00 postage. We welcome unsolicited manuscripts, artwork and photographs, however the publisher assumes no responsibility for submitted work. If the author/artist wishes unused work to be returned a self-addressed stamped envelope must be included. Writer guidelines may be requested by sending a #10 SASE.

The Legend of Johnny Appleseed
  Jan Jablonski 90
Cherry Growing — A Family Affair
  John Enigl 92
Good and Bad Apples 100
The Hill Orchard:
  Continuing A Family Tradition
  Gary Jones 101
The First Cherry Blossom
  Queen 109
A History of the Reynolds
  Preserving Company
  John Enigl 111
"A Beautiful Life"
  Bev Njaa 121
A Cherry Juice Wedding 130
Fruit Grower's Cooperative
  John Enigl 131
Fruit Growing
  H.R. Holand 139
Apple Time at
  Uncle Jerry's 145
Peninsular Experiment Station
  Richard Weidman 148
In Search of Appleport
  Richard Carter 154
A Pig Joke 161

The Art of Winemaking
  in Door County
  Mike Nelson 162
Jim Ingwersen
  Liz Maltman 166
Pangaea Gallery: The Wathalls
  Henry F. Shea 170
Ken Zilisch
  Liz Maltman 174
Tilewood: A Collaboration
  Shirley Nelson 179
County Books and Authors Update
  Harold M. Grutzmacher 182
School Names in Door County's Past
  Conan Bryant Eaton 185
Poetry 191
My Pastoral
  M.E. Sisulak 205
The Fragrances of Autumn
  Lon Emerick 208
Door County: The Winter
  Playground of the Midwest
  Mike Nelson 218
Gallery Guide
  Compiled by
  Evelyn McNamara 221

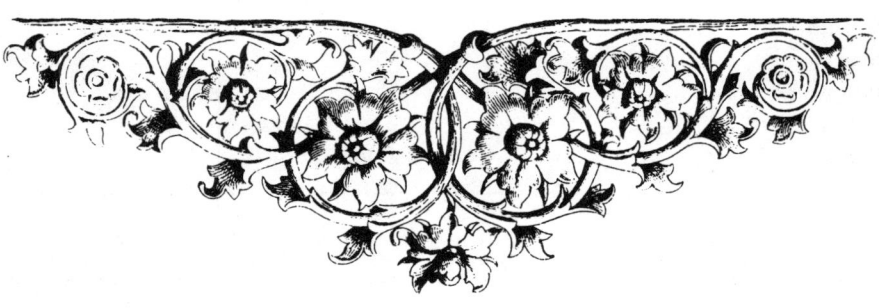

PREFACE

E welcome you back to the Door County Almanak with its second issue. The Almanak now has new publishers and we look forward to a new issue appearing each May. The Almanak will continue to be a regional magazine focused primarily on Door County, but also with its eye on the surrounding areas of Northeastern Wisconsin. The Almanak will be a publication in which to present the history, recent and distant, of Door County and tales of its people, events and folklore in the writing and artwork of all lovers of Door County, residents or visitors.

Each issue will continue to focus on a central theme. This issue's theme is Orchards. It was recognized in the 1800s that Door County's climate and soil conditions were ideally suited for orchard growing. Since then the orchard business in Door County has gone through many changes, and though no longer the county's major industry, it is again on the upswing after a period of decline. While it is true many orchards have been cut to make way for development, in a drive through the county you will see many newly planted fruit trees. The picturesque era of orchards filled with migrant workers may be gone, but it has been replaced with the efficiency of mechanization assuring that the fruit industry will still thrive in the county for many years. We hope you enjoy reading about the orchard people represented here, there are many others in the county too, perhaps their stories can be told in a future issue.

Our thanks to all the contributors to this issue, for they make the Almanak what it is.

Special thanks to Herb Peterson and Bill Tong who provided many of the historical photos. They, along with John Enigl, have organized an exhibit for the State Historical Society and the Door County Historical Society on the cherry industry in Door County. It is one part of a larger exhibit on the diversity of agriculture in Wisconsin. The entire exhibit will be displayed in

Wausau at the "Wisconsin Valley Fair", August 6-11, 1985, then in Janesville at the Rock County Historical Museum from October 1985 - June 1986, and then in River Falls at the U.W. College of Agriculture's Farm Arena from Labor Day to October of 1986. After this the cherry industry exhibit will return to Door County to be displayed in the Door County Museum in Sturgeon Bay. The Museum is a must stop for all interested in Door County's history.

Another event relating to the history of Door County which we should mention is the encore performance of **Porte des Morts**. The theater piece, written by Gibraltar English teacher Gary Jones, tells the history of Northern Door County from the early settlers of the 1850's up to the present. A cast of nearly one hundred fully-costumed people of all ages bring the past alive. The production also features original music.

Many people had to be turned away from the packed auditorium for last February's performance, so two repeat performances have been scheduled for August 2 and 3, 1985, at 8:00 p.m. in the Gibraltar auditorium in Fish Creek. The summer performances of **Portes Des Morts** will launch a fund raising campaign to build a performing arts center at Fish Creek that will serve both the school and the community.

We would like to encourage anyone to submit a manuscript or idea to the Almanak. You need not be a professional writer. We ask only for readable writing presenting informative interesting articles relating to Door County and its surrounding areas.

Our next issue of the Door County Almanak will be focused on **Fishing: Commercial & Sport**. Look for it in May 1986.

Proem

IT was green fruit time. From the cherry trees in the orchard, the blossoms were gone and the tiny cherries were already well formed. The nest, that a pair of little brown birds had made that spring, was just empty, and, from the green laden branches of the trees, the little brown mother bird was flitting to and fro, calling anxious advice and sweet worried counsel to her sons and daughters who were trying their new wings. A bob-o-link, swinging on a nearby bush, poured fourth a tumbling torrent of silvery melody. Beyond him, on the fence, a meadow lark answered with soft, liquid music. A robin, resting for a moment on the top branch of a tree, sang a full throated sweet voiced song.

In the soft, golden sunlight, sifting down through the trees, the blue birds flitted here and there, twittering cheerily the while over their bluebird tasks, while the woodpecker, hard at work in the orchard shade, made himself known by the din of his industry.

The breeze, drifting lazily in from the Inland Sea, softly caressed the birds and the flowers and the new born fruit upon the trees, and stirred the grasses under foot, which formed a luxuriant deep green carpet, studded with pearls from the freshness of the dewy morn.

A pastoral scene, this, and in a country which offers every opportunity to men. A country which produces fruit unequaled, fruit that matures under Nature's careful hand, fruit that knows in its ripening the warm sunshine and cleansing showers, the cool of the quiet evening and the freshness of the morning dew—this fruit alone, I say, has the flavor that is from heaven, and it is grown in only one spot on the universe—

DOOR COUNTY
"THE CALIFORNIA OF THE NORTH"

The Search for Perfection

by Ruth Cook

DOOR County folks are a varied lot, but one common trait is an appreciation of the outdoors — an affinity for green, growing things. My enthusiasm often leads me to a feeling of wild infatuation with whatever plant is currently in bloom, from hepatica and bloodroot on through lilacs, forget-me-nots, lady's-slippers, roses and asters. The warm seasons become one long "high" as I revel in the annual parade.

But inevitably the procession ends, green turns to brown and disappears under white. House plants are tame compensation. Frustrated, I turn again to the outdoors. Fortunately, here in Door County we are surrounded by a great number of trees to keep us company during the winter. Undistracted by gaudy flowers, I then can appreciate anew the lacy patterns of bare branches and even learn to identify the varieties by silhouette alone.

Evergreens comfort me with their assurance of continuing life, but as a child of the temperate zone I do relish change. If I were to choose the perfect plant — one that is outstanding in all seasons — I would quickly narrow the field down to fruit trees.

Not the tallest or sturdiest or easiest to grow, but certainly among the most beautiful in spring and most valuable at time of harvest, fruit trees are desirable as the focal point of home landscaping and as a cash crop for orchardists. Fruitwood is in demand for many forms of woodworking, and even the imperfect parts are useful as firewood.

8

Seen in wintertime, a fruit tree is likely to be symmetrical and bushy. In an orchard the smaller branches will be pruned, and the larger ones may be forcibly spaced apart for higher fruit yield. This can produce a gnarled appearance which, when softened by snow cover, is most distinctive.

Spring's advance is charted in Door County by the development of cherry and apple buds. Fruit trees in full bloom provide such spectacular beauty that they have become a tourist attraction. Seen from a distance, an orchard in full bloom may appear to be covered with magical gauze. The closer you get, the more you will be caught up in the brightness, delicacy and fragrance of the individual flowers and the music of the honeybees. Surely this is the apex of spring!

As summer passes, developing fruit changes the trees with its color and weight. Cherry tree branches sag nearly to the ground by July as the fruit ripens from green through orange to bright red. Finally, the trees seem relieved to shake free of their burden. Apple trees carry their fruit much longer, often into October, and may come to look like Christmas trees decorated with large red or yellow ornaments.

Cherries, plums and pears are all delicious fruits, but my personal favorite is the apple. Its many attractive varieties and endless uses sometimes overshadow how good it is for us.

An apple tree is also most likely to age well. It can be very sad to watch the decline of a cherry orchard which has given so much pleasure to all the senses. Once the peak years of production have passed, the trees quickly fall prey to storm damage and disease. Apple trees have a much longer life cycle and only get more gnarled and dignified with age. Scattered around the county are quite a few solitary apple trees, apparently untended yet faithfully continuing to bloom and produce fruit long after their planters have moved on.

On the basis of beauty, usefulness and durability, my choice for the most perfect plant in Door County is the apple tree.

illustration: Joe Cook

World's First Fruit — "The Apple"

by Kate Dorschel

 IFE eternal, sexual vigor, fertility . . . all these and more are powers ascribed to the apple at some time or place.

In Door County, however, apples mean sweet smelling buds, cider and just plain old good eating. Whether you are an apple farmer, a year-round resident or just an occasional visitor, it's hard not to appreciate the beauty or taste of the Door County apple. McIntosh, Delicious and Cortland make up 80% of this mouth watering crop. There are a few helpers for identifying apples and selecting which are best for your recipes.

The McIntosh, named after a Canadian farmer who introduced this apple to New York state in the early 1900's, makes up the majority of the county's crop. The skin of the McIntosh is green and heavily striped and marked with red. The flesh is tender, sweet and highly aromatic. This fruit is medium sized and ripens in September. It is wonderful in the applesauce recipe below.

Applesauce

4 medium apples, pared, quartered & cored
1 cup water
½ cup brown sugar (packed)
¼ teaspoon cinnamon
⅛ teaspoon nutmeg
4 tablespoons mint jelly
4 mint leaves (fresh)

Heat apples and water over medium heat to boiling. Reduce heat, simmer, stirring occasionally, 5-10 minutes or until tender. Stir in brown sugar, cinnamon and nutmeg, heat to boiling. Then add mint jelly and leaves.

Delicious apples, which are second most popular in Door County, are a large red and oblong fruit. The base of the apple is marked by five conspicuous knobs. The flesh is crisp, fine grained and juicy. The flavor is sweet and mild. This apple can be eaten fresh in salads or out of hand, but does not cook well. Try this rich and creamy coleslaw.

Apple 'n Cheese Slaw

4 cups finely shredded cabbage
 (about ½ head)
¼ cup dairy sour cream
¼ cup mayonnaise
½ teaspoon seasoned salt
2 cups diced unpared apples
½ cup crumbled bleu cheese

Combine apples, cabbage and cheese in large bowl. Blend remaining ingredients, pour over cabbage and toss. If desired, sprinkle with paprika.

The Cortland apple is third largest in population. This apple was created by crossing McIntosh with another apple called Ben Davis. The fruit ripens later than McIntosh, but they resemble one another in shape and size. The skin is yellow with a bit of red. The flavor is sweet and good for desserts or cooking. The Cortland is also nice in salads because its flesh is slow to turn brown after it is cut. Here's a delightful way to end any meal.

Apple Walnut Cake

4 cups chopped apples (with skins on)
2 cups sugar
½ cup oil
2 eggs
2 teaspoons vanilla
2 cups flour
2 teaspoons baking soda
2 teaspoons cinnamon
1 teaspoon salt
1 cup chopped nuts

Mix apples and sugar (will get juicy). Add other ingredients in order and mix well. Put in a 9 x 13 inch pan and bake at 350 degrees for one hour. Cool. Sprinkle with powdered sugar (optional).

Now you have a few fun and tasty recipes to help you enjoy the Door County apple.

How To Preserve
The Fragrance
of Door County

by Jeanne Dorschel

THE art of making sweet pot-pourri is a simple pleasure. In and out of gift shops in Door County, you are tantalized by the delightful aroma of potpourri. Perhaps you have purchased a few to tuck in your linen closets or dresser drawers. But . . . do you know how easy it is to make your own dried perfume? Learn with us.

Potpourri begins in a summer garden or a field of wild flowers. Dried roses and lavender retain their perfume and usually form the basis of potpourri, but many other flowers can be used for texture and color . . . daisies, chrysanthemums, straw flowers, geraniums, marigolds and carnations are just a few of the candidates for potpourri. Any thin petaled flower that can be dried flat or separated into single petals for drying can be used. A deserted orchard can provide apple or cherry blossoms to make your potpourri a genuine Door County treasure.

Gather your petals and spread them singly on a clean window screen or newspaper in a dry, airy place out of direct sunlight. The dehydration process will take about two weeks, depending on humidity and water content of the blossoms you are using.

If it is a particularly damp summer, you can hasten the process by drying them on a cookie sheet in a barely warm oven. Leave the door open so moisture can escape, and be careful **not** to cook the flowers. When they are cereal flake dry, pack them into airtight containers, label and store them in a dry, dark place. We use large coffee cans or lemonade mix containers.

Many herbs can be added . . . mint, basil, marjoram, rosemary, thyme and sage. Dry the herbs as you do the flowers. Pine cones, berries, bark, seeds and even dried chunks of citrus may be used for texture.

When you have about six cups of dried mixture, you are ready to begin. Your spice rack will provide allspice, cinnamon (whole or ground), cloves, ginger or nutmeg. Explore herb shops for unusual herbs, spices and the necessary fixative herbs. Fixatives, such as orris root or calamus root, absorb fragrances and prolong the life of potpourri. Two ounces is sufficient for each batch of herbs and flowers. For a heavy, rich scent, a few drops of flower oils may be used. Oils of rose, lilac, carnation or our favorite, patchoulli, are also nice. These are available at herb shops.

Combine the flowers and herbs in a large bowl of glass or stainless steel. Do not use wood or plastic because fragrances permeate them. Blend the fixative (orris root), spices and oil in a small bowl, and sprinkle it over the flower mixture. Toss lightly with your hands to blend well. Pack it loosely in tight containers, again store in a dry, dark place. Let the potpourri mellow, at least a month, shaking it occasionally before packaging.

Here are a few recipes to get you started.

Summer Garden
2 handfuls mixed dried flowers
2 handfuls herb leaves
3 Tablespoons mixed spices
2 Tablespoons fixative
3-5 drops scented oil
seeds, bark, berries as decoration

Olde Rose
2 cups dried rosebuds
2 cups rose geranium leaves
2 cups dried rose petals
1 Tablespoon whole cloves
1 Tablespoon broken cinnamon
2 Tablespoons orris root
5 drops rose oil

Olde Lavender
2 cups lavender flowers
1 cup thyme leaves
1 cup mint leaves
4 bay leaves broken
3 sticks cinnamon broken
3 Tablespoons whole cloves
2 Tablespoons calamus root

Don't be afraid to experiment, work with the flowers in the nearby fields and your own garden. Try different combinations of herbs, spices and

illustration: Julia Bresnahan

Ellison Bay Pottery
John Dietrich

Open
May thru October

12156 Garrett Bay Road
½ mile from Hwy. 42
Ellison Bay, Wisconsin

oils. The basic proportions are: 4-6 cups herbs and flowers, 1-2 tablespoons spices, 1 tablespoon fixative and about 5 drops of flower oil. Label each coffee can so you can judge which combination is your favorite.

Now, the fun of presenting your special Door County potpourri to friends. Scour rummage sales for interesting containers . . . old sugar bowls, little tin boxes, jam pots, unusual small baskets. If they don't have lids, fashion covers of left over fabric. Seashells are particularly nice for a bathroom . . . wrap these in saran wrap and tie with a pretty ribbon. Of course, you can make sachets of fabric and decorate with bits and pieces of lace. Just remember to store covered and shake occasionally to regenerate.

Memories of sunny days and your favorite flowers are now at your fingertips . . . or should we say . . . tip of your nose?

Enjoy!

M. COVENTRY

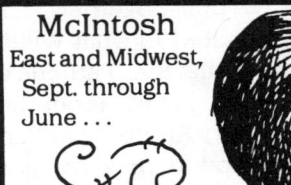

McIntosh
East and Midwest, Sept. through June . . .

. . . good for snacks, salads, fruit cups, sauces, all-purpose cooking (except whole).

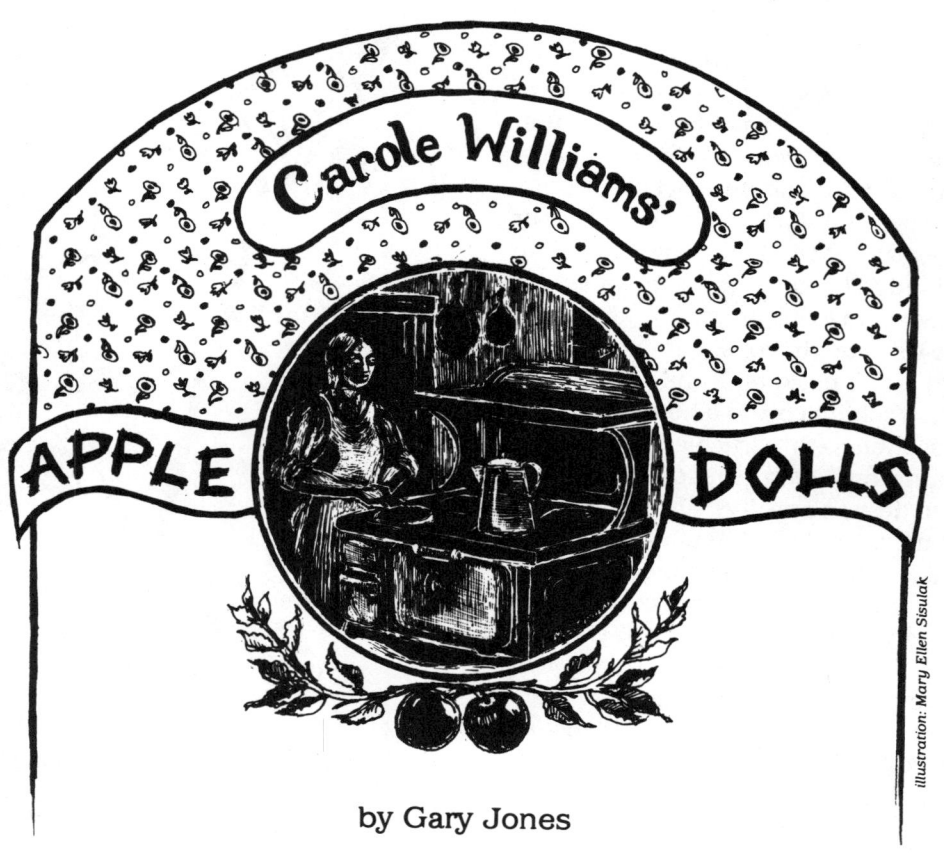

Carole Williams' APPLE DOLLS

illustration: Mary Ellen Sisulak

by Gary Jones

A visitor to the home of Carole Williams might for a moment think he had taken a wrong turn and somehow stumbled into the workroom of a conclave of South American head hunters. For over the wood stove in her living room he will find staring at him the tiny wizened faces of a myriad of shrunken heads strung on strings. A second glance assures our startled guest that these heads once rolled from an apple tree rather than a family tree.

Williams, the lady behind Door County Apple Heads, laughingly concedes that she was probably born into the wrong century. Her old farm house is filled with antique furniture and evidence of her interest in nineteenth century crafts, such as apple head dolls.

Raised in a suburb of Chicago, Williams discovered the magic of gardening and the great out-of-doors after she, her husband, and her children moved to Vermont where they ran an inn. She spun, knitted, quilted, tried theorem painting (stenciling fruit), and, after her family moved to Door County, apple head dolls.

The **Foxfire** books first introduced Williams to apple head dolls. One day a couple of years ago, she assembled her five children and decided to make a doll together. Their first effort resulted in what Williams now smilingly calls the "Pathetic Woman." Her family joked about being the Door County Apple Head People, and driving around in a car advertising the fact.

"My kids never thought I'd really

do it!" she laughed, but she did. And they were involved. She made hundreds of the dolls, assembly line fashion, pressing her children into service during the evening. One night they'd make wire body frames; another, they'd stuff bodies; and legions of orchard offspring filled their house.

She retailed them through shops in Door County, Green Bay, and Chicago. "I was surprised that people bought them," she exclaimed with delight. "But I really do it for the joy of making them. In fact, I give a lot of them away."

"The most fun is working with one and suddenly seeing someone I know. I'll send it to that person, and usually she appreciates it. My mother-in-law wasn't too happy with hers, and my mother refuses to admit that her apple doll looks like her, but they're exceptions!"

As much as she enjoys making the

illustration: Mary Ellen Sisulak

dolls, she also enjoys showing others how to construct them. "I have a problem selling them," she said. "I like demonstrations better. Then people come up and ask questions and don't shy away for fear they'll be obligated to buy one." She especially enjoyed exhibiting at the Gibraltar Area Schools heritage festival a year ago last winter.

She is no longer in the wholesale production of the dolls, though. "Last fall I had to stop," she laughingly explained. "It was too weird seeing all of these faces. You have millions of these things staring at you around the house and you feel like you're starting to lose your marbles!"

But she still makes occasional dolls for enjoyment, for gifts, and for sales. She's also toying with the prospect of creating some male apple head dolls as well, perhaps a chimney sweep or a rustic in bib overalls.

In the past she has worked with two basic apple head dolls. One is the hanging witch, described below. And the other is her domestic doll series. Each is seated on a stool and involved with a household activity: knitting with toothpick needles (Williams actually casts a row of knitting on the toothpick); spinning with a toothpick and cork spindle; holding a basket, a cherry bucket, or a dough trough formed from a walnut shell.

Williams' five children (Ryan, 13; Brett, 12; Tara, 12; Eric, 10; and Erin, 3) keep her involved in her own domestic activities. She tries to prepare all of her meals from basic ingredients, and uses food she has preserved from her own garden. She also finds time to tend a couple of sheep that provide her with raw wool for her projects.

Especially she prides herself in the quality of life she provides her children, and the lessons that they can do anything if they try it. But she good naturedly admits that she has had less than total success. Her son Brett fancies himself a punk rocker. "How do you fight Cabbage Patch dolls and punk rock!" she laughs.

CAROLE WILLIAMS' DIRECTIONS FOR MAKING APPLE HEAD DOLLS

1. Any variety of apple may be used, but golden delicious have the best shape and drying characteristics for making an apple head.

2. Peel but do not core the apple and soak it for a half hour or more in a solution of one tablespoon of ascorbic acid per pint of water. (Lemon juice may also be used.)

3. Carve the facial features, hollowing out the eyes, removing portions beneath the cheeks, nose, and chin, and cutting a slit for the mouth. (Some people pinch the features with their fingers, but Carole finds that a knife works best for her.)

4. String the apple (from bottom to top) and hang it above a heat source which will provide a constant ninety degree temperature for two weeks. When the apple is dry, the seeds rattle, and the string should be removed. (A food dehydrater may be used to dry the apple, but Carole has found the results less satisfactory.)

5. Cucumber seeds dotted with a felt-tip pen are wedged into the eye sockets. Final adjustments to the facial features are made by trimming with a knife.

6. Dip the apple head in satin finish polyurethane sealer and allow it to dry on a newspaper.

7. Using a flexible twenty gauge wire, fashion a stick man type body. A twenty inch piece of wire is doubled and twisted to form a head about two inches in diameter, a twisted torso, and legs. A second ten inch piece of wire is used to fashion the arms. Wrap the arms and legs with a thin layer of polyester fiberfill. (Or, substitute pipe cleaners for the twenty gauge wire.)

8. Cut the head circle so that one piece of wire is an inch in length, and the other, much longer. Run the long piece of wire through the head, entering from the bottom and exiting

the top. Bring the wire down the back of the head and twist the two ends together. (This technique allows the apple head to be replaced should a new one be necessary later.)

9. Dress the doll. Carole makes a t-shirt out of a piece of fabric measuring nine by eight inches, folded in half to measure four by nine. With the fold forming the top of the shoulders and neck of the shirt, cut three inch sleeves with an inch and one-eighth width. This allows for a three inch body. Sew with quarter inch seams, reverse, slit the neck, and place on the doll. Stuff the body of the shirt with fiberfill, and add a skirt fashioned from a piece of fabric fourteen inches wide and six and one-half inches long, stitched in place by hand and belted with a sash.

10. Cut feet (four pieces) from one inch by one and one-quarter inch rectangles of dark felt, and hands (four pieces) from three-quarter inch squares of flesh colored felt. Attach to the doll with fabric glue.

11. Carole prefers to form a wig for the doll from raw wool. She likes the interesting crinkly texture and pieces of hay still embedded in the fibers. For a kerchief, cut an isosceles triangle of fabric with a six inch base and a two and one-half inch height. Carefully tie the kerchief over the apple head gypsy fashion and secure it with stick pins until it can be firmly anchored with needle and thread.

12. Carole's kitchen witch dolls stride a twig of dried lilac seed pods, and are suspended by a length of thread. According to tradition, the doll when hung in the kitchen brings good luck to the homemaker.

Man is incomprehensible without Nature, and Nature is incomprehensible apart from man. For the delicate loveliness of the flower is as much in the human eye as in its own fragile petals, and the splendor of the heavens as much in the imagination that kindles at the touch of their glory as in the shining of countless worlds.
— Hamilton Wright Mabie

Grow What You Eat, Naturally

by Toni Christenson
& Jim Perry

GROWING food at home increases our independence, saves money, provides physically active exercise, and more nutritious meals for ourselves and our families. Natural growing affords us, as local market farmers, the opportunity to eat and sell the healthiest food available anywhere while preserving the natural balance in our most immediate world. In addition, when we buy what we don't grow (like orchard fruit) locally from our neighbors, we strengthen our economy at the most basic level.

Any season is right to begin an exploration of natural growing. Learning to grow food ourselves is a primary survival skill and by **attention** and **practice,** we can all become experts. Any utilization of natural growing skills preserves precious and fragile soil resources, thus contributing to the community in which we live as well as to our own sense of well being.

Whether you have gardened conventionally for years or never sprouted a seed, you can grow a natural garden this season by attending to these practices and guidelines:

FIRST, AND CONTINUALLY, FEED AND BALANCE YOUR SOIL. Natural growers base their work on the premise that balanced soil nutrition leads to balanced plant nutrition. In addition, healthy plants are more resistant to disease and insect attack. Since soil is teeming with hundreds of thousands of microscopic living organisms that eat organic matter, they must certainly be fed. Many culinary possibilities come out of the natural grower's bag of tricks such as colloidal rock phosphate, manure, bone meal, blood meal, green sand, seaweed, cover cropping, mulch, and our favorite and most used: compost. It is so important in the process of our growing that we include here an explanation and how to make it.

ADD COMPOST TO YOUR GARDEN FOR BETTER YIELDS AND HEALTHIER PLANTS. Compost is the end result of a natural system of arranging plant materials to promote decay and structural change. In the compost pile bacteria thrive and multiply by feeding on the pile's raw material. This creates humus, a dark earthy substance that increases the soils ability to hold nutrients and water and makes the ground easier to cultivate.

A Simple Compost Recipe

Gather organic materials all year from among: leaves, straw, hay, manure, garden and kitchen wastes, (excluding meat) pine needles, wood ash, sawdust, grass clippings, etc.

Form your pile in layers of several or all of the above starting with the coarsest material. The finished pile would be 6-10 feet long and 4-6 feet high for high-speed decay.

Sprinkle each layer with a high nitrogen natural fertilizer and water lightly (Possibilities here include blood meal, bone meal, seaweed or fish)

Cover the pile with a thin layer of soil and black plastic or straw.

Turn the pile occasionally with a pitchfork to change the inside with the outside, hastening the decay of materials.

Use the finished compost in several ways. Spring is an excellent time to apply compost directly to your garden area at 25-50 pounds per 100 square feet. Work lightly into the top 3-4 inches of soil. Or use screened compost in your starting-plants-from-seed medium along with equal parts of soil, and a lightener like vermiculite. Placing compost around plants like mulch when transplanted to the garden or side-dressing (placing compost on the soil surface to cover the plant's root zone) when a plant appears to be under stress lends extra energy for growth.

GROW PLANTS IN BEDS TO AVOID SOIL COMPACTION. Since root growth is diminished with the restriction of oxygen to the soil, we grow most of our

21

vegetables in beds which are never walked on. Tight soils also tend to keep water from draining into the soil and run-off can occur. Our beds are 4 feet wide and can be planted, worked, and picked from both sides. Small gardens are especially suited for bed growing. Walkways between beds of any size connect the beds with each other. This visually attractive method of laying out a garden has the added benefit of establishing permanent beds which can be nourished in a concentrated way, thus saving fertilizing resources from year to year.

FEED THE PLANTS THROUGHOUT THE GROWING SEASON. Besides feeding the soil, we continue to support growing plants with an ongoing feeding program. If plants are fed at critical stages in their growth they will yield better, contain more nutrients and resist disease, stress and insect attack.

Foliar Feeding or spraying the leaves and stem surfaces of the plants with a sprayer or mister accomplishes feeding efficiently. An absorption rate of 80% and root stimulation are added benefits. Our basic foliar feed recipe

features 2 tablespoons each of liquid fish and liquid seaweed with ½ teaspoon of a "sticker" like Basic H or Ivory to a gallon of water.

Spray plant surfaces until they drip between 5:00-8:00 a.m. or after 6:00 p.m. so they will accept the spray. Otherwise plants are transpiring. Use foliar feeding at seeding, transplant to the garden, and leafing out time before blossom set. It can also keep vegetables fruiting just a bit longer toward the end of the growing season.

INSECT ATTACK INDICATES AND EXPRESSES THE DEGREE OF YOUR SOIL'S FERTILITY. When the soil is out of balance, natural growers take preventive measures for pest control. Plant disease resistant varieties. Learn your insects. Plant at times which will avoid the insects feeding cycles. Rotate crops. Interplant crops with herbs to repel and confuse easily. Buy and release or encourage natural predators in your garden like lady bugs, lacewings, praying mantis, birds and toads. When prevention must be supplemented by relief for struggling plants attacked by pests try natural plant controls. There are many possibilities among the botanical and biological insecticides:

Contact poisons like pyrethrum, sabadilla dust, safer's soap and diatomaceous earth. **Stomach poisons** like rotenone, nicotine and BT (Dipel or Thuricide). **Herbal sprays** like garlic, eucalyptus, wormwood, tansy, citrus oils, nettle, pennyroyal, etc. **Home remedies** like "bug juice" (make a blended concoction of the offending bugs or worms to spray on the plants), traps, and good old fashioned picking pests off plants.

The best arguments for avoiding chemical poisons lay in toxicity to all forms of animal life including humans and in upsetting the ecological balance. All of the above ideas can be tried **before** chemicals in combina-tion with a wholistic approach to soil fertility and plant health. Cooperating with nature's cycles in producing food for ourselves and our families is rewarding and challenging work.

We believe so strongly in the benefits of local and home-produced food that we provide gardening advice and resources, as well as natural growing products at our farm market open year round. We hope to share them with you in an increasing network of natural growing systems.

HORSERADISH

The botanical name of this well known garden plant and popular condiment is **Armoraciae radia,** a native of western Europe. It is remarkably tenacious of life, and spreads itself without artificial aid, coming up sometimes at long distances from the parent plants in soils adapted to its growth. The root contains an acrid oil similar to, if not identical with, that of mustard, and to the pungent flavor of this oil is due the desire for grated horseradish as a condiment. It is considered medically as a harmless stimulant, of use in dyspepsia, and a sirup prepared from the root is used in colds and rheumatism.

In some cities, the horseradish is grated at the doors of the customers; or dealers stand at the street corners, and grate from the heaped roots a gill, half pint, or more at the call of the customer. All this work is done by hand and is intended to counteract the popular idea that turnip forms a large part of the bottled horseradish. This is not so, for the turnip would turn the horseradish black, or discolor it, and, besides, it costs hardly more to raise horseradish than to raise turnips. The absolute whiteness of horseradish (except the color of the vinegar) is a necessity to its commercial value. This whiteness cannot exist in adulterated horseradish. In the manufacture of the grated horseradish in large quantities the graters must be made of white metal or of sheet tin, as the contact of uncovered iron would blacken the product.

The cultivation of the root is simple. At the harvest, in the autumn, those roots which are too small for commercial purposes--less than a pipestem in diameter--are packed away in sand in short lengths of from four to six inches. In the spring these are planted in plowed furrows by means of a hand dibble, making a hole to plant the slip in, upper end just below the surface. It grows with the commonest cultivation--field cultivation--and is harvested by the plow and the potato digger.

In preparation for the market the roots are freed from sand or soil, and are scraped by hand until every discolored portion is removed. The cleaned roots are then put into a tumbling barrel with water, and thoroughly washed. To be ground, they are fed into a hopper over a cylindrical grinder of white metal with its corrugations like those of a nutmeg grater, and held down to its surface by the weight of a block of wood fitting, like a piston, the sides of a rectangular box into which the hopper leads. The grated root is mixed with vinegar, bottled, and sealed immediately. And herein is the trouble about adulterated horseradish. Exposed in a grated form half a day, the horseradish is tasteless; the aroma goes with the air like a whiff. Nor will dry horseradish retain its strength. Horseradish is like the rose; it must be smelled - or tasted - immediately on its ripening, or it is "scentless and dead."

Scientific American 1885

Recipes

collected by Delphine Johnson

Apple Kuchen

Cut together like pie crust:
1 cup flour, 1 T. butter, ½ cup sugar, ¼ tsp. salt, 1 tsp. baking power. ADD: 1 beaten egg, ½ cup milk and mix until blended. Put in 8 or 9" well greased pan. Slice apples and stick thick into batter. Over apples, sprinkle cinnamon, salt and nutmeg.
TOPPING:
¾ cup sugar, 3 T. flour, 2 T. butter or oleo. Put over apples and sprinkle cinnamon and nutmeg over all. Bake at 350° for 1 hour or less — until apples are done.

Cherry Topsy Cake

7 x 10 coffee cake pan or 10" pie pan
1 cup sugar
1 cup flour
¾ cup milk
2 T. butter
¼ tsp. salt
    Mix first five ingredients and spread in greased pan.
1 tsp. baking powder
1# can of cherries
½ cup cherry juice
¼ cup sugar
    Drain cherries — use ½ cup juice, cherries and sugar — heat until sugar is dissolved. Pour over batter and bake at 350° for 30 to 40 minutes.

Apple Crunch

Peel and slice 6 large apples — put in buttered 2 quart casserole. Cover with ½ cup sugar and ½ tsp. cinnamon.
Mix 1 cup flour, ¾ cup of sugar and ½ cup butter. Put over apples and bake at 325° for 1 hour.

French Pastry Apple Bars

2½ cups flour
1 cup lard
½ tsp. salt
1 egg yolk — mix enough milk with yolk to make 2/3 cup. Divide dough in half — put ½ in jelly roll pan.

Spread 2 handfuls of corn flakes on crust. Put 8 or 10 sliced apples on crust — 1 cup sugar — 1 tsp. cinnamon.

Roll out other ½ of dough and put on top of apples — pinch edges and prick top. Beat 1 egg white and brush on top. Bake at 400° for 1 hour or less. While warm, frost with: 1 cup powdered sugar, 1 T. water and vanilla.

Apple Pie Cake

1 cup brown sugar
½ cup oleo
2 cups flour
2 tsp. cinnamon
2 T. hot water
½ cup nuts or raisins
1 cup white sugar
2 eggs
2 tsp. baking soda
½ tsp. nutmeg
2 cups chopped apples

Cream sugar, butter and eggs. Add dry ingredients alternately with hot water. Add apples, nuts, etc. Bake at 350° for 30 to 45 minutes in a 9 x 13 pan.

Fresh Apple Bread

1 cup sugar
½ cup shortening
2 eggs, beaten
1 cup ground or grated apple
½ tsp. salt
1 tsp. soda
1 cup pecans
1½ T. buttermilk
½ tsp. vanilla
3 T. sugar
1 tsp. cinnamon

Cream sugar and shortening. Add eggs and apple. Mix in sifted dry ingredients to which pecans have been added. Stir in buttermilk and vanilla. Pour into greased loaf pan (10 x 6 x 3 inches). Sprinkle top with a mixture of sugar and cinnamon. Bake one hour in preheated 350° oven. Makes one loaf.

Quick Cherry Coffee Cake

2 cups flour
3 tsp. baking powder
½ cup sugar
2/3 cup oleo
1 tsp. salt
¾ cup milk

Cut oleo into dry ingredients and add milk. Press into well greased 8x10 pan.
FILLING:
½ cup hot cherry juice
¼ tsp. almond extract
2 cups canned cherries
¼ tsp. salt

Make paste with cornstarch, salt and water — add to boiling juice, stirring constantly until thick. Add cherries and extract. Pour over dough.
TOPPING:
¼ cup butter,
⅛ tsp. almond extract
½ cup sugar,
½ cup flour

Spread over filling and bake at 375° for 35 to 45 minutes.

Any kind of fruit can be used.

Dump Cake

1 large no. 2 can crushed pineapple
1 large no. 2 can cherry pie filling
1 pkg. yellow cake mix
½ cup chopped nuts
1 stick butter or oleo

Dump each ingredient in greased 9 x 13 pan, spreading evenly — in order given.

Cut butter into squares and place on top.

Bake at 350° for 1 hour. Serve with cool whip or ice cream.

Wassail

6 cups apple cider or juice
1 cinnamon stick
¼ tsp. nutmeg
¼ cup honey
3 T. lemon juice
1 tsp. grated lemon peel
1 can (18 oz.) unsweetened pineapple
    juice (2¼ cups)
Cinnamon sticks

In large saucepan, heat cider and one cinnamon stick to boiling; reduce heat. Cover; simmer 5 minutes. Uncover; stir in remaining ingredients except cinnamon sticks and simmer 5 minutes longer. Serve in punch bowl; use cinnamon sticks as individual stirrers.

Apple Chiffon Squares

Mix: 1 cup graham cracker crumbs, 3 T. sugar, ¼ cup melted oleo. Reserve ¼ cup and press the rest into a greased 10 x 6 x 2 pan and chill.

1 envelope gelatin
2 T. sugar
¼ tsp. ground nutmeg
2 medium apples
3 egg whites
¾ cup apple juice or cider
3 beaten egg yolks
1 tsp. finely shredded lemon peel
1 T. lemon juice
¼ cup sugar

In saucepan, put gelatin, sugar, nutmeg and ¼ tsp. salt — Stir in juice, egg yolk, and lemon. Cook and stir until it comes to a boil — Cool. Peel, core and shred apples to make 2 cups. Stir into gelatin. Chill until partially set — Stir occasionally. Beat egg whites to soft peaks — gradually add ¼ cup sugar — beat until stiff — fold into gelatin mixture and spoon onto prepared crust. Spread remaining crumbs over top and chill.

Unpeeled Apple Cake

2 cups sugar
1 stick of butter or oleo
   Cream those together.
Add: 2 well beaten eggs.
Mix 2 cups flour, 1½ tsp. soda, ½ tsp. salt, 1 tsp. cinnamon. Sift and add to the above mixture. Add 1 cup nuts and 4 cups unpeeled apples, cut up. It will be thick. Spread in a greased 9 x 13 pan.
Mix together: 1 cup brown sugar, 2 tsp. flour and 1/3 stick oleo and sprinkle on top of cake. Bake at 350° for 45 to 50 minutes.

Apple Sauce Torte

27 graham crackers
½ cup oleo, melted
½ cup sugar
   Line a greased 9 x 13 pan with ½ the crumb mixture and save the other ½ for the top.
MIX:
5 beaten egg yolks
2 cups applesauce
Juice and rind of 1 lemon
1 can evaporated Borden's milk
   Fold in 5 beaten egg whites. Top with rest of crumb mixture. Bake at 350° for 1 hour.

Apple Salad

2 cups diced apples
½ cup raisins
3 or 4 diced maraschino cherries
¾ cup mayonnaise with
2 or 3 tsp. marschino cherry juice.
   Mix with fruit and serve.

Applesauce Cake

Cream together:
¾ cup shortening
1½ cup white and brown sugar, mixed
2 eggs
Add 1½ cups applesauce and beat
Add remaining ingredients:
2¼ cups flour
1 tsp. soda
¼ tsp. nutmeg
½ tsp. cloves
1 tsp. cinnamon
Then add nuts. Bake in 9 x 13 greased pan at 350° for 45 minutes to 1 hour.

Cherry Pudding

Mix with 1 cup cold water:
2 cups flour
1 tsp. baking powder
1 cup sugar
2 tsp. melted butter

Pour into greased 9 x 13 cake pan. Mix: 2 cups cherries, 1½ cups sugar, 2 tsp. butter, 3 cups boiling water and 1 tsp. almond extract and pour over batter in pan and bake at 400° for 30 minutes and then at 450° for 10 minutes.

Black Bottom Cherry Creams

1 stick oleo, melt in kettle, add ½ cup sugar, 2 T. cocoa, 1 egg, ¾ cup flour — mix together and spread in greased 9 x 13 pan. Drain one jar (10 oz.) cherries, cut in pieces, place on chocolate mixture.

Combine sweetened condensed milk to 3 cups grated coconut. Spread over cherry base to cover. Bake about 25 minutes at 350°.

Frost while warm, melt ½ bag of chocolate chips, 2 T. oleo, 1 T. milk, ½ cup powdered sugar. Beat til smooth, add more milk if needed.

Apple Cake

¼ cup butter
1 egg
2 tsp. baking powder
2/3 cup sugar
1½ cups flour

Mix and pour into greased 9 x 9 pan. Peel and slice 6 apples and place on top of batter in rows.

TOPPING: ½ cup butter, 2/3 cup sugar, ½ tsp. cinnamon. Sprinkle over apples and bake at 350° for 1 hour.

Cherry Nut Cobbler

2 cans cherry pie filling
1 white cake mix
¾ cup chopped nuts
¼# butter

Put cherries in well greased 9 x 13 pan — sprinkle dry cake mix over all — put thin slices of butter over this and then the nuts. Bake at 350° for 45 minutes. Serve with whipped cream.

Cherry Pie

Prepare enough crust for a double crust pie.
Mix: 1 cup sugar, 2 T. flour, ⅛ tsp. salt, and about 2 cups cherries and juice. Pour into crust and cover. Bake at 350° for 1 hour.

Pie Topping

Grease pan — put in fruit and put in oven at 350° while preparing topping.
1 cup flour
1 cup sugar
2 tsp. baking powder
2 T. shortening
2 eggs, beaten
Drop onto fruit and bake 1 hour at 350°.

Pie Crust

4½ cups flour
1# lard
1 tsp. salt
1 tsp. baking powder
ADD:
1 egg, beaten
½ cup cold water
Juice of 1 lemon
Will keep refrigerated.

Cherry Tarts

2 cup cake pans and cupcake papers
2 (8 oz.) pkgs. of cream cheese
2 eggs
¾ cup sugar
1 tsp. vanilla
Beat first 4 ingredients — put 1 vanilla wafer in bottom of each liner in muffin pans. Fill each with cheese mixture and bake at 350° for 10 minutes. Serve with pie filling and cool whip.

Rosy Apple Cake

1 cup flour
1 tsp. baking powder
½ stick oleo
1 slightly beaten egg
2 T. milk
Press dough into bottom and sides of greased 9 x 12 pan — fill with apples and sprinkle one (3 oz.) pkg. of raspberry Jello over it.
TOPPING: 1 cup flour, 1 cup sugar, ½ cup butter. Sprinkle over all and bake at 350° for 45 minutes.

Orchards
of Door County

To the People of Wisconsin and the Northwest

In 1910 I accepted an invitation to accompany a party of Wisconsin men through Door County under the guidance of Professor Frederic Cranefield, secretary of the Wisconsin Horticultural Society and after making an extensive and thorough study of the county's natural resources we were requested to make a report to Professor Cranefield.

The commercial orchards of the Door County peninsula show the most intensive and extensive development of high grade fruit culture that I have seen in this state. The most amazing feature of this is the hundreds of acres of cherry plantations in the vicinity of Sturgeon Bay representing all ages and stages of development from one year to twenty, all in perfect vigor and health.

The most interesting and promising thing is however, found in the fact that there is abundant room for further development on equally good land. Northern Door County is certainly the "land of promise" for intensive fruit growing.

Sincerely yours,

Plant Pathology.
University of Wisconsin.

Certainly one cannot appreciate the possibilities of commercial fruit culture of the Door County peninsula by merely reading what has been written about it. Due to a recent trip through that portion of the peninsula lying north of Sturgeon Bay, I am fully convinced that this section is destined to develop into one of the principal fruit sections in the country. Its favorable climatic conditions; well adapted soil and excellent water facilities are all contributing factors which within a comparatively short time must bring about this result.

Respectfully,

Horticulture.
University of Wisconsin.

Orchards

by Duncan Thorp

 HEY almost killed the golden goose when they clear-cut the pine and milled the remaining hardwoods. The somewhat alkaline and shallow soil that topped the Niagara Reef in Door County was poor farm land. But it could grow trees.

Someone found that fruit trees liked the limestone, and dooryard plantings of cherries and apples prospered. Then others found there was a ready market for tart pie and canning cherries and the first orchards were planted. Many trees were planted with a half-stick of dynamite to break up the limestone and give the roots a start in the rock fractures. The trees did well, but frost was a constant threat at blossom time so south-facing slopes and land that sloped toward the water became desirable as orchard sites, since they seemed less susceptible to frost. From 1910 to 1920 hundreds of thousands of cherry trees were planted in and over the rock.

Once in the orchard business with the requisite machinery (sprayers, tractors, discs and ladders) many growers found it practical to combine their cherries with other fruit, and the Door Peninsula produced many tons of apples, pears and plums. Today remnant fruit trees flower among remote woods and fields. Forest birds and animals find a bearing apricot tree or a heavily loaded crab apple in the heart of thick woods, and the motorist or biker encounters a bower of blossom and perfume in late spring.

But the orchards have changed from intensive cultivation to sensible green sod. Now we notice ragged stumps where acres have been abandoned, often replanted to evergreen trees and making a fine crop of second growth conifers.

We used to painstakingly hoe out the squares of grass that the disc wouldn't reach around each truck until a well-kept orchard consisted of tree trunks in an unlimited acreage of finely-tilled soil. And spraying: wearing old coveralls stiff with many fine coats of copper sulfate and lime sulfur, we sprayed with a patient team of horses dragging the heavy rig through the orchard rows. Each spray had a name taken from the stage of bud and blossom development at which the spray was to be applied — dormant, pre-pink, pink, petal, calyx, etc.

Sprays were applied to control blight and coddling moth, about the only enemies our orchards had then, so we didn't need powerful or dangerous toxicants that threatened wildlife or humans. But at blossom time we lived in a cloud of spray with blue haze in our hair or on our whiskers, clothes, skin, and we smelled sulphurous, like creatures born in a volcano.

Once a hired man accidentally blasted one of our horses in the rump with a spray gun, venting 300 pounds of pressure. Sprayer, team and granddad all went for a wild ride to the end of the row.

Much of the picking was done by neighbors. Whole families arrived early in horse drawn rigs with their lunches packed, and put in long days straddling the picking ladders and carrying their bulging 5-quart pails to the checking shed for credit. A champion picker might run up a score of eighty pails. Many of the harvest crew liked to sing, their voices floating across the orchard with popular songs of the 20's, like "Bye-Bye Blackbird", "Beautiful Katie", or "Madamoiselle from Armentieres".

When the orchard got too big for local labor to harvest we tried hiring young girl members of a church camp as an army of pickers. The girls were somewhat intractable. They came with their tiny noon lunches consisting of one small sandwich and sometimes an apple. At one time they revolted and locked their supervisor in the restroom at the camp and made their own lunches, with **two** sandwiches. My mother feared they might starve and brewed vast kettles of soup and other supple-

ments to their meager rations, and the girls picnicked happily at noon.

The day of these colorful cherry pickers passed and the next band of imports were reservation Indians, who were good pickers; then a scattering of "Latinos" from Mexico and Texas. One of our best pickers, a white man who was a sort of hobo, hired a small boy to tote his filled pails to the checking shed, and by starting his day at sunup managed to pick ninety 5-quart pails of cherries in one working day. His record lasted for years but a mechanical shaker would make it look laughable today.

The machines vibrate the fruit off the trees and onto a canvas funnel. Picking is now mostly mechanical. Growers no longer feel they have to have part of their crops in early varieties to attract and hold pickers until the later and heavier-bearing varieties are ripe. The only manual operation left is pruning, which is done in winter when the trees are dormant in deep snow. We often wore snowshoes or skis when pruning.

The land has turned itself around, from the pine forests of the pioneers to orchards, and in many places back to pine again. Time is the great healer. Give the land enough time, and it will heal itself!

C. PETERSON

Aslag's Orchard

by Charles L. Peterson

UST go along the path and listen for the sound of cursing; you can't miss him!"; my wife's pithy instructions to a client who wanted to talk with me on one of the few, now rare, days when I was painting in the field. I had chosen Aslag Anderson's old orchard, a delightful place just across Moravia Street from our home in Ephraim. Normally good for the tired spirit in any season of the year, the orchard as subject for a field study presents a tantalizingly rich variety of color, form and texture which had eluded my best efforts countless times before. And now, on a breezy afternoon in brilliant sunlight, I was losing that necessary edge of detachment as the shimmering patterns of sunlight filtering through the leaves not only brought life to the scene but kep flanking my umbrella and

invading my paper, making impossible the vital adjustments of tone without which no sketch can succeed.

The orchard lies at the eastern end of the long meadow which descends gradually from the old lake shore ridge now occupied by Moravia Street. The path leading to it has been kept open by generations of cows driven by one or another of Aslag's numerous children, replaced, when the Andersons moved to the shore, by deer, raccoons and all manner of domestic pets. In recent years an occasional vehicle has helped hold down the scrub as well (including at least one fire truck on a mission against a late fall grass fire).

Near the bottom of the wooded slope, just before the trees give way to the meadow, the path passes a nearly disintegrated wooden gate marking the place where Aslag's son

Frank tended the pigs, some of his own and a few for his neighbors, the Olsons, whose place was a little too close to the heart of the village. Among the fallen fence posts, a patch of faded green on an almost illegible tin of "Nigger Hair" tobacco, and an ancient clear blue, bubble-flecked bottle, "H. Walker" cast into it's glass base.

One should move slowly as the path leads out into the meadow. On the right is a pond which varies it's acreage according to the level of the water table and which is surrounded by a thick stand of trees. Over the years, these trees in combination with the pond have supplied cover for a wonderful variety of birds; mallards, wood ducks, innumerable song birds, the shy pileated woodpecker, barred owls, and an occasional kingfisher. Fallen trees provide tempting piers jutting out into the pond, upon which turtles sun themselves on warm days, and from which small boys will necessarily fall. In the spring, the chorus of peepers swells in volume

night after night until you simply stop hearing it. One day, standing silently near the pond, my wife Sue was startled by a fox coming out of the woods almost at her feet intent on things other than birdwatchers. The fox carried a young skunk in its mouth, and one imagines his senses may have been impaired.

On the left, crowning a small knoll, a few logs rely on the simple, effective Norwegian log corner notching to resist the final pull of gravity, marking the remains of Aslag's log barn. Inside the foundation; pieces of rusty farm machinery, an old road roller, bits of plaster lathe remain from the aching labor called farming. In winter, the log corner makes a good mark as one skis up the long, gentle slope of Aslag's old hay field. Once past, turn right and glide down the hill into the orchard. Standing there at dusk one winter afternoon, I succeeded in calling a barred owl to the trees overhead. He possibly thought my "who cooks for who?" was so infuriatingly stupid, he simply had to see who would do such a thing. Ghosting silently from tree to tree, he was

C. PETERSON

ultimately looking almost straight down at me. Probably in pity, knowing such a miserable creature could never survive the winter.

Deer and raccoon tracks mark the animal trails among the trees. Signs of the deer's feeding appear here and there in the orchard, and sometimes, as happened last month, a raccoon's meal left unfinished; a muskrat frozen into the pond there under the orchard, hollowed out by a hungry 'coon, leaving a fur-lined hole in the ice.

The orchard is particularly attractive in the fall when the apples are ripe. About every other year, the trees produce a harvest, untended and largely unremembered though they are. Perhaps only five or six of the dozen trees remaining are capable of serious production now, but these bring sweet pleasure to the visitor. There are some obvious variations in size and color, but the real delight comes in the tasting. Tart, sour, sweet, bitter or astringent, they cannot be identified with confidence. But they call to mind names remembered from childhood; Jonathan, snow, duchess, winesap, and they take one back to other times and other orchards, other hopeful farms, and perhaps even a grandmother's pies. I think of Aslag (whom I know only through his sons Adloph and Elmer, his daughter Munda, one of his grandchildren, his great-grandchildren, and his great, great-grandchildren) as I sample his apples and speculate on what they must have meant to him. And I think that little orchard is just right as a memorial to a man and his dreams.

ASLAG ANDERSON

Aslag Anderson was one of the substantial citizens that Norway furnished to Door County. While he has passed away, his influence yet remains and the results of his labors are still felt in the business conditions and the prosperity of this section of the state. He was born in Norway, August 8, 1829, a son of Andrew Halverson, who was also a native of the land of the midnight sun and there spent his entire life. Aslag Anderson was a youth of nineteen years when he bade adieu to friends and native country and sailed for the new world. He did not tarry on the Atlantic coast but made his way at once into the interior of the country, settling in Milwaukee, Wisconsin, in 1848. He afterward removed to Escanaba, Michigan, where he was employed at the millwright's trade for about seven years.

In 1855 he came to Door County but shortly afterward removed to Cedar River, Michigan, and in 1858 he returned to Door County, locating in Ephraim, after which he entered three hundred acres of land. He then concentrated his attention upon general farming and he also built a pier. He remained in business here for several years, working some on Chambers Island and in Menominee, Michigan. Later he operated his farm near Ephraim and in connection with its cultivation he conducted a small store. His business rapidly increased along that line and he later built the present store near the pier. In 1880 a part of the pier, together with his ware house were destroyed by fire, causing him a loss of five thousand dollars. With characteristic energy and determination, however, he at once rebuilt his warehouse and pier and resumed business, in which he remained active to the time of his demise.

On the 18th of June, 1861, Mr. Anderson was united in marriage to Miss Ann Margaret Hansen, a native of Norway, and they became the parents of twelve children, of whom ten are yet living, namely: Lizzie A. and Adolph, who have charge of the business at Ephraim; Julia, the wife of Alex Johnson, of Sturgeon Bay; Munda; Olive; Cordelia, the wife of Martin Hogenson, of Sheboygan, Wisconsin; Alvira, who is the wife of Dr. G.R. Egeland, of Sturgeon Bay; Agnes, who gave her hand in marriage to Samuel T. Torgeson, of Miles City, Montana; Frank, a resident of Ephraim; and Elmer, employed in a bank at Green Bay.

The death of the father occurred August 5, 1892, while his wife had passed away February 23, 1890. His political endorsement was given to the men and measures of the republican party and he served on the town board in Gibraltar. His religious belief was that of the Moravian church and his faith guided him in all of life's relations. He was a man worthy of the respect and confidence of his fellow citizens and during his long residence in the county he won a very extensive circle of friends who ever entertained for him the highest regard.

from H.R. Holand's History of Door County 1917

The Names in the Orchard

by Tom Davis

HE shape of the conversation remains the same. Its timing varies only slightly from year to year, beginning as an offhand remark in midsummer, by September swelling in proportions like an apple tree loaded with fruit, then dropping off gradually, like windfalls, through the autumn. It is heard in grocery stores, at hairdressers, in laundromats and after church services. Usually the participants are women, most often wives with the clear-eyed gaze of people who have come to terms with living in the country. The talk is of Cortlands, Macs and Red Delicious, of pies and sauce and pickles, of cold storage on the summer porch, of the proper blend for cider. There are discussions of canning and putting up apple butter. The dialogues end abruptly: there are apples to be peeled and cored, there is cooking, sweet aromas twining through the house, and there are spaces to be cleared in the freezer, cupboard and cellar.

Door County is orchards. The fragrance and delicacy of blossoms in the springtime, the delight of children scrambling to fill their pails with fruit, the rightness of sipping strong cider on a crisp afternoon in October, the stark, orderly resilience of the bare trees in their winter theater of snow: the offerings of the orchards are as reliable - and changeable - as the seasons.

But it is the fruit itself that focuses attention. One doesn't need to know the name of an apple variety to enjoy its taste, but newcomers in the county may feel bewildered by the names that are everyday vocabulary to natives. In fact, there are relatively few varieties of fruit grown today in Door County, and five months of study is enough to memorize them all.

The fruit upon which the county's fame hinges is the cherry. The first commercial plantings were made in 1896, with the number of trees increasing slowly until 1910, when the industry boomed. Early Richmond and Montmorency were the preferred varieties, both tart red cherries used primarily for cooking. The orchards steadily expanded, and the Montmorency became the favored cherry. It was larger and firmer than the Early Richmond, its fruit making for a superior "pack." By 1959, there were 1,122,340 cherry trees in Door County, placing it first in the nation in cherry tree population, and the only county in the USA with over a million trees. Over 95% of these were Montmorencies. From this peak in 1959, the number of trees declined due to poor economic returns, diseases and pests, and the high capital investment costs associated with the rapid mechanization of the industry, until only 351,100 trees were reported in 1974. This mechanization - primarily in the form of powerful shakers which have replaced the armies of laborers formerly needed to harvest the cherry crop - spelled the end of the Early Richmonds, for their soft flesh could not stand up to the rigors of shaking and rapid processing. Cherry acreage has increased lately due to recent high prices, but changing land use patterns dictate that the mark of one million trees is unlikely ever to be reattained. But there will always be plenty of Montmorencies hanging heavy from the trees in summertime, waiting to be placed gently in a bucket held by a small, eager boy or girl, or popped straight into the mouth, the sour juice screwing a bright face into an amazed wince.

According to an article entitled "Cherries and Door County," published in 1948 by Alice R. Reynolds in **The Peninsula**, the periodical of the Door County Historical Society, it was the Jonathan apples of Joseph Zettle that led to the establishment of commercial orchards in the county. The taste and appearance of Zettle's Jonathans, on display at the 1891 Wisconsin State Fair, intrigued Professor E.S. Goff of the University of Wisconsin and A.L. Hatch, a member of the State Board of Agriculture and himself an orchardman. They questioned Zettle, and he spoke in glowing terms of the

climatic conditions and soil, which together created an ideal environment for the fruit trees he had begun planting in 1862. The county's reputation in that era rested on its lumber and sawmill industry; little was known of its potential for cash crops. Persuaded to visit the county, Hatch offered this testimony to the Wisconsin Horticultural Society in 1892:

> The modifying influence of the waters and ice of Lake Michigan and Green Bay gives the peninsula a cold, backward spring. It is generally considered that this retards bloom until the frosts are over. The fact is rather that it prevents a rapid, tender growth that would not be sufficiently hardy to endure subsequent frosts.
>
> Further south there is too little steady cold; fruit trees burst quickly into bloom with the advent of warm days, and the tender growth succumbs to subsequent frosts. In Door County the buds come on very slowly; often it is several weeks from the time they first swell until full bloom. During this time they strengthen and become hardy.

Hatch also recognized that the loose limestone soil was well suited to the nutrient demands of fruit. It was the interest of Hatch and Goff, and later of Hatch's son-in-law Delbert E. Bingham, that virtually created Door County's orchard industry.

Jan Jablonski

As the acreage devoted to orchards soared, cherries occupied about twice the land area planted to apples. The **Soil Survey of Door County**, published in 1919, estimated that 1700 acres of apples existed in the county. The Jonathans that had so impressed Hatch and Goff, and had led indirectly to the Door's orchard explosion, were no longer a significant portion of the county's apple crop. The **Soil Survey** reported "The apples grown most extensively on a commercial scale are the Wealthy, (Duchess of) Oldenburg, Fameuse, McIntosh, Dudley, Northwestern (Greening), Toman and McMahon." A census made in 1959 ranked Door County 32nd in the country with a population of 144,612 apple trees. It is thought that this figure has remained relatively stable since that time.

And what of the apple varieties most prevalent in 1919? The McIntosh, the large, deep-red, crisp yet juicy apple that originated on the Ontario farm of John McIntosh in the early 1800s, has retained its popu-larity. The McIntosh-type apple is probably the county's most widely grown, the Cortland, a member of the McIntosh "family" of apples, is also extremely popular. The Northwestern Greening, which originated in Wisconsin's Waupaca County and is called "the original pie apple" by veteran Door orchardman Charles Krowas, is still grown on a minor scale, the green early-ripening fruits favored for their cooking qualities.

But the other apples - the Duchess of Oldenburg, imported from Russia, the Wealthy from Minnesota, the Fameuse or Snow Apple from Canada, the McMahon which originated in Richland County - are no longer of any commercial significance here. All agriculture has experienced increasing specialization in this century, and the growing of apples has been no different. In "Just How Good Were Those Old-Time Apples?," an article by Lewis and Nancy Hill in the April, 1981 issue of **Country Journal**, the demise of many of these varieties is blamed on a decline of the apple's importance to the average American's diet, a proliferation of new varieties which forced storekeepers and nurserymen to stick to a relatively few kinds, and increasing reliance on pomologists - literally, apple scientists - to determine which strains bore the most fruit, required the least attention and could stand rough handling.

The "old-time" apples are undergoing a renaissance of sorts among hobby orchardists, and neglected survivors from aged plantings are undoubtedly scattered about the county in abandoned orchards and forgotten farmyard. But in 1984, only three varieties accounted for more than 80% of Door County's apple production, according to University of Wisconsin Horticultural Extension Agent Cliff Ehlers: the McIntosh, Cortland and Red Delicious. These names are familiar to those who have never laid eyes on an orchard, for they are commonly stocked on supermarket shelves, where they become the pies and snacks of urbanites. This 80% will go almost entirely for fresh use, while the Northwestern Greenings are normally sold as processing apples for commercial sauce. New varieties of minor importance include the Paula Red and the Viking, the latter developed by Dr. Fred Gilbert at the Door County Agricultural Experiment Station as an early-ripening, red apple. The visitor to the county should sample them all, deciding for him or herself which tastes best after a bicycle tour, which holds its flavor under melted cheddar cheese in a deep-dish pie, and which make sauce as tangy in February, taken from the jar, as it was the day it was put up.

The poor sister to Door County's cherries and apples is the plum. Hatch and Goff counted plums among their first plantings, and by 1919 the county contained 200 acres of the deep violet fruits. But it was not until the early 1960s that plum growing "took off." The Door County Fruit Growers' Association announced plans to begin canning plums for regional distribution, and the orchardmen responded. Unfortunately, the plans never materialized, and most of the plum orchards were bulldozed and planted to other crops. Only two growers, the Krowas and Martin Orchards, still raise plums commercially, the Stanley Prune variety which, as its name implies, dries into prunes in arid southwestern climes. The Door County plums are marketed fresh, because the humidity here usually induces rot before the drying process is complete. However, it is possible in winter to find a few true prunes hanging from the trees, the cold having "freeze-dried" them to the desired consistency.

Those are the names: the Montmorency cherry, the McIntosh, Cortland, and Red Delicious apples, the Stanley Prune plum. That's not too many to remember, but keep in mind that the names are only labels. The fruits have the same wonderful tastes, produce the same luxurious blossoms, and grow in the same grand country, no matter what they're called.

What a place to be is in an old library! It seems as if all the souls of all the writers that had bequeathed their labors to these Bodleians were reposing here as in some dormitory, or middle state. I do not want to handle, to profane the leaves, their winding-sheets. I could as soon dislodge a shade. I seem to inhale learning, walking amid their foliage; and the odor of their old moth-scented coverings is fragrant as the first bloom of these sciential apples which grew amid the happy orchard. —Charles Lamb

photo: Museum Collection

Door County's First Cherry Cannery
Prevented Fresh Fruit Spoilage

✤✤✤✤✤✤✤✤✤✤✤✤✤✤✤✤✤✤✤✤✤✤✤✤✤✤✤✤✤✤

by John Enigl

HEN were the first cherries processed in Door County? By what company? Who headed the processing operation? Fortunately, the man who can answer those questions with authority is still living. Capt. Edward S. Reynolds, now 93 years old, organized Company F, of the Thirty Second Division of the U.S. Army, in Sturgeon Bay during World War I. How he came to can the first cherries ever canned in Door County is interesting, for he was in France, engaged in furious battles, when that event was first scheduled to occur.

Lougee Stedman, who was manager of the Fruit Growers Cooperative at the time of his death in 1948, wrote a

history of that organization shortly before he was killed in an airplane crash along with two other prominent figures in the cherry industry. The article was carried in an industry publication, **The Wisconsin Canner,** and it explains how the first cherries came to be canned:

"The Fruit Growers Canning Company was organized by a group of cherry growers in January, 1918, and purchased the pea canning factory of the Reynolds Preserving Company. At the same time there existed the Door County Fruit Growers Union which actually controlled the disposition of raw cherries. The Canning Company was organized for the purpose of creating another outlet (in addition to fresh fruit sales) which would be in the hands of cherry growers themselves.

"The first president of the Fruit Growers Canning Company was A.W. (Gussie) Lawrence (who was also president of the Fruit Growers Union). E.S. Reynolds, Sr., was the first manager. After two terms as president, Gussie Lawrence was succeeded by H.W. Ullsperger. E.S. Reynolds, Sr. died in 1919, and for a few months, his brother, Will Reynolds, acted as manager. In April, 1919, Ed Reynolds, Jr. became manager, and occupied that position until February, 1924, at which time H.W. Ullsperger became manager."

The Fruit Growers Canning Company had originally planned to can cherries in 1918, but the crop was short that year, so that caused the plans to be cancelled. In the meantime, Edward S. Reynolds, Sr., the plant manager died unexpectedly, and someone was needed to run the plant in the 1919 season. Young Capt. Edward S. Reynolds, Jr. was still in the army, but he was the man the company wanted for the job. An appeal was made for his release, and it was granted. He came home to find a partially completed plant, with the prospects of a bumper fruit crop, and the canning season only a couple of months away.

The June 26, 1919, issue of the **Door County News** (later purchased by the **Door County Advocate**) tells about that first canning season:

"The Fruit Growers Union on Saturday started up the canning factory and canned strawberries.

"There was a slump in the market price of the fruit and the fact that it was coming in faster than it could be shipped out in good condition, owing to the following day being Saturday. It was deemed the proper thing to preserve the fruit.

"Consequently a crew was put to work on Saturday and about 5000 quart cans of the fruit was put up, the factory running until nearly midnight.

"On Saturday there was a carload of strawberries shipped to outside points by the Union."

The article suggests the important reason for the building of the canning factory. Many fruit crops, cherries and strawberries ripen quickly so the picking season is rather short. In those days, as today, the crop was sold as fresh fruit; but then it could not be shipped around the country as quickly. So, although all the crop might be picked on time, the market was flooded, and some of the fruit spoiled before it could be shipped

photo: Milwaukee Journal, Sun., Aug. 1, 1937

SORTING THE "STRAW FROM THE CHAFF," only this time it's undersized and spoiled cherries from the good ones on the conveyor at a Sturgeon Bay cannery.

and sold. Therefore, a method of preserving the crop so it could be sold later was developed. Housewives had already been canning fruit and making jam and jelly at home for years by then, and it only took the development of machines to do the job in a factory to permit the preservation of fruit commercially.

The July 10, 1919 issue of the **Door County News** sang the praises of the new **Fruit Growers Canning Company** factory:

"A great help to the growers is the canning factory. The fruit that is too ripe for shipment is just what is wanted for canning purposes. As a

Children enjoy picking cherries in Door County orchards.

"A potent power, subtly strong,
Controls my senses as I lie
The morn is eloquent with children's song,
And the earth seems yearning to the sky."

result the factory is kept running practically every hour of the day. It has been found necessary to put a double crew on to handle the output. Women at the factory are being paid the rate of 25 cents an hour for their services and the supply is not equal to the demand."

By July 17, 1919, the **Door County News** waxed eloquent about the new canning plant:

"That the residents of the city and county do not fully appreciate what they have in the local canning factory is quite evident.

"Warren B. Jones, merchandise broker of canned goods, whose headquarters are at Chicago, was in the city the latter part of the week looking over the local factory and he expressed the sentiment contained in the above paragraph. 'People here do not realize what they have in the cherry cannery', he said. 'Why, this is the largest factory in the United States, double the capacity of any other single factory. Where the next largest only operates four machines, this one is operating nine.'

"Another impression that seems to be abroad among the uninitiated is that inferior cherries only are used in canning. This is just the opposite of the truth. It is the cream of the crop that is used for canning. These are the cherries that are ripe. The riper they are, the better they are for canning purposes and only those are received and accepted at the factory. Consequently, the fruit that is being canned is bound to make a reputation for itself when placed on the market.

Hauling cherries, picked "on stem", to the train depot in Sturgeon Bay to be shipped to market.

43

"Owing to the season being further advanced than usual on account of the warm weather in June, there will be more cherries available for canning purposes than was estimated early in the season.

"This is a fine thing for the growers, for if they did not have the factory to can the fruit that is too ripe for shipping a long distance, they would suffer a loss.

Mrs. Don Pegnovich smiles like the champion she is. She holds the record at the orchard where she works.

photo: Milwaukee Journal, Sun., Aug. 1, 1937

"There is a ready market for the canned fruit and the buyers have been here making contracts for the output at good figures."

A week later, on July 24, 1919, the **News** reported that members of the state county agents association had toured the canning factory and were highly complimentary of the operation.

The manager of that first cherry processing plant, Capt. Edward S. Reynolds, Jr., is now a resident of the Dorchester Nursing Center. He was interviewed for this article in December of 1984. In his cheerful, sun filled room, this man who still has the proud bearing of a military man, told of that first year.

"I recall that one of the problems we had was with the de-stemming machine. All the cherries were picked with the stems left on in those days, for the fresh fruit market. The cherries that were canned by the hot pack method had to have the stems removed. But many of them came through the machine that was supposed to remove the stems with the stems still on, so we had to have workers remove them by hand.

"Our brands, Sturgeon Bay Cherries and Pathfinder became particularly well-known in the Southwest, especially in Texas and Oklahoma in the oil fields. We had a big market and the sales went very well.

"The old pea canning factory, which my father converted to a cherry cannery, was a three story building which ran down to a dock along the shore. We would store the completed product down near the shore where it would be hauled away by boat.

"I had to put a new floor in the factory after I came home from the army in April of 1919. As for the canning machinery, a steam bath had been developed. The no. 10 cans were filled full with the raw cherries and passed through the steam bath and then the cans were sealed. That's all the cooking they needed, and fortunately everything was successful. The can had a double seal and used closing equipment made by the American Can Company.

"When the crop came in, we had crates of fresh cherries standing all over the place! We were working around the clock to take care of them, but somehow managed to get through with the crop. As a result, the quality of our no. 10 water-packed cherries became known everywhere."

When asked about the personnel who packed that first crop at the Fruit Growers Canning Company, the first name to come to Capt. Reynolds'

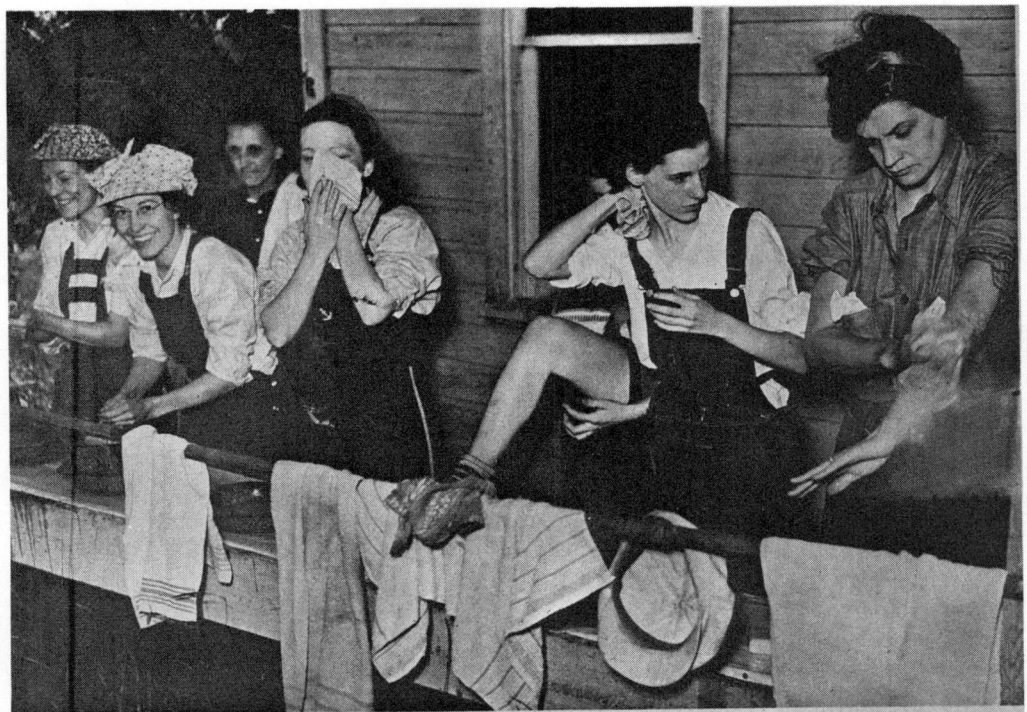

THE DAY'S WORK IS DONE and this group of girl cherrypickers is cleaning up for supper at Boyce's orchard. The girls at the left feel quite gay, but it's serious business for the young ladies at the right.

mind was that of Bow (pronounced "bough") Augustine.

The Wisconsin Canner book, **The Story of Wisconsin's Great Canning Industry,** quoted before and published in 1949, gives us the background of Bow Augustine.

Clarence Plummer, who had worked in a cannery in Davenport, Iowa, was hired to set up a pea cannery for the Reynolds Preserving Company after the company was organized in December of 1895. Although he had never packed peas before, the plant was set up and running by the summer of 1896.

Charles "Bow" Augustine went to work when construction began and became superintendent of the plant when Plummer left after 1897.

"It is interesting to note," the book states, that 'Bow' remained with the Reynolds factory and with the Fruit Growers through several different managements, and as of 1949 was still in charge of the factory, making

fifty-three straight years of service in one plant."

Nearly a quarter century after Capt. Edward S. Reynolds, Jr., left the Fruit Growers Canning Company to go with American Can Company, Lougee Stedman spoke of the difficulty of running a cherry factory and the service of "Bow" Augustine:

"The many changes in managers indicates the severe strain on men in executive positions. It is a killing pace, and grower-membership in a co-operative enterprise contribute their share of grief. On the other hand, we have found it of advantage to introduce new methods and ideas through such changes. It is hard on men, but good for the association. The one exception of which we are very proud is the unusually long term of service of our plant superintendent, 'Bow' Augustine, whose detailed knowledge of the canning industry and whose wholehearted devotion to succeeding managers contributed mightily to our success. We hope that he will retain his health and for many years to come will continue to be the solid foundation of our enterprise."

The author of the article in which the quote from Stedman was included further states: "Mr. Augustine holds a unique record, certainly in Wisconsin and possibly in the nation, of having continued employment without interruption in one plant under several reorganizations and changes of management from the beginnings of operations in Reynolds Preserving Company, in 1896, up to the present, November, 1949, and is still active as general superintendent. He attended the convention in Atlantic City, in January, 1948. Surely fifty three years in one and the same plant must be an outstanding record."

The Fruit Growers Canning Company was not the first company to can cherries in the United States, Capt. Reynolds says.

"Cherries had been canned in a small way in New York State," he says, "and Michigan had several canning factories.

"I want to stress that the Fruit Growers Union and the Fruit Growers Canning Company were two separate organizations. The Fruit Growers Union was a cooperative; the Fruit Growers Canning Company was a corporation. The Canning Company had a contract with the Union to process cherries at a fixed rate. The first year we made too much money, so we had a hard time! But we had spent a lot on rejuvenating the plant and putting in new equipment.

"The next step in plant improvement was putting in tanks of water in which the cherries were soaked. In doing that, the cherries were cooled down and became more firm and pitted out better. Also, they took on weight, so they were worth more! The quality improved in addition, for

cherries in crates suffer a good deal of spoilage."

The next year, Reynolds states, he had to increase plant capability 100%. Cherries for the hot pack canning process were then picked without the stems, a practice much easier on the hands and fingernails than picking them on stem.

Quoting from the before-mentioned book, "In a June, 1922, news item, it was stated that manager E.S. Reynolds, Jr. has the big plant all tuned up ready for the start on red sour cherries. The capacity of the factory has been increased from 250,000 cases of fresh fruit to 425,000 cases. Twelve additional pitters have been installed, making thirty-three pitters in all." A later report in August, 1922, said, "The Fruit Growers Canning Company this season just completed August 1st, canned a total of 9,280,000 pounds of cherries."

After the 1924 canning season, when his father's five year contract was completed, Capt. Reynolds left Sturgeon Bay to begin a thirty year period of employment with the American Can Company on the East Coast. Upon retirement, he moved back to Sturgeon Bay, where he had two sisters.

The Fruit Growers Canning Company plant later became the Fruit Growers Cooperative canning plant. In the 1960's it was sold to Peterson Builders, Inc. and torn down for the shipyard's expansion program.

The Canning Industry

In 1896 the Reynolds Preserving Company started their large pea cannery. This was one of the first three canneries in the state and the first one to introduce the vining system. Other factories at this time had no provisions for vining the peas. At first the vining was done at the central plant, but later a number of vining stations were established. The first factory was a part of the present Goodrich warehouse. Two hundred thousand cans were put up the first season and about fifty persons were employed in the factory. In 1907 the output was 3,309,000 cans and about two hundred persons were employed in the factory.

The canning company used to rent a great deal of land on which to grow their peas. The lowest rent paid was $8 per acre. In 1907, 2,200 acres were rented at a cost of $22,000. All the work was done by the company. The crop is uncertain, however, only one in four having been found satisfactory. One year 2,500 acres were sown by them of which only 1,000 acres yielded sufficiently to induce cutting.

Because of these and other uncertainties the Reynolds Preserving Company is not pushing the canning of peas as energetically as formerly. Moreover, in order to improve the quality of the output the vining stations have been discontinued.

In 1917 the canning company began to can cherries. Thirty-three thousand crates were contracted for. The Reynolds Preserving Company has a capital stock of $100,000.

In 1902 Louis Reichel started a cannery in Sawyer under the name of the Door County Canning Company, which later was purchased by the Van Camp Company. The largest output of this cannery was 2,000,000 cans in 1907. This cannery has had a rather checkered existence and was finally closed up. In 1917 the Van Camp Company opened it again as a factory for condensed milk.

H.R. Holland
History of Door County, 1917

Winesap Mid-Atlantic regions, Nov. through July . . .

. . . good for snacks, salads, baking whole, all-purpose cooking.

Packing shed of W.I. Lawrence Orchard on Highway 17, July 28, 1924

photo: Museum Collection

Pickers Camps:
Once a Necessary Part of the Cherry Growing Scene

by John Enigl

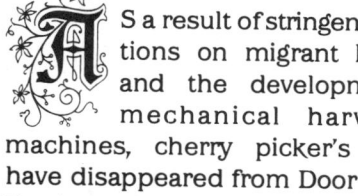

AS a result of stringent restrictions on migrant housing, and the development of mechanical harvesting machines, cherry picker's camps have disappeared from Door County. But in 1919 they were an important part of the local scene, as was reported in the now-defunct Door County News.

From these news articles, preserved on microfilm in the Door County Library, we learn about these temporary homes where boys and girls were discretely kept apart, where their values were expanded and improved, their intellect devel-

oped, and blacks and Indians had separate and **almost** equal treatment, if in a condescending way.

The objective, of course, was to get the cherries picked within the very short season when that fruit is at its best, and that meant it was necessary to keep the workers happy so they did not abandon that mundane task and go back home. But in these stories of long ago, we can detect the beginnings of a concern for the welfare of the worker, and for those of other races than white.

To begin with, the cherry crop of 1919 was a large one; that fact had been predicted early in the season, so arrangements had been made to recruit pickers and bring them in by train and steamboat. With the new cannery operated by the Fruit Growers Canning Company, a large amount of cherries could be handled in a day, a larger amount than when the fruit was sold only in the fresh form. There was a need for a large number of pickers.

Consequently, the county fair grounds was opened up as a picker's camp. E.W. Brandenberg of Milwaukee, active in the state Y.M.C.A., directed the operations of the camp. (The only name similar to that in the Milwaukee telephone book is Brandenburg; the News may have used a phonetic spelling.)

Half of the four hundred boys in the camp came from Milwaukee, and the others came from Madison, LaCrosse, places in the Fox River Valley, and one came from Winona, Minnesota. A spin-off of the cherry-picking experience is that some of the pickers eventually came back as tourists, and some became property owners, once captured by the charm of Door County.

"The boys are brought here for their own welfare, as well as for the benefit of the cherry growers," the article in the News stated. "They are taught all that is elevating and patriotic."

The article continues, "They are divided into groups of one hundred each, there being one hundred in each of the three barracks, and one hundred in tents. The one hundred groups are divided into groups of twelve. In each of the groups is organized a baseball team which plays among themselves. The winner of each group plays in the finals for the championship of the camp. There are also other athletic contests as well as contests for picking cherries, cleanliness, behavior, etc. Flags are being awarded the group winning the picking contest each day and the one winning the most gets the flag at the end of the season.

"Every evening sixteen of the groups play ball; eight engage in track events; four prepare for the stunts that take place at the conclusion of the athletic events; four have the evening off to write letters home,

Typical cherrypickers—
young and not so young, tall and short, boys and girls line up with their buckets, ready to go on the job in the orchard of the Sturgeon Bay Fruit Co.

photo: Milwaukee Journal, Sun., Aug. 1, 1937

wash their clothes, etc. Every morning and evening there is a flag raising and a vowing of allegiance to their country."

There was a charge for the meals and lodging at the cherry picker's camp of 40¢ a day. On the average the pickers earned about $1.35 a day, and some earned as much as three dollars a day. The amounts may seem small, except when we remember that these were the times when you could buy a new Chevrolet sedan for $490, and a Ford touring car for as little as $290. Try multiplying everything times forty to get comparative values.

The **Door County News** writer tells about a problem at the camp:

"Naturally in the handling of so large a number of boys there will be found some who will find fault. They get lonesome and start stories in order that they may be able to go home. Mr. Brandenberg, when asked concerning the feeding problem, stated that anyone who has even two boys in their family can understand the difficulty of satisfying 400. Naturally there may be some who will not like the menu on a given day. It is impossible to serve an individual order for each person."

We can get an idea of the kind of fare the boys were offered by the list of some of the groceries consumed by the 400 during a week: 1650 1½ pound loaves of bread; 210 pounds of butter; 425 pounds of meat, or about a pound per week per boy; 72 pounds of cheese; 1500 quarts of milk, or about a gallon per boy per week; various canned fruits; 200 pounds of sugar, probably much less than children consume today. That amounts to only a half pound per week, perhaps accounting for the fact that children were so much less hyperactive years ago than they are today.

How did the boys get from Mil-waukee to the picker's camp at the fairgrounds, in the days before Wisconsin developed its hard-surfaced highway system? Just as many tourists got here, even before the turn of the century, by boat. In this case, they traveled to and from Milwaukee on the Goodrich steamers, Arizona and Georgia, on a roadway built by nature, Lake Michigan. There are hundreds of old timers still alive in the Milwaukee area who remember the days when they picked cherries in Door County and traveled to and from here either by steamer or by train, since we had passenger service until the mid 1930's.

Another camp for cherry pickers was operated by the "cooperative", as the **Door County News** called it.

Of this camp, the **News** said: "While this is called a camp it is in reality a regular little village. All the cherry pickers that are employed here **with the exception of the camp of Indians**, are housed in fine buildings that were built especially for the purpose.

"There are about 450 pickers employed steadily at this orchard. They are all girls and women, who came from all parts of the state. The company does not keep boys for pickers; that is, they do not board them the same as they do the women folks."

photo: Milwaukee Journal, Sun., Aug. 1, 1937

PICKER MARY LA GUARDIA (left) adds another pailful to the crates as Evelyn Ullsperger checks her.

Today, of course, that policy would arouse cries of discrimination, and a demand for housing of the boys in the same dormitories as the girls. But this was 1919, the year that Andrew Volstead was drafting an amendment to the Constitution to stop everyone from drinking alcohol, the wistful times when it was thought that you could legislate morality.

"This is possibly one of the most interesting places to be found in the United States," the article continued. "This is the largest single orchard in the county and in the world, as is known to our readers. The company has between 700 and 800 acres and they figure on harvesting between 40,000 and 50,000 cases of cherries.

"The girls in this camp are a wonderfully bright and interesting lot on the whole. They are their own entertainers, readers, talkers, singers, musicians, etc. Evenings are spent in a most enjoyable way, the pickers having a large room in which there is a piano, a place to dance, and a large and roomy porch on which to lounge if they so desire. There are baths for thirty at one time and the cuisine is of the very best. One pays for what she eats on the cafeteria plan. Everything is sold at actual cost.

"On Friday and Saturday evenings there are special doings at the Cooperative. This consisted of a couple of lectures and a dance."

A lady who had helped war orphans from the just-concluded communist revolution in Russia spoke of saving Russia from Bolshevism and starvation, terms probably not familiar to the innocent, well-fed girls from Milwaukee.

Said she, "It is Americans on whom depends the resurrection and development of Russia. It is American morale, American food, and American merchants who will develop the marvelous resources of Russia and

photo: Milwaukee Journal, Sun., Aug. 1, 1937

Dancing in Cherryland, Henrietta Kosobucki plays the concertina for other young cherry pickers.

Siberia." (That turned out to be wishful thinking on her part.)

The speaker was also an expert on Indians, "but found comparitively few **aborigines**," the reporter said. "Aborigines" is really not a degrading term, a synonym of "savages", but actually means first resident or native of an area. She had a wide acquaintance among various tribes of Indians, and apparently had good intentions.

Another speaker "defended" the Indian, according to the reporter. She said that the Indians picking cherries at the Cooperative Orchard were highly educated and really in no need of advice.

The Cooperative Orchard was located about three miles north of Sturgeon Bay, on the present-day highway HH. Just loosely called a cooperative, organized by James G. Martin, it was owned by a group of investors who reaped the profits, if any. Changes in laws determining what was a true cooperative and what was not caused the company name to be changed to Martin Orchards, a corporation. Pepperdine Golf Course is now located on part of the land. In the early 1980's, the mess hall and chapel building, referred to in this story, and used in World War II by German prisoners of war, Luftwaffe veterans, who picked cherries for Martins, was torn down. One of the original buildings still remains as of 1984.

The Reynolds Orchard to the north of the Cooperative Orchard consisted of 200 acres of cherries in 1919. The trees were small, being six and eight years old. Their cherry picker's camp consisted of 165 boys, under the charge of W.S. Reynolds. They were Chicago boys, "an exceptionally fine lot of boys," according to the reporter.

He goes on to say, "In this camp there are nineteen colored boys from Chicago, who have quarters of their own." One wonders if there was something special about these "colored boys," that they had a camp of their own. But when you consider the times, perhaps it was a step forward in race relations just to give these blacks a chance to leave the big city and earn some money, the same as anyone else.

For entertainment, the boys played baseball and swam in the bay, just a mile or so from the camp. Another sport was snipe hunting. The **Door County News** reporter explains:

"Picking out some unsophisticated youth who has never seen green fields before, some of the boys inform the green one that they are going snipe hunting and invite the victim to partake in the sport. If he 'falls' for it, they give him a large sack and tell him when the shades of evening fall, it is an easy matter to catch snipes. All that he has to do is sit at a certain spot which is generally located a mile or so from camp in some lonely place. The other members of the party form a circle around the boy with the bag and drive the snipe into the open mouth of the bag. The snipe, being scared by the yells of the drivers, rush for the opening

for a hiding place. This must be done just as night is falling, of course.

"The lad with the bag takes his The snipe, being scared by the yells of the drivers, rush for the opening for a hiding place. This must be done just as night is falling, of course.

"The lad with the bag takes his position after they have walked him as far away from the camp as possible and the others start yelling in the woods. At a preconcerted signal, they all come together and return to camp, leaving the victim alone, holding the bag, for the snipe never come.

"One night one of the lads did not return to the camp until four o'clock the following morning, having waited until daylight to find his way back."

Reassuringly, the writer continues: "Great care is taken in seeing that the boys do not get into any bad habits, and of course with a large crowd it is hard to avoid getting one 'black sheep'. No gambling of any kind is allowed, and the boys are permitted to indulge in only clean, manly sports."

Cedric Dreutzer, whose orchard was on the Bay Shore north of Sturgeon Bay, had a large picker's camp, consisting of ninety girls from Milwaukee and Escanaba. He hired a young lady from the University of Madison, a journalism student, who was also a good cook and activity leader to tend the girls. Under her direction, talent shows were held, and she taught them camp fire songs and group yells. They also went bathing frequently, since Ced's camp was close to the beach, not far from where Bay Shore Inn is located today. Dreutzer's neighbor and close friend was fellow orchardist, John Miles, who found time in later years to get away from his cherry orchard and act as secretary for the Door County Fair.

A.C. Templeton had a camp of thirty pickers from Milwaukee. Among his 700 cherry trees was one that had the reputation of having the largest amount of cherries of any tree in Door County.

The Sturgeon Bay Fruit Company, D.A. Larkin, manager, had a camp of eighty five boys, in charge of a Milwaukee school principal, Mr. Snell. "A large shack was built (at the orchard) for the accommodation of the pickers, who have excellent quarters", the **News** reporter said. (No doubt they were furnished with those inexpensive but nonpolluting little houses "out back" to take care of their sanitary needs.)

The Peninsula Fruit Farm had planted 110 acres of cherries in 1912 and in 1919 they were ready for harvesting. Thomas Boyce, the manager, had set up a camp for seventy girls, many of them Milwaukee school teachers. For entertainment, they put on musical and theatrical productions; one Sunday, Mr. Boyce took them all to Idlewild, a resort area, to spend the day. Taps were sounded at ten o'clock every night and the girls were expected to be in their bunks at that time. (The advent of the automobile changed things. Julius Haroldson, who worked in Sturgeon Bay about ten years after this, recalls that the girls would be lined up along the road, waiting to get a ride into town.)

Many people prominent in Door County history had gone into raising cherries by 1919. Some families are still in the business of raising fruit today; some later followed other pursuits. R. Fellner had eighteen acres of cherries that year, and also raised plums. Frank Borchert had twenty acres of cherries, and had his crop picked by the Boyce pickers. (In years to come, it would become common for the smaller growers to contract for picking with the processor who bought their cherries, such as Reynolds Brothers. The smallest orchards were picked by the grower's family, and a few neighbors.)

Richard Gilbert must have been one of the early planters of cherries, for he had one orchard that was thirteen years old. His camp consisted of twenty Milwaukee girls. Henry Hahn, well known as a furniture dealer, undertaker, promoter of a Door County fair the year the county

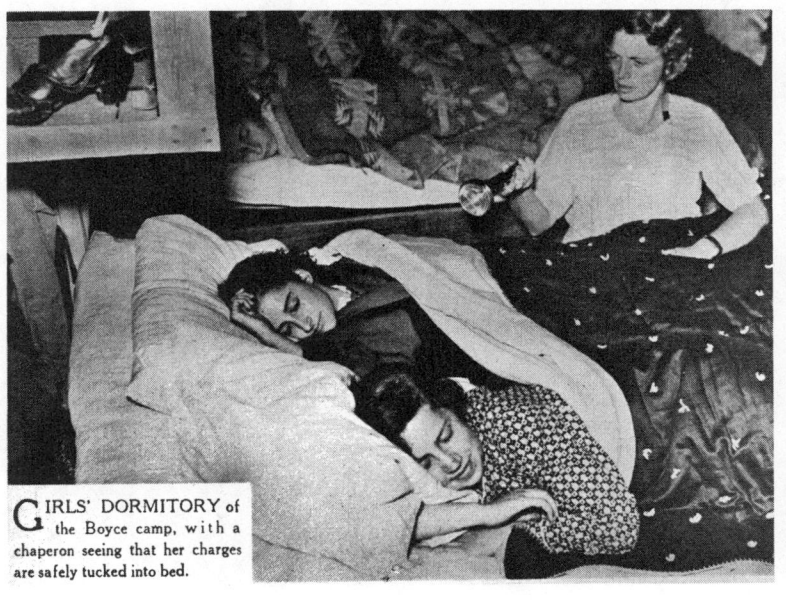

GIRLS' DORMITORY of the Boyce camp, with a chaperon seeing that her charges are safely tucked into bed.

photo: Milwaukee Journal, Sun., Aug. 1, 1937

board decided not to have one, owned ten acres of cherries. His camp consisted of fifty five children from a Catholic orphan asylum at Green Bay, who were in charge of a couple of sisters. "They have come to this farm for the past three years," the **News** reporter said, "and enjoy the outing immensely, having excellent quarters on the Hahn farm, which is under the management of Henry Tipler."

Among other well known names of Door County people in the business of raising cherries, some of whom had picker's camps, were Moulton Goff, D.C. Bingham, Roy Marshall, Peter Simon, and Lester Birmingham, as well as A.L. Hatch, who had the first cherry orchard in Door County, now owned by his grandson, Frank Ullsperger.

In later years, as times got better, it would become more difficult to recruit city people, especially whites, to pick cherries and live in the drab barracks built as temporary quarters for the pickers. Spanish-speaking Mexican-Americans from Texas filled the gap, and some growers recruited poor Indians from the reservations to pick their fruit.

Children from St. Joseph's Orphanage in Green Bay picked cherries under the direction of nuns.

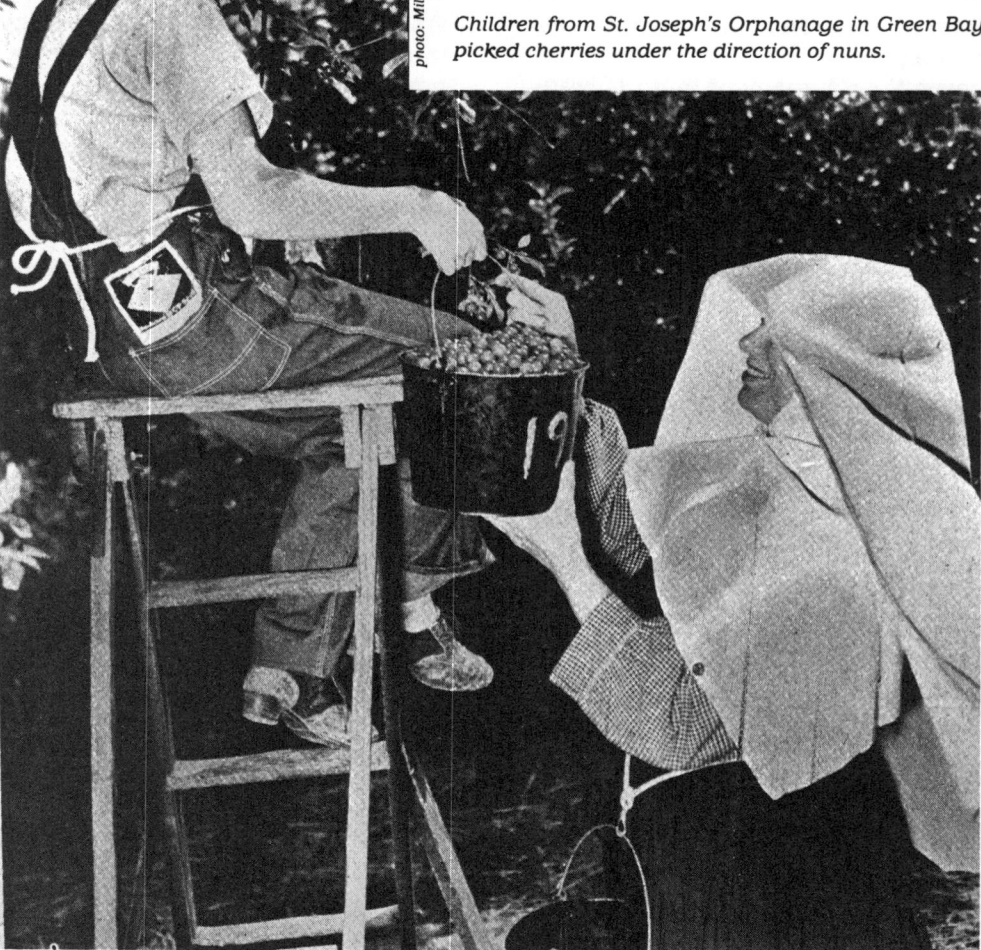

photo: Milwaukee Journal, Sun., Aug. 1, 1937

World War II provided better jobs than picking cherries even for the disadvantaged Mexican-Americans and Indians, so pickers of African origin were recruited among the poor of the British West Indies, including Jamaica. The B.W.I.s continued to come to some of the Door County camps until the early 1960's.

The cherry picker's camps, never intended to be permanent structures, continued to deteriorate, so that when a migrant agency was set up, some growers were told that their camps would be condemned if not renovated drastically. Rules for the building of new migrant camps were so strict that the buildings could serve as motels, and some growers considered going into that business, since Door County is a tourist area.

What really spelled the doom of the picking camps was a crude device called a "donkey", used experimentally in a Michigan orchard in 1945. It consisted of a gasoline engine fastened to a frame, with one end high up on the trunk of a cherry tree, and the other end on the ground. The "donkey" would shake the tree trunk and then the cherries would fall off the tree onto a catching frame of canvas.

By 1957, the Gould company had perfected a reasonably effective cherry shaker, eliminating the need for hand pickers and cherry picker's camps.

In the last years of the cherry picker's camps, Catholic and Protestant churches provided religious training and supervision for the children of migrant cherry pickers. The Migrant Ministry and local merchants provided a radio program with Spanish music on the local radio station. The program was called Saludos, Amigos and was broadcast on WDOR.

Finally, the number of Spanish speaking and other migrants had dwindled so much that the Catholic and Protestant churches and migrant agencies joined forces to provide for their needs. The last such joint effort, before the migrants became a thing of the past, was based at the St. Joseph Novitiate at Kangaroo Lake, the Calvary United Methodist Church of Egg Harbor providing a Spanish-speaking minister to help out.

The picker's camps of the past produced a desirable side effect for the residents of Door County. No one who grew up here in the days of the cherry camps and the migrant worker is bothered or surprised by the sight of a face of a different color, or the sound of people speaking a different language than their own.

photo provided by John Engl

Blacks from the British West Indies at Reynolds

The Milwaukee Apple

The variety Milwaukee was originated by George Jeffry of Milwaukee, from seed of the Duchess. It was a clear yellow, marked with bright red, but was too tart for a dessert apple. The tree was quite hardy and a good producer, but the variety never became popular.

Published in One Hundred Years The Wisconsin State Horticultural Society 1968

illustration: Rosemary Utzinger

Reflections of an Apple Baron

by Anonymous

NO one knows the exact means by which **Pyrus Malus** became established in the new world. The American "apple belt" stretches from the counties of Upstate New York, across the Great Lakes into Michigan, Wisconsin and Minnesota, ending in the Pacific Northwestern states of Oregon and Washington. This geographical region provides the ideal climate for this ancient fruit to really come into its own. The apple is a European fruit with domestic roots in the beginnings of agriculture. Botanically, it belongs to the family of roses. The common root-word for apple among the Celts, Germans, Lithuainians and Slavs indicates its domestic origins in the lands inhabited by these peoples. The Greeks and the Romans brought the apple with them to the British Isles. But,

how did this beautiful fruit become established in our area? For that answer, we must look to the very early establishment of the English Colonies in America.

It is said that some inhabitants of the Massachusetts Colony brought the first apple seeds and saplings with them from Europe in the early 1600's. The first apple orchards in North America were planted by the English in Boston and the French in Quebec. With the homesteading of New England, the apple spread as trees became a familiar sight around the pioneers' cabinsite. The cultivation of apples was also quickly adopted by the native American agriculturists. The apple's spread westward may have been by any one of many routes. Perhaps they traveled westward with the expansion of white settlers across the Alleghenies and then down the Ohio River Valley into the fertile heartland of Indiana, Illinois and Iowa. The popularity of the apple certainly had a powerful push in the form of the itinerant John Chapman, more commonly known as "Johnny Appleseed". It would have been through this heartland up the Lake Michigan shore past the military forts of Dearborne and Howard that the apple traveled to our region. Perhaps a bit earlier, apple seeds or saplings might have found their way into a French Voyagers cargo canoe leaving out from Montreal in early Spring to visit some fur-trading outpost on the far shores of Lake Michigan. Or even less likely yet, passing from the dark-skinned palm of one native American to another until that appleseed found root in the land of the Potawatomi. None the less the apple arrived and established itself in our area as the crop of economic importance well over a hundred years ago.

Here is where my roots lie. In the apple country of Northeastern Wisconsin. Glorious autumn mornings in the crisp air of the orchard are unforgettable memories. Our eighty acres are planted in a variety of apples, mostly the commercial types — Jonathans, Delicious, Winesap and McIntosh. However, we have a few trees of the outstanding types like Northern Spy and Spitzenburg which are the pride of the family homestead.

The Northern Spy is purely an American apple. It was developed in New York and by the 1840's, it was gaining attention throughout the Northeast. The Spy is a rather large apple with a somewhat thin and tender skin of dull yellow streaked with red. It ripens late and its juicy, tart, yellow flesh is unforgettable to taste. This apple is just as good cooked as eaten raw. Our stand of Spy's is just east of the house with

only nine of the gnarly old trees left, the greater portion having succumbed to the elements and the years.

Our other pride and joy is the Spitzenburg and stands out behind the machine shed. This apple has almost disappeared and it, too, originated in New York State. The Spitzenburg apple is medium in size and is ribbed. Its skin is pale yellow merging into bright red with small yellow dots. Its flesh is crisp and aromatic but not as juicy as the Northern Spy. This apple is one parent of the Jonathan and was favored by Grandma above all others for her delicious strudel.

We also have some greens scattered throughout the orchard. They are a good cooking apple and provide a distinctive taste to applesauce.

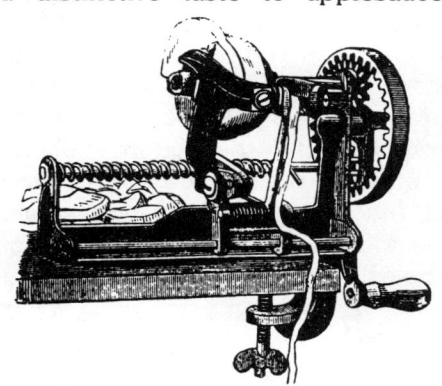

APPLE PARER

Things haven't changed much as long as I can remember. There is still pruning in the Winter, spraying in the Spring and, of course, the harvest in the Fall. Most all of the crops go to the Co-op now so we can avoid the tedium of sorting, but the picking is still done by hand with ladders and the old apron basket. The new chemicals and machinery have made spraying easier and less frequent unless you should happen to spray shortly before a good rain. I remember a time when we had to spray eight or ten times a season with a horrible smelling "lime sulphur". Of course, the ever present threat of a late frost can still easily put you to ruin.

It always seemed that "schooling" interfered with my apple harvest, but I'd rush out to the orchard where the crews were working as soon as I got home. Dad was adamant about keeping the windfalls picked up from under the trees and this was my evening chore. The bad apples were sent to the vinegar mill and the better ones went to the evaporator where they were cut up and dried. The apples we kept for the family were packed away down in the fruit cellar between layers of straw.

Cider making was a real family affair with aunts and uncles, brothers and sisters. Grandpa would say "You gotta grind them apples as uniform as possible, and slowly. That's the trick to the makin's of a good cider". The product you buy at the roadside stand is apple juice. The prospects of finding real hard cider have been complicated by the modern era. Most good wood presses are the property of antique dealers. The best ciders are a blend of different varieties of apples. The Delicious, Cortland and

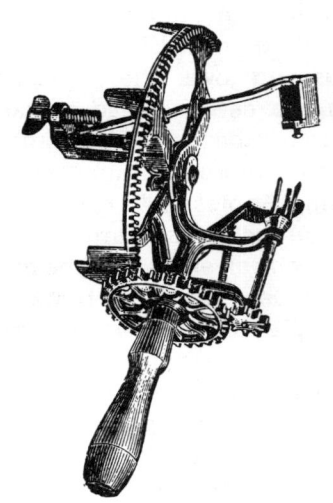

SLICER

Rome Beauty will yield a sweet dry tasting cider. For a slightly tart and mildly acid tasting cider, use the Winesap, Jonathan, Northern Spy and Greening varieties. Delicious and McIntosh will give an aromatic fragrance and flavor. The crab apple varieties of Red Siberian, Transcendant and Martha apples will procure an astringent taste.

The cider mill provided the family with hours of warmth and mirth long after the autumn sun had set.

Cortland
Northeast and Great Lakes regions. Sept. to early spring . . .

. . . good for snacks, salads, fruit cups, baking, sauces, all-purpose cooking.

Golden Delicious
Most regions across the country. Sept. through June . . .

. . . good for sauces, snacks, salads, fruit cups, baking, all-purpose cooking.

The California of the North

"Here in the sifted sunlight
A spirit seems to brood

On the beauty and worth of being,
In tranquil, instinctive mood."

(These 4 pages excerpted from the book "Door County The California of The North" published in 1914)

To that vast multitude of loyal men and women, who, by sheer strength of will power and braun and muscle have hewn a beautiful kingdom out of a wilderness where once ran only the trails of the Indian, and where one now finds the white, broad, smooth and well drained macadamized roads of higher civilization, which lead one through beautiful vistas of sweet smelling orchards where it is hard to visualize the primeval forests of old—

To those men and women who love and cherish all things growing and goodly that foster this life and breed—the immortal flower of wisdom from out of the mortal seed—

To those men and women who braved the dangers, difficulties, disadvantages and hardships and gave their strength, efforts, ability and at last, even their lives in the founding and building of this beautiful commonwealth

TO THE PEOPLE OF DOOR COUNTY
THIS BOOK IS SINCERELY
DEDICATED

Door County Horticulture
The California of the North

INTERESTING tales have been told of the great grain and cultivated grass producing lands which are situated at nearly every point of the compass and as great and gratifying as are their returns, they are but as a mere pigmy when brought into comparison with the revenue gained from successful fruit raising.

The development of horticulture in Door County during the last few years is a matter of contemporaneous history. It is a story so vast, so marvelous, that any attempt to review it must indeed prove futile. Suffice it that Door County has shared to the full in this movement that, in so short a time, comparatively speaking, has made this particular section of Wisconsin one of the foremost fruit raising sections in the United States. Especially in the production of the cherry, the emperor of fruits, has Door County taken her place in the forefront of the great cherry producing sections in the country, operating the largest cherry orchard in the world.

It is not a question of possibilities or probabilities. It is not only what Door County *can* do in the cherry, apple and small fruit industry; it is what Door County *has* done and *is doing,* and pre-eminently, what Door County *will do.* Her fruit is proven and known in the markets of the world. In the finest retail grocery store in the Twin Cities Door County cherries command the highest market price of all cherries throughout the entire season. The name, Door County, is seen repeatedly in the lists of first prize winners at the great fruit shows throughout the country. Her horticulture has long passed the questionable, the experimental stage; it is certain, proven, established—and her slogan is "Door County Does."

Door County Cherry Culture

THE continued success of the cherry culture in Door County is now attracting national attention. During the past twelve years Door County cherry orchards have produced cherries by the train loads, giving excellent crops each year. Behind this is a record of forty years past without loss of orchard fruits by spring frosts, a situation counteracting so emphatically what so often occurs in the rest of the country that many intelligent men, well informed in horticulture development and fruit growing are not only "sitting up and taking notice," but are investing in Door County lands and planting cherry orchards.

The first question which arises is: what are the conditions which make this famous fruit region of Wisconsin contrast so sharply with the widely advertised fruit lands of the west and south? Are they reliable and permanent and do they possess opportunities for investments of city bred men? In purchasing land we shall assume that the investor desires to acquire land which, when under cultivation will produce for him a living income, or land on which he may establish a home for his family and through cultivation derive a competent living, in a section of the country where he may feel absolutely assured of sharing in the increase in land values of future years and thereby increase the invested principal itself.

Granting that Door County, now possessing and operating the largest cherry orchard in the world, produces certain varieties of fruit better than any other fruit region, this question must be answered: can it be done profitably?

Door County Climatic Advantages

IN answering this question we must first go back and consider the two primary conditions which spell success in the development of all horticulture, soil and climate. Here it is well to review the peculiar conditions Door County possesses with such marked advantages for horticulture. The modifying influences of the waters of Lake Michigan and Green Bay gives the Door County peninsula a cool backward spring. It is generally considered that this retards the blooming of the trees, while the fact is that it prevents a rapid tender growth that would not be sufficiently hardy to endure subsequent frosts. In Door County fruit buds come out very slowly, it is often several weeks after they first swell until they burst into full bloom. During this time they increase their strength and become hardy. Further south there is too little steady cold. Fruit trees burst quickly into bloom with the coming of warm spring days and the tender growth often succumbs to late frosts. This is also true in what we consider garden vegetables like the cabbage, tomato, onion, beet and potato, which are often destroyed by frosts owing to their rapid growth during the spring season.

In the fall of the year Door County possesses still another climatical advantage gained from the warm waters of Lake Michigan and Green Bay. These great bodies of water so modify the temperature as to prolong the growing season considerably and there is a long period in the fall when frosts are not severe enough to destroy the leaves on the trees, but allows them to do their work of ripening the twigs, storing a surplus food supply for spring use, hardening and perfecting the buds to the fullest extent; which results in a fruit of exceptionally fine texture and flavor, with excellent keeping and shipping qualities.

Profits Realized From Door County Orchards

IN the growing of fruit we expect the largest returns from the land so that the number of acres required to support a family is much less than that of other forms of soil culture. Fruit farms in Door County will average from five to twenty acres and this acreage is found sufficient under proper cultivation to yield highly satisfactory returns. Let us consider the profits derived from this small acreage. Each year train loads and boat loads of cherries are shipped to Chicago, Milwaukee and Twin City markets from Door County. One single orchard of less than five acres produced over fifteen thousand sixteen-quart crates of cherries in the past three years. Another five-acre orchard produced in the last two years 7,380 crates of cherries, which sold above all cost of picking and crates for $8,246.00 A single acre of cherries has produced $836.61 in one year. Figuring on matured trees, one-half of some of the yearly crops of Door County cherries would capitalize the land at from $3,000.00 to $4,000.00 per acre on an interest basis, and each year this basis increases with the natural increase in land values.

Door County frosts do not usually kill foliage until the middle of October and this gives a full six weeks advantage in fall growth over many of the famous fruit districts of the west. In a very beautifully illustrated western magazine published in Oregon, advertising and exploiting Oregon's famous valleys for fruit raising, one may find many different kinds of orchard heaters. These heaters, burning crude petroleum and other smudge fuel are used to prevent injury from untimely frosts to the fruit bloom. Lake Michigan and Green Bay have served for many years as heaters for Door County orchards, and for the past forty years they have not failed the fruit grower. Smudge-pots are unknown in Door County orchards.

Profitable Crops Grow in Young Orchards

IN establishing a young orchard in Door County there should be no loss of revenue from the land while waiting for the trees to reach a bearing stage. Profitable crops should occupy the ground space from the very beginning of tree planting until the space beneath the trees is actually required for the care of the fruit.

A variety of crops can be planted to advantage. Strawberries have proven very profitable and come into full bearing in one year from planting, producing as high as $700.00 and $800.00 per acre. Peas, beans, cabbages, potatoes and onions thrive on Door County soil and their cultivation fits nicely the needs of a growing orchard.

Currants and gooseberries are grown in considerable quantity in Door County and have demonstrated their ability to produce $500.00 per acre.

Door County soils are exceptionally well adapted to horticulture for several reasons and it is a matter of statistics that they are of such nature as to produce the bearing habit to a very striking degree. The warm, strong, stony, clay loam soil of Door County, underlaid with lime rock, forms a combination of soil food which is extremely helpful and beneficial to young growing trees. This strata of lime rock comes up to within one to four feet of the surface, is full of seams and is so broken that it drains the land in wet weather and holds the moisture better than underlaid tile, while in dry weather it gives up the moisture which the trees need for nourishment and fruiting. In the fall, snow comes early and protects the roots of the trees from freezing. In no other section of Wisconsin and in fact in few parts of the entire United States, does the soil and climate together produce conditions so near the ideal for horticulture as does the soil and climate of Door County.

Door County Fruit Trees Bear Very Young

THE bearing habit of fruit trees in Door County, due from the effect of soil and climate, is worthy of comment. Fruit trees in Door County bear very young. Cherry trees planted four years often yield fifty to sixty crates of cherries per acre and it is nothing unusual to find single branches with five and six feet of fruit buds growing thickly and continuously along their length. Trees reach their full bearing capacity at twelve years of age and continue to produce, under proper care, full twenty years more. Not only is this bearing habit shown in tree fruits, but also in shrub fruits.

HARVESTING CHERRIES

In harvesting Door County cherry crops there is no danger of loss from inability to get fruit picked at just the proper time as Door County is within easy reach of a thickly populated district from which an abundance of competent pickers can be obtained at small expense.

MARKETING CHERRIES

Each year the cherry crop of Door County is handled by the Door County Fruit Growers' Association and is sold to the highest bidder, F. O. B. cars or boats at Sturgeon Bay which does away with the peddling or consigning of fruit. Some idea of the steadiness of demand for Door County cherries and the profit there is in them may be gained from the table of prices at which sixteen quart crates sold during the past ten years, as shown by the official records of the Door County Fruit Growers' Association, which gives a price range from $1.34 up to $1.58 per crate.

Wink Larson:
Orchard in His Blood

by Gary Jones

ERE'S the story of how Wink bought the orchard," said Audrey Larson, as she, Wink Larson, and I sat in the spacious living room of their Sister Bay home perched on a bluff, the hazy waters of Green Bay provide a background for the chickadees and goldfinches competing for birdseed just outside the window.

"Wink was in the real estate business then," Audrey continued, "and found out that one of the last really big parcels of land left in Northern Door County was for sale, 740 acres of orchards. He bought the land, planning to develop it, but a Sturgeon Bay cherry processor talked him into running the orchard and cherry plant, at least temporarily: '$35,000 of easy

money for two weeks of no work.' " Audrey laughed. "Wink tried it, and probably lost $35,000, but he fell in love with the land. He decided that there were too many tourists here already, and his family had been in the orchard business for years." And so the Larson Orchard came into being.

Wink Larson — orchardman, real estate developer, former Democratic Party Precinct Chairman — is a colorful local character. A bit of the devil lives in Wink, especially when it comes to dealing with mindless bureaucrats. But more of that later.

The Larson Orchard is a family concern. Wink's son, Mitch, like the three generations of Larsons who preceded him on the Northern Door Peninsula, makes his living as an orchardman.

63

Like her husband, Audrey Larson is a Door County native. Her family founded and still manages Bunda's Stores in Sister Bay. Audrey presides over the salesroom at the orchard, along with her mother-in-law, Hazel, wife of the late Everett Larson who lived at Appleport. Hazel, a native of Newport, has the strong, weathered face of an orchard matriarch.

Wink Larson's daughter, Lisa, has not been bitten by the orchard bug, but rather makes her living as an assistant vice president for Banco in Duluth.

The Larson Orchard has a history every bit as colorful as Wink himself. In 1910, two partners, Bingham and Lawrence, founded the orchard. Wink introduced me to Louis Koessl, who at age 87, remains a living volume of orchard history. A dignified man who has retained a Germanic manner and speech pattern, Louis Koessl spoke of the early days of what is now the Larson Orchard with an encyclopedic assurance, recalling dates, names and figures with ease.

"I worked the old Ellison Bay Orchard for Bingham and Lawrence in 1913, 1914 and 1915. All the other men who worked there then are dead," Koessl recalled. He worked a sixty hour week, was furnished room and board, and was paid thirty dollars a month.

Spraying was accomplished with a fifty pound pressure sprayer drawn by a two horse team. One man was required to stand on the rig, and another to walk behind as the outfit progressed slowly through the orchard.

Three mule teams worked up the land between the rows of trees where oats were broadcast by hand, and when ripe, cut, cradled and bundled all by hand. A horse walking in a circle furnished the power for threshing the oats, which in turn were used to feed the horses and mules required for orchard work.

Cherries had to be picked by the stems in those days, Koessl remembered. His job was to haul the filled boxes from the orchard to a shed where they were weighed. He added or removed cherries to maintain a 28 pound weight per box. At 6:00 p.m., the boat arrived at the Ellison Bay dock to pick up the cherries. On the way to Sturgeon Bay, stops were made at Sister Bay, Ephraim, Fish Creek and Egg Harbor. At Sturgeon Bay, the cherries were transported by rail to their destinations.

But not only were wages considerably less back in the early part of this century. In 1912 or 1913, Koessl recalled, a boat stopped with a load of mixed fruit trees which sold for eight cents a piece, quite a bit cheaper than the current $5.00 per tree cost. Orchard growers bought extra trees which were planted closely together in a trench and were transplanted later as necessary to replace trees that had died.

Spraying was not the investment then that it is now, either. Today it would not be unusual to pay $115 for a gallon of spray. Koessl remembers mixing a spray of lime, arsenic of lead and blue vitriol. The lime cost 35 cents per 100 pounds; the blue vitriol was two cents per pound.

Of course, fruit commanded a much lower price then than it does now, too, only two or three cents per pound.

The Tipperary section of the Larson Orchard is now one of the most productive plots. Louis Koessl remembers when he and Harold Gename cleared that land of timber and planted a field of oats for the horses.

Koessl and Wink Larson talked of pruning trees, and agreed that apple trees can withstand the most vigorous of pruning. Koessl spoke of fruit trees that he tends which are nearly as

old as he is, but still bear apples. "The harder you prune, the better apples you get," he said. After a long life of hard work, Louis Koessl is still vigorous and alert; one suspects that if the adage is true for apple trees, it may be true for men as well.

During the 1930s, the Bingham and Lawrence Orchard became the Ellison Bay Orchard Company which fell prey to the depression and was bought after foreclosure by a wealthy Chicago attorney, Art Friedlund.

Under Friedlund, the orchard enjoyed its heyday. Approximately 350 acres were devoted to cherries and another 300 to apples. Over a million pounds of cherries were produced, and over 50,000 bushels of apples. Ten full-time employees lived on the orchard, including a superintendent, foreman and head mechanic. 300 pickers were employed during the cherry season, and a regular village was created for them. Friedlund maintained a company store for the workers (the blackboard outside the door remains yet today), and a tent city, enough sixteen by sixteen foot concrete slabs to accommodate forty tents. Two houses, four

apartment buildings, plus migrant worker row houses and apartments in the main complex of buildings, provided housing for the army of workers which assembled to take part in the harvests each summer and fall. A fleet of a dozen tractors and as many trucks replaced the horses and mules of earlier years.

An artifact which testifies to Friedlund's industry and willingness to invest money in his orchard survives yet today. He commissioned a Chicago surveying company to prepare a huge "blueprint" of the orchard. This tree census graphically accounts for every living fruit tree Friedlund owned. A legend listed the abbreviations used for twenty-five varieties of apples; a U marked those trees whose varieties had not been established.

But the Friedlund Orchard was not the only one to prosper during the forties. The Martin Orchard, located just north of Sturgeon Bay, boasted 750,000 trees, the largest cherry orchard in the world at that time. A neighbor, the Reynolds Orchard, tended 550,000 cherry trees. Ironically, a good season during the 1940s produced 400 million pounds of cherries in the U.S., all of which sold; present day growers produce 300 million pounds of cherries, and can not sell all of them to a much larger population. The reason? Today's high prices, orchardmen agree.

Despite his apparent success, Art Friedlund maintained that the only time the orchard made him any money was when he sold it in 1950 and bought stock in American Canteen. The new owners called their enterprise the Rolson Orchard, combining the names Roen and Olson. One of the co-owners, Captain John Roen, was a Norwegian immigrant who ran a big maritime salvage operation and was at one time half owner of the Sturgeon Bay Shipbuilding and Dry Dock Company, now Bay Shipbuilding Corporation. Doc Olson, the orchard partner, was a prominent physician in Sturgeon Bay with patients that attributed his doctoring skill to a sixth sense.

Cap Roen was at the helm of Roen Orchard alone from 1953 until Sam and Sadie Goldman purchased the property in 1958. The orchard flourished under their hands, but unfortunately, with the end of the marriage came an end to the orchard partnership. In 1968, the orchard was managed by a trust established through the Bank of Sturgeon Bay.

And shortly after, in 1970, Wink Larson decided to try his hand at orchard work.

Audrey recalled that first year. "It was a hassle," she said. "We still owned the ski hill, and I ran that while Wink took care of the orchard." The Omnibus ski hill, located south of Fish Creek, is no longer a Larson property. And the orchard runs more smoothly now. At least when the bureaucrats stay away. But that comes later.

The Larson Orchard is smaller than it was in its prime. Of the original 740 acres, only 450 remain. "I can't afford to keep it," Wink explains. "Land assessors make you a millionaire, except without any money. I tell the assessor I couldn't sell it for half of what it's assessed at."

Despite his grumbling, Wink Larson is not headed for the poor house. While he plans to continue to sell off parcels of the land, he will keep at least 250 acres for orchard production. And the business will continue under the direction of Wink Larson's son, Mitch, when Wink hands over the reins. Presently Mitch and Dale Seaquist own and manage a cherry processing plant located on the Larson Orchard. (John McCool, an owner of twelve processing plants in Michigan, jokingly called Wink "the meanest S.O.B. of a father in the world" for selling Mitch the plant.)

But in the meantime he has plenty to do to keep himself busy. The Larson Orchard consists of 120 acres of apples and another 40 acres of cherries. At the peak of the season, he hires as many as 40 workers, many of the same people year after year.

The Cortland continues to be the number one apple at Larson's. "It's the best all-round apple," Wink explains. "It's firm, it keeps." The

DOOR COUNTY CHERRY CAMP ✦CIRCA1940☜

illustration: Ken Zillisch

second most popular apple is the Delicious, a favorite eating apple for many people. The McIntosh, which used to be extremely popular, has fallen to third place, probably because it is softer than a Cortland and breaks down faster.

Other varieties to be found at Larson's Orchard include Jonathans, McMahons, Northwest Greenings, Patton Greenings, Dudleys (an old, early apple), Wealthies, and Yellow Transparents. No, he does not grow the popular Granny Smith apples. "They're just a greening apple," Wink laughed. "There's nothing special about it. I think it's just popular because of the name."

About seventy percent of the Larson apples are sold locally through their outlet store. The remaining apples are sold to Michigan processors and the Krier Preserving Company in Sturgeon Bay for sauce or juice.

Two of Wink Larson's touches have made the retail store a popular place. At the end of the driveway sits a huge barrel filled with free sample apples. And inside the store sit a jug of cold cider and an urn of hot cider (freshly pressed at the orchard), again free samples. It is very difficult to sample orchard produce and then leave empty handed.

A showroom full of produce belies the effort and the headaches involved in nurturing and then harvesting the crop. While the cherry industry has become largely mechanized, apples still have to be picked and graded by hand. However, growers of both fruits have come to rely heavily on the findings of horticulturists, such as Dr. Gilbert at the experimental station operated by the University of Wisconsin just north of Sturgeon Bay. Clifford Ehlers, the Door County Horticultural Agent, serves as a clearing house, providing up-to-date recommendations regarding sprays

and fertilizers and time of application that he has gathered from researchers. Sprayers, high pressure affairs using air rather than water to disperse the chemicals have improved, too. Some growers prune with hedging machines, but because they are expensive and not as effective as hand pruning, Larson doesn't use them.

Planting has changed, also. Wink recalls a time in the past when the least productive portion of a farm was reserved for the orchard. He remembers helping his grandfather, John Larson, plant cherry trees. "We'd use a crowbar to chip away at a crevice and then stick in a half stick of dynamite with a wick fuse, light it, run off, and let it blast away just to get a hole to plant a cherry tree in." He laughed. "Then the tree was supposed to grow in that hole!"

One of the biggest problems apple growers face is that the price of apples has not kept up with inflation. Every year the cost of equipment and chemicals escalates, but the $5.00 per bushel wholesale price has remained constant for the last ten years. "It's killing the business," Wink claimed. "With a $40,000 assessment on a 40 acre tract, there is no way you can get a return on your money. You might as well sell off in five or ten acre plots and let people build houses on them."

The productivity of Northern Door soil is a problem, too. It is difficult

illustration: Jan Jablonski

for the peninsula's thin, rocky turf to compete with the rich orchard soil in Michigan.

And, ironically, the mechanization which makes the cherry industry so efficient is also working to kill it. "Imagine how you'd feel if your feet were set in concrete, and then someone came up with a cherry shaker and fastened it onto your leg. It cuts the lifespan of a cherry tree from about 35 years down to 20, and when you remember that it takes six or seven years for a cherry tree to get into production, you're left with only ten to twelve years of production."

While it's difficult for Wink to laugh at the financial worries that plague orchardmen, he can chuckle now at another concern: the intrusion of the bureaucracy into the orchard business. Posted on a wall in one of the administrative offices at the orchard is an eight by ten glossy photo of Wink standing atop a step ladder in front of a Larson Orchard semitrailer. In one hand was a Federal Marketing Order form that he was required to complete. Its twelve foot length fluttered to the ground. In his other hand was a twenty-three foot DNR form which stretched onto the ground in front of him like a bridal train. This photo was distributed via the AP wire service in 1976 and earned Wink national attention.

On another wall is a yellowing news story clipping about bureaucratic visits to the orchard. It seems that fifteen to twenty federal and state inspectors always chose the busy months of summer to make their calls. They would bring along their families or their secretaries,

and mix business with pleasure, at the inconvenience of the orchard growers.

One lady inspector from the Wisconsin Department of Industry and Labor had a physical handicap as a result of a canning factory accident during her youth, and was less than objective and considerably less than pleasant on her summer visits. Wink pointed out to the state that she transported her family to Door County in a state car and dropped them off at the beach on her way to hassle him. As a consequence, she lost her job.

Every year between the fifteenth and twentieth of July, Wink could count on a three or four day federal wage and hour audit. But his last midsummer visit from an auditor was about six years ago. The inspector had arrived on a bad day. Wink already had someone from the DNR sitting at one desk, someone from

"Wink" Larson with his 50 year old apple peeler which peels and cores apples.

OSHA at another, when in he walked, ready to mix business with pleasure. "Get your ass out of here and come back in October when I have time to talk to you!" Wink shouted, shaking his fist. The man left hurriedly, and the two remaining bureaucrats shifted nervously in their chairs.

Two seasons ago three workers that Wink had hired turned out to be, in his estimation, useless and as a consequence, he fired them. The men took advantage of a federal legal aid organization to bring a suit against Wink, and he was forced to pay a settlement to them. Wink wrote out the check, but he also presented the men with a custom built hog trough as a reminder that the bureaucratic "trough" will soon be empty, and then they'll have to fend for themselves.

With the headaches and the diminishing financial return, why would anyone stay in the orchard business? "I don't want to see all of Door County become a subdivision," Wink answered. And he enjoys watching the fruit trees go through their seasonal changes. "They look like they're dead in the winter. Then in spring, you see those little green sprouts, and then the blossoms, and then the little fruit." Anyone who has tended crops or even a garden knows what he means. "I like being a part of nature. It's a clean-cut, fresh life. Other then when you're spraying," he adds with a laugh, "and you finally become immune to the spray dope."

"I like all of the good people you meet in the store," Audrey added, and Wink agreed. Many of the same people come back year after year. "And you get the winters off," Audrey laughed.

However, Wink is not the sort to sit around and relax. He has maintained a broker's license for years, and has recently become more active in real estate work. And he is toying with the idea of making cherry and apple wine at the orchard. "We have the cherry and apple juice," he said, "and the equipment — a German press, vats, pumps, and piping. We just have to go through the legislation." He'd also like to plant some grapes, as a "way to keep some land from being developed as condos."

Of course, Wink still finds time for politics. But while still a Democrat, he is no longer Democratic Party Precinct Committee Chairman, a position he held for many years. He laughed remembering the frustration that accompanied such a job in a county predominantly Republican. "No one wanted to admit to being a Democrat," he laughed. "It used to be a dog could run on the Republican ticket and win by a landslide. But it's changed now."

I asked Wink if he saw any changes coming in his own life, if he was considering retiring from orchard work. "I always said I was going to retire when I was fifty, but I didn't."

illustration: Mike Judy

He laughed. "Of course everyone around here says I've been retired for fifteen years. I'm lucky to have a hard working wife and a hard working son." He laughed again. "No, I have no plans for retirement."

Louis Koessl comes to mind again, animated with memories of orchards from the past. It is said that sailors get the salt sea spray in their blood, and never really leave the seas until death. I suspect that the sap which surges every spring through the limbs of apple and cherry trees gets into the blood of orchardmen as well.

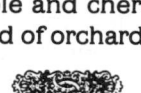

illustration: Jan Jablonski

A portrait of Louis Koessl today

Delbert E. Bingham

Delbert E. Bingham is extensively interested in fruit lands in Wisconsin and his prominence in this field of labor is indicated in the fact that he has been honored with the presidency of the State Historical Society. His knowledge and experience are such as to give him place among the leading fruit growers, and the work that he has performed has constituted an example that many others have profitably followed. A native of Richland County, Wisconsin, he was born on the 21st of August, 1873, a son of George Elisha and Anna (Cheeney) Bingham, who were natives of New York and of Vermont respectively. As young people they came to Wisconsin and in this state George E. Bingham followed the occupation of farming, but at the time of the Civil War he put aside all business and personal considerations and responded to the country's call for troops. His father, George Bingham, also enlisted in defense of the Union and laid down his life on the altar of his country.

Delbert E. Bingham acquired a public school education and when but a boy became interested in fruit growing. He was employed by A.L. Hatch from 1891 until 1895 and in the spring of the latter year came to Door County, where he took charge of the fruit farm which Mr. Hatch was here developing. He started with sixteen acres of European plums and one acre of cherries, planted in 1893. The following year a large number of plum trees were added to the orchard and in 1895 three acres more were planted to cherries. In 1897 he set out ten acres more in cherries and in 1896 he planted twelve acres of

apples. He continued in active connection with Mr. Hatch until 1898, at which time he had developed about forty-five acres of tree fruit and twenty acres of small fruit. The following year Mr. Bingham started out independently as a fruit grower, purchasing fifty acres near Sturgeon Bay. He took over one forty-acre tract of the Hatch & Bingham orchards, which had covered eighty acres. He now has thirty acres in fruit at his home place and he also has large interests in several hundred acres of fruit land, of which he personally manages four hundred and twenty acres. From the beginning he has closely studied every phase of fruit growing relative to soil and climatic conditions as well as nursery stock, and his broad knowledge enables him to speak with authority upon what can best be produced in this section of the country with the most desirable results. His fruit has taken many prizes in county and state fairs and his crops rival any that are produced in Wisconsin. Mr. Bingham was one of the organizers and directors of the Fruit Growers Union, an organization which was formed for marketing the fruit. This phase of the business he has also studied and is perfectly familiar with the best methods of handling the crops. In 1911 he was elected president of the State Horticultural Society, in which position he continued for two years, and his work in behalf of that organization has been a strong feature in its success, for he brought to bear the broadest possible experience and sound judgment.

On the 20th of August, 1895, Mr. Bingham was married to Miss Musa

Hatch, a daughter of A.L. Hatch, and they have become parents of two children, Gale and Murray.

Mr. Bingham belongs to the Knights of Pythias fraternity and his religious faith is evidenced in his membership in the Congregational church. Politically, while he usually votes independently, he has leanings toward the republican party but he does not seek nor desire office, preferring to concentrate his undivided time and attention upon his business affairs. He has done farmers' institute work for nine years and every winter he lectures all over the state, being regarded as one of the fruit experts not only of Wisconsin but also of the country. Not only has he gained broad knowledge of horticulture in its every phase but also gained success by the wisdom and enterprise which he has displayed in fruit raising and is today one of the prosperous residents of Sturgeon Bay.

H.R. Holand's History of Door County 1917

The S.S. Telfers
of Driftwood Farms

In a beautiful setting near Ellison Bay in upper Door County is Driftwood farms, orchard and home of the Sid Telfers, now in its third generation with grandson Lee just home from Service.

Sid Telfer, Sr., has made many contributions to fruit growing in Door County and to the Wisconsin State Horticulture Society. He was on the Board of Directors of the Society for a number of years, was Vice President and President. He was awarded the Honorary Recognition Certificate for his contribution to fruit growing in 1944. In 1943 he was one of the Committee of nine appointed by the Society who met at Green Bay to organize the Wisconsin Apple Institute.

Sid Telfer, Jr., who is now president and manager of Driftwood Farms, is a member of the Board of Directors of the Wisconsin Apple and Horticultural Council and its vice president for 1968.

Sid Telfer, Sr. developed a life-long interest in horticulture at an early age. He attended high school in Ft. Atkinson and worked part time at the Coe, Converse and Edwards Nursery. After studying horticulture at the University of Wisconsin, he and his wife came to Ellison Bay and for 25 years managed the large Ellison Bay Orchard Co. However, in 1932 he started his own orchard.

Driftwood Farms has increased in size considerably since that time by adding other farms and orchards. Beef cattle have been one of the "side lines". Parts of the cherry orchards have been removed, but more apple trees have been planted. Varieties of apples now being grown are principally McIntosh, N.W. Greenings, Cortland, Delicious, Jonathan and a few new varieties.

Marketing the apples is principally in 4 pound bags, sold through the Badger State Apple Corp. of which they are members.

Those who remember the large cherry picking camps and army of pickers in Door County in by-gone years will be interested in this observation by Sid Telfer, Sr., in August 1968: "Have just visited an orchard where they were "shaking" cherries mechanically at the rate of one tree per minute or better. Hand picking of cherries may soon be a thing of the past."

Mr. Telfer was a member of the Board of Directors of the Door County Fruit Growers Cooperative from 1935 to 1962 and was president from 1955 to 1962. The manager of the Co-operative writes: "Under Mr. Telfer's direction, Fruit Growers Co-operative, a grower owned processing and marketing corporation of cherries and apple products, has remained a dynamic force in the nation's food business complex. It is today a growing company and is numbered among the oldest of the canning companies in the State of Wisconsin. The success of the company can be attributed to intelligent, constructive action by the officers and directors.

Published in One Hundred Years
The Wisconsin State Horticultural
Society 1968

Almanacks

THE word Almanack is derived from two Arabic words which mean 'to count'. In one form or another their use is very ancient, but the precise date at which they were first used amongst us is not known. The Library of Lambeth Palace is said to contain an almanack written in 1460. The first printed almanack was published at Buda, and for it the compiler received a handsome present from the King of Hungary. Richard Pynson, in the year 1497, was the first to issue a printed almanack in England. Predictions soon began to be one of the chief features in them, owing, in a great measure, to the success of Michael Nostradamus, who in his almanack was supposed to have predicted the deaths of Charles I of England and Henry II of France, the fire of London, and other great events. Some almanacks are still printed which try, but with little success, to rival his fame.

from Chatterbox 1882

illustration: Martha Coventry

"You've Got To Work It": The Krowas Orchard

by Tom Davis

ARRANGED in neat blocks of cherries, apples and plums, the Krowas Orchard lays atop the height of land west of Kangaroo Lake. It had been a family dairy farm of over 100 acres since shortly after the turn of the century, but Charles Krowas - born there on the place in 1914 - found dairying a struggle simply to make ends meet. "Too many rocks" is how Charles Krowas explains the dairy's demise: it ceased operation in the early 1950s, when the herd and the milking equipment were sold at auction. Krowas hired on at the Christie Corporation shipyard in Sturgeon Bay, working in the yard maintenance crew. He retained ownership of the farmland, his aim being to convert its fields and pastures into orchards when finances allowed.

Charles Krowas is a gentle, amiable man, quick to laugh, with the proverbial twinkle in his pale blue eyes. But he possesses a powerful determination, leaving no doubt he will accomplish whatever he intends. The Krowas Orchard was founded in 1956 with a planting of 500 cherry trees, the tart Montmorency variety used primarily for pie filling, and virtually the only cherry of com-

CHARLES KROWAS ORCHARDS
BAILEYS HARBOR, WIS.

photo: Tom Davis

73

mercial significance grown in Door County. (The Early Richmond cherry was once popular here, but its small size and relative softness proved disadvantageous with the advent of highly mechanized picking and processing.) The orchard was steadily expanded, until a full 20 acres of cherries - about 2,000 trees - had been planted by 1959. In the fall of 1960, 200 Stanley plums, the same variety which dry into prunes in California's more arid climate, were planted in response to plans by the Door County Fruit Growers' Cooperative to begin canning plums. Soon thereafter the Cooperative became defunct, forcing Krowas to create his own market for the fruit, which characteristically he did, through "pick your own" and occasional sales to the Door Peninsula Winery in Carlsville. Apples were first planted in 1961, when 75 McIntosh and Red Delicious trees went in. After more Macs, Red Delicious, and a block of Cortlands had been established, Krowas was among the first to try the Viking apple developed by Dr. Fred Gilbert at the University of Wisconsin's Door County Agricultural Experiment Station located just north of Sturgeon Bay. Named for the Lawrence University Vikings, it is derived from the Jonathan, Red Delicious, Williams Early, Early McIntosh and Star varieties, and is unique because it is a red apple that ripens early (most early-ripening varieties are green.) The orchard's most recent planting, other than the replacement of the played-out cherries (25 years is the maximum useful life of a commercial cherry tree), is a block of Northwest Greening apples - Krowas calls them the "original pie apple" - planted in 1982.

From the first 500 trees in 1956, the Krowas Orchard has swelled to some 5,000 cherry trees covering about 50 acres; 1200 apple trees and approximately 500 plum trees. The number of plum trees has dipped dramatically over the past few years due to a bacterial infection. Unfortunately, knowing only that diseased limbs must be removed immediately if the tree is to survive, the bacteria was unwittingly spread by the saw used to trim infected branches. Not until this past summer did an extension scientist suggest that the saw be sterilized after each use: this practice has apparently helped control the outbreak of the disease.

The orchard's produce is marketed through normal channels. Other than a small coterie of repeat customers who return annually to pick their own cherries, the tart Montmorencies are delivered to the Northern Door cherry plant outside Baileys Harbor or to the Egg Harbor Orchard. Both facilities are connected with Cherry Central in Michigan. Apples are sold directly off the orchard, although in the past some have been distributed through local grocers. Whatever apples are left go to Krier Preserving in Sturgeon Bay to be made into sauce or juice. Plums are strictly a pick-your-own proposition, except when the winery needs a few.

Charles Krowas has tended his orchard lovingly and well, with the help of his wife, Dorothy, and their eight children. Some of the early years were lean, but fortunately Krowas held his position at Christie until the corporation closed its doors in 1969. Considering the day-to-day demands of running an orchard, especially one continuously being enlarged and diversified, it is remarkable that he was able to beautifully maintain his trees and still work full-time elsewhere, even with his family's assistance. The orchardman's year has no definite beginning or end: there are always chores to be done, whether the exciting rush of harvest or the seemingly endless drudgery of pruning. Krowas' philosophy of operating an orchard is simple, straightforward and yet terribly difficult to adhere to. "You've got to work it," he insists. "You can't wait until the prices are good. Every year, regardless of the market, you have to take care of your trees. If you don't, you won't be able to take full advantage when the prices are up. There's no such thing as a quick buck in this business. Success takes time and a lot of work."

That Charles Krowas' words command quiet authority is evident in the outlook of his son Dan, 29 years old and, since 1982, the owner of Krowas Orchard. Dan has inherited much from his father: the manner of speaking, sense of humor, the sense of commitment and responsibility. If anything, Dan's dark eyes betray an inner intensity exceeding Charles'. After two years of training in Green Bay, Dan worked for two years as a draftsman with Appleton Structural Steel, and then two years in the same capacity with Therma-Tron-X of Sturgeon Bay. He enjoyed his work, but the dream of running the orchard recurred too often for him to ignore. While still employed by Therma-Tron-X, he began buying into the orchard, finally deciding in 1978 that it was sufficiently profitable for him to devote his full energies to it.

If the ownership has changed in title, the management of Krowas Orchard has continued in substantially the same fashion. Soil tests are conducted annually, dictating the exact amounts of fertilizer required, virtually on a per tree basis. The fertilizer is measured and applied by hand, perhaps a more time-consuming process than mechanical application, but one that Charles and Dan agree assures the proper portions without waste. The Krowases are also advocates of foliar feeding, applying liquid fertilizer directly to the leaves. Some argue that it is too expensive, but the elder Krowas admits "We never saw it that way. We always gained with it." Dan adds that foliar feeding is especially important in dry years, when the ground-applied fertilizer cannot be absorbed by the root system. Plant micronutrients, elements such as zinc, copper, iron, manganese and magnesium which in very small amounts are vital to a healthy tree, are applied via the foliar method. Pruning takes place throughout the winter and early spring; although the "experts" claim it should wait until March and April, it is physically impossible to prune the number of trees in the orchard in just two months time. The harvest season begins in late July when the cherries ripen, and extends for about three months through the early apples, plums, and late apples. The last two years have seen the harvest officially conclude on October 27.

It is obvious that there is "always something" to do on the Krowas Orchard. But in what Dan and Charles call their "spare time" - usually in winter, when it just doesn't pay to buck the cold and the snow to get in a few hours' pruning - they sequester themselves in their shop to ready implements for spring and summer use. Like the corn producer in Iowa, the orchardman places a tremendous burden of reliance on his equipment. Pronounced changes have occurred over the last 15 years in the technology of orchard operation. The trend, as elsewhere, has been to attempt to generate economies of scale by employing sophisticated, efficient machinery. If the Krowases still insist on doing some jobs the hard way, such as applying fertilizer by hand, they have nevertheless been among the leaders in utilizing and **developing** equipment designed to save time and labor. A great part of the Krowas genius lies in the ability to envision a better technique for accomplishing a certain task and to bring this vision to reality through the application of industry and expertise.

The Krowas machine shop bears little resemblance to the workbench of the weekend tinkerer. The array of tools is staggering, from the familiar wrenches, screwdrivers and drill bits to implements unrecognizable to the uninitiated. Even more impressive, however, is the orderliness: each item seems to be in the correct place; nothing is strewn about haphazardly. But somehow nothing less would be expected of these men. Predictably, Dan assents "Oh, there are a few things it would be nice to have. There's a jointer we've been thinking about."

Charles Krowas starts the portable welder

photo: Tom Davis

Prominent in the shop is a portable arc welder fabricated by Charles. The wheeled frame is built to house a 1930 Chevrolet automobile engine which powers the generator. It goes without saying that the engine starts quickly and runs smoothly. A current project is a log splitter; by no means something ordered in kit form, but a unit being assembled from the ground up. At its heart is a burly Wisconsin engine which will ferociously turn logs into firewood.

One of the first implements Charles Krowas made explicitly for use in the orchard was a tree hole digger he machined in the shop at Christie shipyards. He chuckles when he calls it "a little government job." The business end looks like an anchor with the flukes cut down to half size. It mounts on a three-point tractor hitch, and still performs admirably.

Tired of having to spray each tree with a hand-held gun, Krowas next focused his talents on a tractor-drawn sprayer. He purchased a second-hand sprayer to scavenge the pump, bought a tank, tooled a frame and mounted the entire works along with a Wisconsin engine for power. He added a boom to give the unit the needed reach. The result was a rig incomparably more versatile and efficient than the old method. As the orchard expanded, Krowas built a second sprayer along the same lines. These pump-driven outfits sprayed under about 600 pounds of pressure. Alert to findings that low-pressure spraying (approximately 200 pounds of pressure) provides better coverage on the leaf surface and results in less spray carried off by winds, the unit currently in use depends on a blast blower to drive the spray through twin booms. Solenoid coils - electro-magnetic switching devices - were installed to facilitate independent control of each boom. Despite their technological wizardry, Dan and Charles admit somewhat ruefully that very small trees still require hand spraying.

One of Charles Krowas' less glamorous innovations is nonetheless one of the most important in terms of saving time. For years, the only way to clear prunings and windfalls was to gather them by hand, one by one. This cleanup is a must, not only to allow for navigation but because rotting wood may host unwanted insects. Krowas credits Bill Zahn, the long-time manager of the neighboring Kangaroo Lake

illustration: Jan Jablonski

Orchard, with the idea of using a buck rake designed to pick up windrowed hay to clear brush. Mounted on what Krowas calls a "car tractor" (naturally, he'd made it himself), in one afternoon it cleared apple brush that would have taken a week by hand. He took his "invention" around the county, hiring out to orchardmen tired of handwork. "Not much money in it," he says. Dan laughs "But a lot of fun." Virtually every orchard in Door County now possesses a similar piece of equipment.

When confronted with his achievements, Charles shrugs and talks as if anyone with a mechanical bent and a little knowledge could do the same. "I gained a lot of experience at the shipyard," he says. "I worked in yard maintenance, so I learned about everything: welding, metalwork, plumbing, compressed air, you name it." He conveys the impression that any man not wanting to spend money for an "off the shelf" item, or having an improvement or two in mind, would build his own as well. Only the barest hint of pride or satisfaction emerges when he and Dan discuss their handiwork.

A person swayed by his false modesty would immediately return to his or her senses upon examining what is truly the Krowas's masterpiece: a completely self-propelled cherry tree limb shaker. Before shakers came into widespread use, cherries were picked by hand. As many as one hundred laborers, both local residents and migrant Amerinds, were hired at Krowas Orchard primarily for the cherry harvest. Hand picking took at least three weeks, and labor costs depressed profits dangerously near the break-even point. The mechanized limb shaker was a revelation, but Charles Krowas was still dissatisfied with the normal set up: the shaker itself, a claw-like apparatus which attached to one of the main limbs, was typically mounted on a tractor hitch, while the canvas nets used to collect the fruit were positioned manually around the tree. Krowas was determined to combine these functions in a single unit, and in 1969 designed and constructed his first self-propelled shaker. It had two engines, one strictly to power the shaker, another for locomotion and to drive the elevator, a flat belt located between the two halves of the net used to channel the cherries into boxes or tubs. The shaker could be steered down a row of trees, and the wing-like net halves could be adjusted hydraulically to fully encircle the trunk; "Like an upside-down umbrella," is how Dan Krowas puts it. Dorothy Krowas helped out too: the yards and yards of vinyl-coated nylon that went into the netting were sewed by her on her home machine. The shaker not only cut picking time in half, but labor costs were reduced to practically nil.

This shaker served with distinction for about eight years, but as the trees grew larger the net area proved too small. A new shaker, with more netting, was fabricated in 1977. Nets and hydraulic equipment were purchased new, but much of the unit is made of materials salvaged from a nearby junkyard. The first shaker has been dismantled, but the later version still occupies a large space in the machine shed. Its folded wings suggest a huge katydid composed of a wilderness of engines, drive shafts, gearboxes, hydraulic hoses, connecting rods and framing. It tests the imagination to believe that two men in a backyard shop could produce such a machine - unless you know Dan and Charles Krowas.

The second shaker harvested two seasons' worth of cherries - "It paid for itself," Dan says - when, for once, technology progressed more rapidly than the Krowas' ability to keep up. The trunk shaker came into vogue. Whereas the limb shaker must be repositioned three or four times to grasp each main branch, the trunk shaker need only be placed in a single stance. Dan purchased a trunk shaker from a Michigan firm, and harvest time was again cut in half: some 2,000 bearing trees were picked in five days.

But the purchase of the trunk shaker afforded new territory for invention. The previous shakers had deposited the fruit into boxes or tubs, which were dumped by hand into trailer tanks for transport to a processing facility. With the trunk shaker it became possible to run the cherries directly into a pallet tank which could in turn be loaded onto a flatbed. The only practical method for placing a full pallet tank (weighing a ton) on a flatbed is by using a forklift. Commercially available forklifts were running about $15,000, so in 1978 Dan and Charles built their own. It is a more elongated vehicle than the upright, boxy-looking units seen in warehouses and loading zones. Appearing something like a low-to-the-ground armored car, its white sheet-metal body is trimmed in red. Charles concedes "It was a little tricky to make": what to him is

photo: Tom Davis

Forklift #1

a "little tricky" would halt most mechanics in their tracks, if not send them spinning in an irreversible nervous breakdown. Their second forklift is now ready to roll, not as a replacement to the first but as a complement. They feel even more efficiency can be obtained with two forklifts hauling tanks to their flatbed and fifth-wheel trailers.

What do Dan and Charles Krowas attempt for an encore? They're considering installing a "cooling pad," where cold water could be continuously circulated through tanks awaiting delivery to the processor. Cherries must be cool to enable pitting, and prolonged exposure to warmth can cause the fruit to deteriorate. It's not a question of "if" they'll get it done, simply "when."

In spring, the mild breezes from Kangaroo Lake will open the cherry blossoms on Krowas Orchard a few days earlier than on other orchards, and this same warmth may hold off a damaging late frost. The fruits, invigorated by careful fertilization and the lime found in Door County's rocky soil, will swell and ripen. The Krowases will have worked their orchard hard, not only with machinery but with their hands, and the payoff at harvest will be in more than mere dollars. It will be in the knowledge that what the orchard is giving up is no more - or less - than what they put in.

ᔇᕀᙅᕀᔥ

John Enigl's mother and aunts picking cherries.

A Family Background
In The Cherry Industry

by John Enigl

HE story of my family's involvement in the cherry growing business is probably typical of that of any small grower, except that in my case, I was suddenly thrust from the ranks of a small grower into that of a fair-sized grower. Fortunately, with the help of my newly-wed wife, who had some experience in the cherry growing business, and some neighbors long involved in the industry, we were able to turn the orchard into a profitable venture. Another friend, whose family pioneered in cherry growing, helped greatly.

Mainly, this story will tell you how cherries were handled in the days of hand picking, which is the system we still use with the few cherry trees we have left.

Our orchard was planted in the early or mid 1920's, when a market had already been established for cherry products, both fresh and canned. Many farmers planted a few acres of cherries, just enough so that their own family could pick them for a little extra money.

Some say that my dad planted the three acres of cherries behind our pig and chicken house by plowing a furrow down each row and placing the tree in the furrow and covering up the roots. Whether he did it that way or not, I can't say, since that was about the time I was born. But I must say he got the rows pretty straight, so that we could work up the ground between the trees in both directions, with the horses and drag, and later on, with the old steel-wheeled Fordson tractor. The orchard was about eight trees wide, and about forty trees long, which followed the old rule of one hundred trees to an acre, the trees being about twenty feet from each other. That allowed you to work with an eight foot wide drag between the rows on each side of the trees, without getting so close to them as to chance taking off some bark from the trunks. That would be enough to kill the tree.

Fertilization of the trees was easy enough; no complicated formulas to follow. We used barnyard manure from our twelve or so cows. Some say that still is the best fertilizer to use. We'd pitch the well-rotted manure into the horse or tractor drawn manure spreader and throw the spreader in gear as we entered the orchard. The back wheels of the spreader were geared to the big forked roller in the rear of the spreader, and to an apron or conveyor belt that carried the manure back to the roller. Today when I see a farmer headed out to an orchard with a manure spreader, on a rainy day, or on wet ground, I think to myself, 'You'd never do that in the old days. The draft of the back wheels would get both spreader and tractor mired down." But today, with power take-off spreaders, there is no drag except for the weight of the load. Still they get mired down at times.

Besides working the orchard with the old Fordson and the drag and the disk, the first job I can remember in the spring was spraying the orchard.

The first sprayer we owned was one you pumped by hand, much like the old fashioned well pumps. This pump was mounted on top of a 55 gallon wooden barrel, and it created enough pressure to expel a fine mist from the nozzle of the hand spray gun attached to the pump by a rubber hose. The unit was mounted on a sledge pulled along the ground by one of our horses.

While the cherry trees were still in bloom, we sprayed the trees with a fungicide to combat what we call today cherry leaf spot. We called it yellow leaf then, not knowing the fancy name already given the disease by the Extension Service of the Wisconsin Department of Agriculture.

I can recall that preparation of the spray material was not as easy as it is today. We used a fungicide known as Bordeaux Mixture. It was composed of a chemical called blue vitriol, which I learned later in chemistry class in high school was copper sulphate. (I found it could be used to copperplate iron.)

CHERRY STONER

In those days (the early 1930's) the copper sulphate came in crystals, and it had to be soaked in water overnight before it could be used in the Bordeaux Mixture. As anyone knows who has taken a chemistry course, the slowest way to make a solution is to use the crystals of a chemical and cold water. So later on, you could buy the blue vitriol in crushed and powdered form, each progressively easier to dissolve; we "learned" this later in chemistry class. Just one of those things that I learned on the farm that made college, university, and engineering school meaningful to me in later years, and that helped me in my teaching career.

The other ingredient of the Bordeaux Mixture was lime. Today you buy slaked lime, a powdered

"Farmer Bill" Lawrence spraying apples, 1921.

hydrated calcium product, in a bag. Then, in the late 1920's and early 1930's, you bought unslaked lime, a chunky white rock like substance made from limestone rock that had been baked in a lime kiln until all the water had been driven off.

To make the Bordeaux Mixture, you had to mix the unslaked lime with water. We never knew about the danger of the fizzing, foaming compound you got when water was added to the unslaked lime. (The reaction from changing calcium oxide to calcium hydroxide produced a good deal of heat and splashed out into the air.) A mason who built the house where my wife lived before we were married never got to see the house, because he was blinded by the lime he was going to use for mortar for the stone blocks in the foundation.

While the trees were still in bloom, you didn't use anything but a fungicide on the cherry trees, because an insecticide would kill the bees which helped so much in pollination. In the second spray, we would use arsenate of lead, a very powerful insecticide. Again, we got no training about the danger of using this poison. But we got some idea that it would not be smart to eat it, and when the play, "Arsenic and Old Lace," came out, we knew what the playwright was talking about.

About 1940, our trees were becoming quite large, and it became quite a chore to spray them with the old barrel sprayer. So my dad decided to exchange my labor with a neighbor, Albert Kroll, to get our orchard sprayed in a faster way.

Al had a fair sized orchard of ten

81

(l. to r.) John Enigl, Al Kroll, Frank Kroll next to 1923 Meyers Sprayer on the Kroll farm 1940.

or fifteen acres on a farm about a mile north of our place, which is near Carlsville. The Krolls and Enigls had known each other in Austria, so we were good friends. Al owned a Meyers sprayer built about 1921, with about 200 gallons capacity, with a single cylinder gasoline engine to power it, and a Meyers pump. The pump developed about two hundred pounds of pressure, which gave quite adequate coverage of the trees.

The sprayer was originally designed to be pulled by a team of horses, but, as with many such units of farm machinery, the pole had been cut off and fitted with a hitch for a tractor. Al's tractor was a later model Fordson than ours, and I always marveled that it started with the first lift of the hand crank. His model had a high-tension magneto, where ours had the old Model T Ford system with a timer and four ignition coils, which always gave trouble. He would let me drive the tractor, while Al and his brother, Frank, would handle the spray guns on top of the sprayer. That is, until I clipped off one of the small trees by making a too-tight turn. After that, I got to handle one of the spray guns, which meant that I got full of the spray material which coated Frank and me with a white film.

With the kind of equipment we had, the job took a couple of days each time. What I enjoyed most, was the good meals Marie Kroll, Al's wife, had ready for us promptly at noon. There was always plenty of delicious meat, raised on the Kroll farm; hot mashed potatoes, and fresh vegetables from the Kroll garden, topped with cake and strawberries as dessert.

Those days I spent helping the Krolls spray their orchard were pleasant ones I shall always remember fondly. The young couple, Al and Marie, had an ideal farm life, it seemed to me, with a nice herd of dairy cows as well as the orchard. (Very few people depended on cherries alone for a living.) Al was to die at the young age of 51, his funeral ending just as the first news of the death of President Kennedy was announced to some of the mourners. Marie and Frank are gone also. But for a while they had it all.

In return for my labor, Al would come over and spray our three acres of trees, which didn't take long. Starting in 1941, we pulled the sprayer with our new John Deere tractor, which impressed Al so much by its ease of operation, that he went out and bought one himself.

Al's tractor was a model with the wheels wide apart in the front, which worked much better for making turns than our tricycle model. Some orchard owners bought orchard model tractors, which had special skirted fenders over the wheels that would allow the branches to pass over the wheels without being pulled off the trees.

Picking cherries in our orchard was done mostly by our family members until the 1950's. My mother's sisters from Chicago and their children would assist. This would give the sisters a chance to talk together in Norwegian about all the happenings of the past year. That was very convenient for them, because they could busy themselves stripping the cherries off the trees and putting them into the five quart pails unique to Door County, and we children wouldn't know what they were talking about. In my brother Charles' and my case, having an Austrian father, we never learned the language. (He's learned it now, in anticipation of a trip to Norway.)

Cherry picking time was a time for getting to know our cousins better, and broadening our view of the world.

Cousin Charles Mueller would come from Chicago; I first recall picking cherries with him in 1932,

and his telling me about his young friend, George Goebel, who played and sang on the National Barn Dance on WLS. From Charles we found out about the World's Fair in 1933. Through the years my brother and I became fast friends with cousin Charles, a friendship started in those cherry picking days. In September of 1939, I went back with him to Chicago, and he showed me all the sights — the Museum of Science and Industry, Field Museum, Chinatown. Then one day we saw the headlines in the Chicago Tribune telling of the beginning of the war that changed all our lives. Charles' college plans were to be shelved for a career in the army that was to last into the 1970's.

Other cousins, from Pennsylvania, would come to visit and help with the cherry harvest; World War II ended their visits, too. By that time my brother and I were big enough to be able to harvest the crop pretty much without outside help since our parents picked too.

One incident I remember from the 1930's, in the midst of the Great Depression, concerns picking cherries with the stems on. One morning a man came into our orchard and offered to buy a large amount of cherries if we would pick them on stem, as they were sold in the fresh

Sorting cherries in the orchard.

fruit market.

We worked hard all day, my Aunt Inga and cousin Charles assisting, to pick the cherries on stem which requires a special twist of the fingers to remove the cherries from the branch. After this tedious labor, the man returned at the end of the day to pick up the cherries.

But he had no money! He wanted us to give him, a perfect stranger, the load of cherries and he would return with the money when he sold them.

My parents wouldn't go for that, but the man thought he had us over a barrel. However, we told him it was no deal, and he left. Then we spent the next couple of hours picking off the stems so the fruit could be taken to the Reynolds factory. I can recall all of us working on that thankless job, out by the barn, grumbling about the man who had almost bilked us.

A typical cherry season in the old days started with the working and fertilizing as well as spraying the orchard. But the fall or winter before, the trees were pruned.

Pruning is an operation whereby unwanted branches are cut out of the trees. Either Grandfather or Dad did this important job. The recommended procedure was to trim the cherry trees for an open center. If not pruned, a cherry tree will grow straight up, with a central trunk, and little branches will stick out from the central trunk.

That is a poor way for a cherry tree used for fruit to grow, for the tree will be too high to pick. Also, the cherries will ripen better if the center is kept open. So in pruning you cut out the central trunk and train the branches to grow out from the trunk to the sides at about a 45 degree angle. You also cut out any branches that rub on each other.

I never learned to prune cherry trees at home. I learned at Sevastopol High School from my vocational agriculture teacher, Glem Habermann, who I consider one of the best and most influential teachers I ever had.

Glem had a philosophy about pruning. He felt that one should cut branches heavily, so that you ended up with three or four limbs coming out from the center. He felt that the added room would allow smaller branches to form on the limb, and that you would thus have more spurs to produce cherries.

Well, one day I came home from school and decided to prune the orchard, and I got through about 35 trees before my dad found out what I was doing. I got bawled out for doing what my teacher suggested; but those 35 trees survived for many years after the rest of the trees died, the last one living for over 50 years. The average life of a cherry tree is 30 to 35 years. The pruned trees produced well, too, since their energy wasn't put into growing limbs.

In 1941, the federal government tied up the entire crop which had been canned by the processor to whom we took most of our cherry crop, Reynolds Brothers. Their source of funds frozen, the family reorganized the company, even mortgaging some of the stockholder's homes, in order to keep the company going. Then the government announced that it would buy all the cherries Reynolds could can, for the armed forces, assuring them a ready made market for the duration of the war.

1946 and 1948 saw the resumption of cherry product sales on the civilian market, and also two years of the highest prices, coupled with big crops, ever seen in Door County. I remember the 1936 crop, when only the bottom limbs of the trees that had been covered by snow to protect them from the harsh winter had cherries. In that depression year, we only got 1¢ a pound for the crop. I think the price in 1948 was 16½ cents a pound. That year, the farmers chuckled over the fact that the fruit they hauled in was worth more than the truck itself. (You could buy a new pickup truck in 1948 for about $800.)

The prospect of better prices for cherries, and the fact that we had some land too rocky to grow anything else, prompted my dad to plant 500 cherry trees in a new orchard in 1945. This orchard he laid out in a pattern I didn't recognize until long after he died and the trees were quite large. Every fifth row was a little wider than the rest, to allow access with a truck. Yet you could work the rows either north and south, east and west, or crossways, diagonally, with an eight foot wide drag or disk, the rows were so straight.

In 1952 Dad added another 500 trees, making a block of ten acres.

Even after I attended college and started teaching, I couldn't get away from the cherry industry.

My first teaching position had been on Washington Island. For a summer job in 1950, I converted my car into a tour cab, and picked up fares at the ferry dock, even though I had moved on to teach in another community by then.

One day, tired of going along with the tourists through the Island museum each day, I took a walk down a nearby road through the woods. I passed the cabin once owned by world reknowned economist, Thorstein Veblen, and met a distinguished older gentleman on the road. He explained that he was a psychiatrist from Milwaukee.

He told me that he owned an orchard on the Island, a cherry orchard, near Boyer's Bluff. He said his son had run the orchard that summer, but had been concentrating so much on having a good time, that

he neglected to spray the trees with the proper spray materials at the proper time. Consequently, all the cherries were found to have a little worm inside of them, the worm being known as the plum tree curculio.

I told the doctor that I had grown up with cherry orchards, and he asked me if I would like to have the use of the orchard free for two years if I would only take care of it. Having found the tour business lots of fun, but not too profitable, I decided to take him up on the offer.

So in the spring of 1951, I left for the Island, taking with me a young lad that had just graduated from eighth grade a few days before, from a local parochial school. I had met him at his brother's high school graduation party and told him about the wonders and profitability of cherry picking, so he agreed to come along with me to care for the orchard.

I had cut down a 1933 Ford Model B to use as a farm truck, making the transformation in the school shop. (The vehicle was a rare four cylinder model, as most '33 Fords were V-8s; I was told there were only 2000 of them made at the beginning of the production year. But it was just a vehicle for a job to me, so I cut it down, and threw the rest of the body away after I put in a truck box. A few years back, I sold the truck to a car buff in Oshkosh, along with an extra body that I had bought when I thought I would have the ambition to restore it.) Quite a few small cherry growers used to build these converted vehicles, usually out of Model T or Model A Fords, to serve as a cherry hauler for the one time during the year they had need for a pickup truck.

When school was out, I took my young friend up to the Island with me. We arrived there in the evening, with plans to spend our first night on the Island in Dr. McCoy's garage, where he said we could stay. There was a loft up above the place where he kept his sprayer. He told us if he wasn't on the Island (sometimes his patients' emotional needs demanded that he stay in Milwaukee) we should get the key from Jens Jacobsen, who owned the museum next to McCoy's cottage.

The museum was closed, so we went over to Jacobsen's house to get the key to the garage, but Jens was reluctant to give it to us, since he knew only the barest details of the deal I had struck with McCoy. He finally agreed to go along with us to unlock the garage; but due to the late hour, and in consideration of his advanced age, (in the eighties) we told him we would make other arrangements for the night.

So we went down to the McCoy property at Little Lake and pried the lock off the garage and cleared a place in the loft where we could sleep for the night. Locks were an unnecessary thing on the Island anyway, and carelessly installed. The Islanders didn't bother to lock their doors or take their keys out of their cars. They were so honest with one another that they figured that if anyone wanted to use their car or enter their house without their knowledge, it must be for a good reason. We knew we had a right to be where we were, anyway.

The next day, we decided it would be better to set up our headquarters right at the orchard, which wasn't far from Little Lake, but which had to be reached by a round-about route. My young helper had brought along a tent, and there was a little storage shed at the entrance to the orchard with a cot in it. I cleared out the shed and made room for my things.

We cooked our meals over a campfire, and I made good use of my self-taught training as scoutmaster of the Island scout troop for the two years before. We had to buy food frequently, since we had no refrigerator. Living was cheap; Hans and I would go out to Jackson Harbor and catch as many perch as we thought we could eat and come back and fry them while they were fresh. Later on, when I brought some boys up from my school to pick cherries, we divided up the cost of food, and it came to two dollars a week.

My young friend Hans and I found the orchard sprayer in McCoy's garage, and filled it up at Thorstein Veblen's well. I had brought along the spray materials I needed, not any of the new stuff which I thought might have been responsible for young McCoy's having a crop of worms. I brought good old fashioned copper sulphate and lime, both of them powdered, which enable them to go into solution more easily than in the old forms I mentioned before. For the insecticide, I used arsenate of lead.

The trees did well that summer, with no sign of worms. Instead of working the orchard, I had a farmer come in and cut the grass before picking time. For the three sprayings, I pulled the sprayer through the orchard with my cut-off 1933 Ford. I had painted it pea-green, like a John Deere tractor, and the Islanders called it the "Green Grasshopper." But after the first spraying, it became coated with the light blue copper sulphate spray, which was almost impossible to remove, from iron as well as hands and faces. The same thing had happened to our brand new John Deere tractor in 1941. There was nothing you could do to prevent it.

When it came time to pick the crop, I went down to the town where I was teaching at the time and picked up the rest of my cherry picking crew. I found that the only processor that handled the few cherries coming off Washington Island was the Fruit

Grower's Cooperative in Sturgeon Bay.

I was a bit wary of any dealings with the Co-op, for my father had told me that when the Fruit Grower's Union, its predecessor, had gone under in 1932 or 1933, anyone who owned stock had to pay up for part of its losses. You automatically became a stockholder in the Co-op when you sold cherries there.

Because of the cooling effect of Lake Michigan, the trees had bloomed about two weeks later than those back in the home orchard in Egg Harbor, around the first week in June. In this most northern of all the orchards in Door County, and therefore in all of Wisconsin, the crop was ready to harvest around the first of August. This worked out fine for me, because in the meantime, between the first spraying and picking, I took off for summer school in Oshkosh. When summer school was over, it was just about time to pick the crop.

My imported boys thought it would be great fun to pick cherries, and I recruited a few Island boys to help. But the Island boys were fishermen's sons, and not used to such a mundane way of earning money, compared to the adventure and danger of helping out a fish tug. After a few days they disappeared and could not be found.

My crew from the town where I taught couldn't quit as easily, because they were far from home, and had no way to get home except if they finished the job.

They did have a little fun, though around the campfire at night. One night I took them "up the road" as they call it on the Island, and left them over at Tom Nelson's pool hall to attend a party over at Freddie Mann's to which I had been invited.

Several hours later, being unsuspecting and in my twenties, I had fallen under the spell of Freddie's dandelion wine to a small degree. I went to pick up my boys, Gunnar Nelson complained that I really shouldn't have left the boys alone in the pool hall that long; but the Island boys did it all the time so I had thought it was o.k.

We'd pick the cherries in the usual five quart black pails, and at the end of the day, the boxes into which we put them into my truck. We'd haul the boxes down to the ferry dock, where they'd be loaded for their trip across to the mainland. From there they'd be sent to Fruit Grower's factory to be canned, in Sturgeon Bay.

A sidelight is that the Fruit Grower's always took a long time to pay. You would get a little bit the first year, to pay the pickers. The next year you would get a little more. It might be three or four years before you would get it all; it depended on how fast the manager sold the crop. He didn't have to hurry; the members, it seemed, were happy to wait, knowing it was their own company they were waiting on. To me, it seemed that this was a funny way to do business, and I wouldn't have dealt with the cooperative if it hadn't been the only processor to take the Island cherries. Many other growers felt the same way, (although most co-op members were fiercely loyal), and after the Fruit Grower's Cooperative finally broke up, many growers were still wary of the name. A new business, a corporation, Door County Fruit Growers, still has to explain to growers that it has no connection with the old Fruit Grower's Cooperative. I still have some worthless Fruit Grower's Cooperative stock which I was obliged to take instead of money.

My boys and I finally got the crop off, although the last day, my pickers had gotten so homesick that they asked their parents to come up and pick them up at the ferry dock on the mainland. I had to finish picking the crop all by myself. That is the only time I picked forty pails of cherries in one day.

I operated the McCoy orchard one more summer, and then abandoned the Island venture. During the next few summers, I pruned the home orchard, which had fallen into neglect since my dad had gone to work again in the shipyard. For the summer of 1954, I worked in the Reynolds factory as a manual laborer, and in 1957, I was timekeeper for all the factory workers.

In 1957, both my parents died suddenly, and I bought out my brother's share of the farm. Two years later, I married a lady whose family also had a good deal of experience in the cherry business. With the help of a former teacher of mine, Sarah Daubner, and her husband Marvin, we learned how to handle a large orchard. For many years, another friend, Fred Berger, did most of the orchard work for us while I was teaching, and we took care of the summer work and picking.

The home orchard now has been reduced to somewhere around 100 trees, but Mary Ann and I still look forward to cherry season and all the fond memories it has for us.

ARTHUR L. HATCH

Arthur L. Hatch, deceased, was one of the best known horticulturists of Wisconsin and one of the first three men in the state to receive recognition from the State University for services rendered in the development of horticultural and agricultural interests here. He well merited the honors which were conferred upon him, as his life was one of great usefulness and constituted a contributing factor to that progress of which Wisconsin has every reason to be proud.

Mr. Hatch was born in Sherburne, Chenango County, New York, March 25, 1846, and his life record spanned the intervening years to the 19th of February, 1916. His parents were W.A. and Amanda (Stewart) Hatch. In the maternal line he was a great-grandson of Oliver Stewart, a Revolutionary war soldier. His father was a blacksmith by trade and after spending a goodly portion of his married life in the Empire state he brought his family to Wisconsin in 1856, settling at Lloyd, Richland County, where he engaged in blacksmithing and also cleared up a farm. There he resided until his death, which occurred when he had reached the very venerable age of ninety-four years.

Arthur L. Hatch was a little lad of ten summers at the time of the removal to this state and he attended the public schools of Lloyd, the high school of Richland Center, Wisconsin, and the schools of Sextonville, this state. He afterward took up the profession of teaching, which he followed for a few years, and in 1871 he turned his attention to the nursery business at Ithaca, Wisconsin, in connection with S.I.

Freeborn. He remained in that business for about twenty years and also owned a large fruit farm there, which he cultivated for a few years after disposing of his nursery business.

Mr. Hatch came to Door County in 1891 to investigate the possibilities for fruit growing in this district and the following year he purchased a tract of land in Sevastopol township in connection with Professor E.S. Goff, of Madison. Upon this land he planted the first cherry trees in Door County and proved that this industry could be profitably carried on here in a commercial way. As a result of his labors and influence there are thousands of acres of cherry orchards now in Door County. In 1893 his son-in-law, D.E. Bingham, took up his abode upon the place and began its development, which was continued under the supervision of Mr. Hatch. The latter in 1898 sold his home in Richland County to Professor Goff and purchased the latter's interest in the farm in Door County, to which he removed. Mr. Hatch had long been a close student of questions relating to Wisconsin's development as a horticultural state and came to be recognized as an authority upon fruit raising in Wisconsin. He successfully instituted many experiments and, basing his work upon scientific knowledge, experience and sound judgment, these were attended with success. He was one of the first three men in Wisconsin to win recognition from the State University, a recognition that was similar to the degree of L.L. D. when conferred by colleges upon men eminent in public life. He was very active in instruction work for the State University and was again and again called upon to address public meetings upon questions in

which he was deeply interested. He made a scientific study of the soil and climatic conditions and of the best methods of producing fruit and other crops in this state, being thus able to give expert opinion upon such questions.

On the 26th of January, 1873, Mr. Hatch was married to Miss Clara E. Taplin, a native of Canada and a daughter of R.G. and Evaline (Cilley) Taplin. Their children are Musa, the wife of D.E. Bingham, of Door County, by whom she has two children, Gail and Murray; Bernice, the wife of F.M. McCullough, of Pittsburgh, Pennsylvania; and Eva, the wife of H.W. Ullsperger, of Door County.

Mr. Hatch gave his political endorsement to the republican party, but was never ambitious to hold office. He was president of the Door County Park and Driveway Association and he was interested in all phases of public life affecting the general welfare of city, county and state. He was ever a man of action rather than of theory. His opinions were never hastily given, but were the outcome of careful consideration and as a horticulturist his contribution to the world's work was indeed valuable.

H.R. Holand's History of Door County 1917

Joseph Zettel

Prominent among the early settlers of Door County was Joseph Zettel, who was one of the first to turn his attention to fruit growing in this region, and in that line of endeavor he met with most excellent success. He was born in Canton, Lucerne, Switzerland, on the 26th of November, 1832, and was a son of Joseph and Mary Josepha (Rosly) Zettel, who spent their entire lives in that country. The father was an innkeeper and he also served as judge of the circuit court and as captain in the reserve army. When our subject was seventeen years of age his mother died and his father subsequently married again. When a young man he came to the new world, leaving his old home on the 27th of March, 1853, and landing in New York after a trip of fifty-three days. For the following two years he was employed in railroad construction work and on farms in various places.

It was in 1855 that Mr. Zettel arrived in Door County, Wisconsin, and for some time he worked in sawmills and lime kilns, but in the spring of 1857 begain clearing a tract of land which he had purchased on section 11, Sevastopol township. Later he sold this tract, however, and bought other land on section 27, the same township. In time he cleared this tract of timber and underbrush and converted it into a very desirable farm. His first buildings were of a primitive character, but these were subsequently replaced by excellent farm buildings. He soon discovered that the soil was adapted to fruit growing and planted apple, pear and other fruit trees. Under his scientific care they flourished, and in 1892 his orchard yielded three thousand bushels of apples. At the World's Fair in Chicago his displays attracted great attention. His orchard at that time was the largest in the state and he was the first fruit grower in Door County. It was his success that inspired others to engage in the same occupation until now fruit growing has become one of the most important industries of the county.

On the 28th of July, 1861, Mr. Zettel was united in marriage to Miss Christina Lorch, a native of Germany, born December 9, 1842, and a daughter of Christof and Margaretha (Leonhardt) Lorch. Her father died in Germany but in 1855 her mother came to the United States and located in Door County, Wisconsin. The children born to Mr. and Mrs. Zettel are as follows: Christina, the deceased wife of James Aznoe; Philip A., a resident of Sturgeon Bay; Joseph, of Milwaukee; Alfred, of Sevastopol township; Henry, of Sturgeon Bay township; Jacob, of Sevastopol township; Julius, whose sketch appears elsewhere in this work; Mrs. Catherine Grass, of Door County; Mrs. Louisa Strom, of Milwaukee; Mina, a resident of Door County; and Lillian, deceased.

Mr. Zettel took an active interest in public affairs and by his ballot supported the men and measures of the democratic party. His fellow citizens, recognizing his worth and ability, called upon him to fill a number of township offices, the duties of which he discharged in a most capable manner. He was one of the county's most successful men and was held in the highest esteem by all who knew him. After a useful and well spent life he passed away on the 11th of March, 1904, at the old homestead, and his wife died there December 27, 1915. Both were laid to rest in Bayside cemetery.

H.R. Holand's History of Door County 1917

FREDDIE AND THE CHERRY–TREE.

FREDDIE saw some fine ripe cherries
    Hanging on a cherry-tree,
    And he said, " You pretty cherries,
Will you not come down to me ? "

" Thank you kindly," said a cherry,
    " We would rather stay up here ;
If we ventured down this morning,
    You would eat us up, I fear."

One, the finest of the cherries,
    Dangled from a slender twig,
" You are beautiful," said Freddie,
    " Red and ripe, and oh, how big ! "

" Catch me," said the cherry, " catch me,
    Little master, if you can,"
" I would catch you soon," said Freddie,
    " If I were a grown-up man."

Freddie jumped, and tried to reach it,
    Standing high upon his toes ;
But the cherry bobbed about,
    And laughed, and tickled Freddie's nose.

" Never mind," said little Freddie,
    " I shall have them when it's right."
But a blackbird whistled boldly,
    " I shall eat them all to-night."

POETRY FOR CHILDREN.

The Legend of Johnny Appleseed

John Chapman was born in Massachusetts as near to 1775 as can be reckoned. Legends soon grow out of half-known truth about ordinary people, but in this case, the man was genuinely one of a kind and deserved to become legend.

He had a sincere wish that all persons in the west would be able, at some point in their lives, to partake of an apple. To eat a sweet, ripe fruit off an apple tree like they did in the east, free of charge, wherever their circumstances led them.

So he devised a plan. Just himself on his short legs would travel the back country, and when possible, plant apple seeds. The country being so new made Johnny's task a formidable one, considering the back country was all lands west of the Shenandoah Valley. But he set out, barefoot, with only a sack slung over his back filled with the seeds from the cider mill, and his cooking pot stored neatly on his head.

Apple seeds needed special care, so whenever Johnny happened to meet some pilgrims settling in, and if they were interested, Johnny would show them how to care for the tiny trees. He'd carry the saplings in small deerskin sacks tied with a cord. He'd investigate the soil, dig a hole with any available stone, and lovingly nest the trees in the ground. He'd stay for weeks, teaching them how to nurture the new orchard. Johnny could tell many a wise tale from his travels,

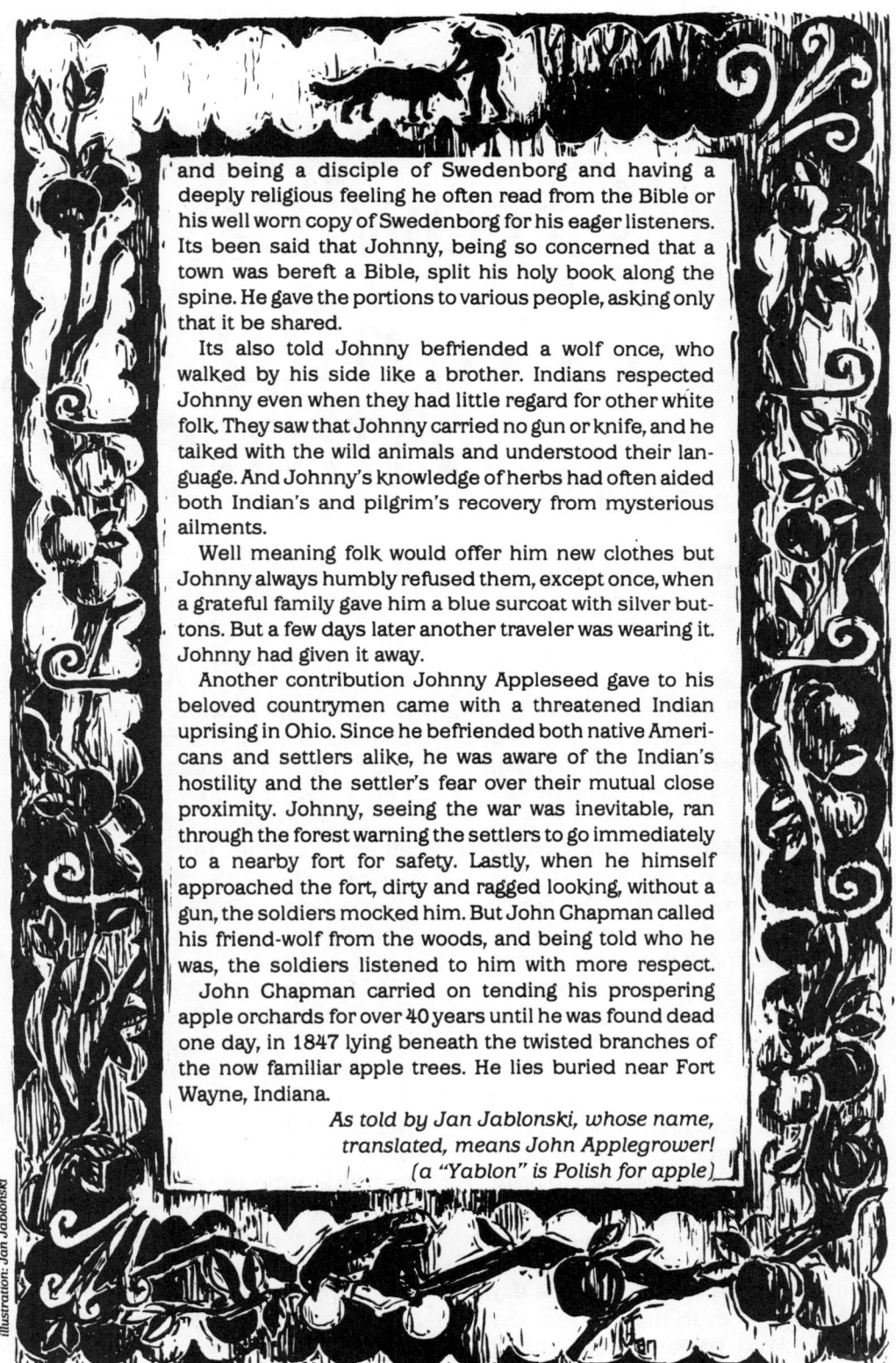

and being a disciple of Swedenborg and having a deeply religious feeling he often read from the Bible or his well worn copy of Swedenborg for his eager listeners. Its been said that Johnny, being so concerned that a town was bereft a Bible, split his holy book along the spine. He gave the portions to various people, asking only that it be shared.

Its also told Johnny befriended a wolf once, who walked by his side like a brother. Indians respected Johnny even when they had little regard for other white folk. They saw that Johnny carried no gun or knife, and he talked with the wild animals and understood their language. And Johnny's knowledge of herbs had often aided both Indian's and pilgrim's recovery from mysterious ailments.

Well meaning folk would offer him new clothes but Johnny always humbly refused them, except once, when a grateful family gave him a blue surcoat with silver buttons. But a few days later another traveler was wearing it. Johnny had given it away.

Another contribution Johnny Appleseed gave to his beloved countrymen came with a threatened Indian uprising in Ohio. Since he befriended both native Americans and settlers alike, he was aware of the Indian's hostility and the settler's fear over their mutual close proximity. Johnny, seeing the war was inevitable, ran through the forest warning the settlers to go immediately to a nearby fort for safety. Lastly, when he himself approached the fort, dirty and ragged looking, without a gun, the soldiers mocked him. But John Chapman called his friend-wolf from the woods, and being told who he was, the soldiers listened to him with more respect.

John Chapman carried on tending his prospering apple orchards for over 40 years until he was found dead one day, in 1847 lying beneath the twisted branches of the now familiar apple trees. He lies buried near Fort Wayne, Indiana.

As told by Jan Jablonski, whose name,
translated, means John Applegrower!
(a "Yablon" is Polish for apple)

illustration: Jan Jablonski

Cherry Growing A Family Affair

by John Enigl

LTHOUGH my brother and I had grown up on a farm with a cherry orchard, I never expected to own an orchard of my own. But, suddenly, with the death of both of our parents in 1957, I was plunged into a larger orchard operation than my parents or I ever realized it was going to be.

My dad and mother had planted their first cherry orchard of three acres in the mid-1920's. The family had always been able to handle the care and picking of the orchard, since the harvest season was extended over a two or three week period. That little orchard, even with the low price of cherries in the 1930's, often paid the taxes for the whole farm. So as the cherry trees got older, with the prospect of them producing for ten years or so more, our folks decided to plant a new orchard. A piece of land too gravelly to farm economically was selected for that purpose. My dad pointed out the spot to me one day as we drove over the field in the Model A Ford, back in 1944.

The higher prices of cherries during the war years and immediately thereafter encouraged our parents to go ahead with the project. In 1945, our dad planted 500 Montmorency cherry trees, and, in 1952, another 500 trees. At 100 trees to an acre, that made two five acre blocks, not a large orchard, but not a small one either. Since it wasn't my orchard, I suppose I never gave it a thought that it would require considerably more time and effort to operate than the old one.

When our parents died, my brother Charles and I inherited the farm. He decided he wanted to sell out his share, so I bought it.

A few years before, during my summer vacation from teaching, I decided to prune all the 1000 trees properly. The 1945 trees were then nine or ten years old and somewhat neglected because my father had been called back to the shipyard and had little time to farm. So I pruned all the trees into the proper open center shape, and repaired the old Meyers orchard sprayer.

The sprayer was a model from the 1920's with wooden slats covering the sides of the engine, and a wooden tank holding about 100 gallons of water. The original one cylinder engine had been replaced by the previous owner with a 1928 Chevrolet automobile engine. It was common practice to do this sort of thing when you built a saw rig or power supply for a hammermill or even a welder. A homemade governor, either one controlled by the wind from the fan, or one which had flying balls and worked by centrifugal force would give the engine more gasoline if the speed slowed down. There were commercial units built as power supplies, but most farmers soon found out how to make their own more cheaply than if they would buy one. Times were tough in the 1930's and you found ways to do things more cheaply than in better times, or do without.

By the 1950's, it became difficult to get parts for a 1928 Chevrolet engine, so I converted the sprayer pump engine over to a Model A Ford engine. Even in the mid-1950's, Model A Fords were beginning to be a collector's item, with at least 30,000 in use at the present time, so parts availability was very good then and is even better today.

Cleaning cherry boxes

In 1955, my dad had planted a large acreage of hay, and that led to a solution to a problem that came up with the planting of the new orchard. We had about 2000 bales of hay out in the field, we didn't look forward to loading all those on the wagon and hauling them into the barn, especially in the hot July sun.

We had just started our arduous job, when a little Nash Metropolitan drove into the yard carrying five Indians and a white friend of theirs. They asked if we had any work that needed to be done. We told them we sure did, and by the afternoon all the hay was safely under cover.

At supper that night, the Indians told us if we needed cherry pickers for the orchard that was now getting quite large, they had relatives in the area that could help us out. So that summer of 1955 we hired several Door County Indian families, all related to one another, to pick the remaining cherries in our old orchard and in the young five acre plot planted in 1945. The 1952 planting wasn't ready to be picked yet.

One of the Indians who worked for us was old Dan Wayse, who was considered somewhat of a grandfather figure by his relatives. He was the son of an ordained Baptist minister. Very dark, a huge man, Dan charmed us with his stories of his father's efforts to bring Christianity to his fellow Indians, some of whom still followed the worship of the Great Spirit as practiced by their forefathers. For a while, he lived with my parents in their garage and ate with them, and helped around the farm.

Years later, in the 1960's, after I bought my brother's share of the orchard, a Texas state patrol car came out into our orchard, complete with two Texas Rangers. They told us they were looking for illegal aliens, "wetbacks." They looked suspiciously at our darked-skinned friends, and asked if we had employed any "Mexicans".

I said, "You don't hear anyone speaking Spanish, do you?"

All our workers were long-time Door County residents (certainly they weren't the immigrants.) Their ancestors hunted on our land hundreds of years before the white man

came; we found an arrowhead to prove that.

The summer after our folks died, in 1957, being unmarried, I lived in the house alone. I was hired as time-keeper for the Reynold's Preserving Company, a job which required being on duty from 18 to 20 hours a day. Therefore, I had no time to get a crew together so I had Reynold's crew come to harvest the cherry crop. That summer the final details were worked out for the purchase of my brother's share of the farm, a decision I have never regretted.

Shortly thereafter, I contacted a friend, Fred Berger, to roof the barn, a job my folks had asked him to do. Working on the roof led to my asking Fred to take care of the orchard, too, while I was teaching. He was 60 years old when he first started working for me, and he continued to work in the orchard until he was almost 80 years old, when he decided he should take it a little easier.

1947 Chev truck loaded with cherry ladders

In 1959, I married Mary Ann Notz, who was a teller at the Bank of Sturgeon Bay. Her mother and dad had come from Oconto to Door County during World War II. He had worked in the shipyard and his wife had managed a rooming house for shipyard workers. After the war, they bought a farm with a small cherry orchard. Gust Notz, whom I never met, died while he was a guard for the Reynolds Preserving Company in 1949. Before we were married, Mary Ann lived with a sister at Fred Fleischmann's, where Sturgeon Bay's Park Du Chateau subdivision is now, and where Fred had a large cherry orchard. So Mary Ann brought along some valuable background in the cherry business.

We left the orchard in charge of Fred Berger, while we took a wedding trip to Wyoming, Nevada, Utah, Arizona, and Mexico. We returned after about three weeks to find we had a large cherry crop, in beautiful condition thanks to Fred's diligent work and good weather, with the price the lowest it had been in years.

The price that year was projected to be four cents a pound, barely enough to cover the cost of picking, if we had Reynolds Brother's come in with their crew. The only way we could make a profit was to pick and haul the cherries ourselves. So Mary Ann and I decided to buy a truck we had looked at at John Pelke's Shell station in Kewaunee, when we took off on our wedding trip.

Purchasing the truck for $300, we set out to gather up all the cherry pails and ladders we could find around the farm. We still had the problem of getting pickers.

Sarah Daubner, a neighbor and former grade school teacher of mine, heard about our plight and came to see us. She explained that the orchard she and Marvin owned was in its last years, and they wanted to find a place for their pickers, who had been very loyal to them. She asked if they could come over to our orchard after they were done at Daubner's. Not only that, Sarah offered to let us use their pails and ladders if we needed them.

We relied on the help of our friends, the Daubners, and that of Fred Berger, to get started in the orchard business, since neither of our fathers were living to give us advice and help. Not many young couples start out that way; but we were both in our thirties when we were married, so we were accustomed to making decisions on our own.

By the early 1960's, our 1000 trees had grown so much that we had to look for more pickers, so we again contacted our Indian friends for help.

After that, we probably had members of every Indian family in Door County working for us at one time or another. Nearly all of them are related.

The patriarch of the families was a gentleman named Ben Huff. Ben was grandfather to many, including our own children, who never knew a grandfather of their own. Ben was a heavy-set handsome dark-complexioned man with a gruff but friendly voice. He'd chide the children so they would keep on picking. It was always a pleasure to see him each year; and now that he is gone, he is missed.

The Indian families worked quietly; they made their children behave, and stick to the job. There wouldn't be any cherry throwing or fights. You didn't have to tell them to fill their pails; sometimes they delighted in putting so many cherries in a pail that you couldn't put another one on top. Despite a little fun, they were fast pickers. Even if some of them found better picking in another orchard, they would see to it that you had enough pickers to harvest your crop.

Eventually, as Native Americans came more and more to get a share of the American dream, cherry picking became more of a summer outing and a chance for the relatives to get together than an economic necessity. Some found good jobs locally; others moved to the big city. Many bought homes here and elsewhere and began to set down roots in the community where they lived. Some became active in Native American history groups. But they would arrange their vacations so they could come back to our orchard to help us with the cherry crop.

We employed up to 75 pickers during a season, although we didn't have more than thirty or so working at one time. In handling this large number of workers, my wife, Mary Ann must be given the credit. Besides checking in the cherries and dumping them into the crates, and

MORE THAN 500 INDIANS, who live on Wisconsin reservations, are picking cherries. Mrs. White Thunder (right) of the Winnebago tribe is preparing a stew at her camp at Martin's orchard. The youngster doesn't seem to like the camera.

photo: Milwaukee Journal, Sun., Aug. 1, 1937

also helping load them on the truck, she did the bookwork every night, so that if anyone wanted to draw out money, everything would come out right. And then, of course, was the matter of handling seven children, who were born within eight years.

All our children except one grew up in the cherry orchard. John was born in July of 1961, and spent some of his very first days under the shade of a cherry tree. Bill was born the next year shortly after the cherry season ended. Jimmie was born in 1963 just as President Kennedy was being buried, but Jimmie died in April of the next year, so he never got to see a cherry tree in bloom. David was born the following year in January, so it was his turn to be in the crib under a cherry tree in the 1965 season. It was Constance Rebecca's turn, at age three months, in 1966.

But Richard came at the most interesting time — August 4, 1967. Mary Ann had spent the day as usual during the cherry season, checking and dumping cherries, with the kids begging for a cookie or a drink, or indicating that their pants needed to be changed. She had survived figuring out the checks for those who wanted to be paid at the end of the day, as pickers sometimes did. We had picked the largest amount of cherries we ever had that day, about three and one half tons. (The price was low, however.)

Then, about ten thirty at night, she told me it was time to go to the hospital. Immediately after we arrived, Richard was born, even before Dr. Hobson was able to get there, and he is fast.

The next day we picked four tons of cherries, the most we have ever picked, but it took my sister-in-law and me to replace Mary Ann in the orchard. In addition, my mother-in-law was down at the house taking care of the kids.

John and Mary Ann Enigl filling cherry boxes

My mother-in-law has taken care of all of our children while Mary Ann was in the hospital giving birth to another one. That's how we became the first, and for a long time only, orchard to use citizen's band radio.

Citizen's band two-way radio first started in 1958, when the eleven meter radio amateur band was turned over to business radio use. Knowing we would have a newborn boy down at the house most of the time with Grandma taking care of him, I decided we needed some form of communication between the house and the orchard. So I bought two Heathkit c.b. units and wired them up in time for cherry season. I put one in the house and one in the 1948 Ford truck.

Back in 1961, when I still thought c.b. was strictly for business as the law said, I used it to find out how our son John was doing back at the farm. C.b'ers didn't use "handles" back in those days, but "Grandma" was who I asked for, and it became a commonly used handle a few years later.

Our pickers sometimes arrived before I got out in the orchard — at 5:30 a.m. By the time I got there at 7:00 a.m., some of them would be ready to check in what they had picked.

By 9:00, Mary Ann would be in the orchard. Some days, I would be almost ready to take a load to the factory. Usually, Mary Ann would help load the boxes into the truck (oftimes when she was pregnant.)

Noontime was always the hardest time for Mary Ann, especially if I wasn't home from the factory. Just before lunch she would call the pickers, by either yelling "dinner time!" herself, or letting one of the children do it. The pickers would line up with their pails to be checked in. Meanwhile, the kids would be getting out the lunch, arguing with each other, or in case of the younger ones, crying for a bottle or to have their diapers changed. Generally, the kids were pretty good, looking out for each other, and becoming a great deal of help at a very early age. By age of eleven or twelve, they were able to drive the old truck or tractor around the orchard, but only if there were no strangers around to get in the way.

Mary Ann took all the work and confusion into stride and ran everything in an organized way. She always kept her cool, and dignity. She hadn't been a bank teller for many years before we were married for nothing; she knew how to handle stress.

At the end of the season, as the last cherries were turned in, we always had a party for the pickers. The day before, we would buy the ice cream cups and put them in the freezer, buy cases of soda and put them in the basement to cool. While Mary Ann finished out the final tally of pails picked by each person and made out the checks, the crew would enjoy the picnic. Some would use the swimming pool.

But that wasn't the end of the cherry season. We still had to go through the orchard and pick up all the pails, ladders, and any picking belts left lying around. Then, with a little pruning, and one more spray, the orchard was left until the next spring.

After I took over the orchard, and later on got married, we had to buy a bigger tractor. The little John Deere Model H just didn't have the power and speed to cover the ground fast enough and do a good job of working it up. Fred Berger worked the orchard most of the time, and he used his big 10-20 McCormick Deering instead of our little tractor.

In 1961, Fred found us an Oliver 70 tractor, which had tremendous power and speed, and a road gear for traveling along the highway. That got the disking and dragging done much faster. I think it cost us $100, plus our old John Deere, and the Oliver had been completely overhauled.

1947 Oliver with 1946 sprayer, spraying apple trees

Our old sprayer required at least two people to operate, so in 1965, I started looking for a different one that could be operated by one person. John Miles had stopped growing cherries in 1961 and had laid up his sprayer. It was a Friend, which he had purchased new in 1946, the first model to come out with a steel tank after the war. His neighbor, Blaine Dreutzer, a friend of mine I had met in college, told me about it and we went to see John.

The sprayer had an engine no longer manufactured but for which parts were available. Otherwise, it was in good shape, John said. He wanted $500 for it, but when we said we only had $300 to spend, he agreed to take that.

So we had a perfectly good one-man sprayer. We thought the engine had a knock, but a friend took it apart and found that the knock was only backlash in the reduction gears.

We were able to get along with used equipment at low cost. That's important in the cherry business, for some years you don't make a profit. We bought several new trucks, but they served other purposes, too.

We bought a cherry shaker, one built on the principle of a chain saw, but it was too hard on the operator to be practical. We stick to the old hand picking method even today, which is the only practical method for the few trees we have left.

Now, with only a hundred or so trees left, we're not sure if we will start a new orchard. But we'll never get away from the cherry business entirely even if we have to go out and pick cherries for someone.

It's Harvest Time in Vast Orchards of Door County Cherryland

The cherry harvest is on in the orchards of Door County and hundreds of people, young and old, are busy picking what growers call a "good normal crop." Nearly a dozen huge orchard camps are occupied by the pickers, who will be on the job for a total of nearly six weeks. They receive 7½¢ a pail and most workers gather from 20 to 40 buckets a day.

photo: Milwaukee Journal, Sun., Aug. 1, 1937

Good and Bad Apples

Robert Hall was a bright and interesting little boy. He was the youngest of fourteen children. His parents loved him very much; for he was merry, and frank, and truthful, and affectionate, and industrious.

But one day, Robert's kind and considerate father saw him playing with some boys who were rude and wicked. He had seen, for some time, a change for the worse in his son, and now he knew the cause. He was very sorry, but he said nothing to Robert at the time.

But one day, Robert's kind and considerate father saw him playing with some boys who were rude and wicked. He had seen, for some time, a change for the worse in his son, and now he knew the cause. He was very sorry, but he said nothing to Robert at the time.

In the evening his father brought from the garden six beautiful, rosy-cheeked apples, put them on a plate and presented them to Robert. The son was much pleased at his father's kindness, and thanked him.

"My son, you must lay the apples aside for a few days, that they may become mellow," said the father. And Robert cheerfully placed the plate, with the apples on it, in his mother's storeroom.

But, just then, his father asked him to bring back the fruit, laid on the plate with the others a seventh apple, which was quite decayed, and desired him to allow it to remain there.

"But, father", said Robert, "the decayed apple will spoil all the others."

"Are you quite sure, my son? Why should not the six fresh apples rather make the bad one fresh?" And with these words, he requested Robert to return the apples to the storeroom.

Eight days afterward, he asked his son to open the door and take out the apples. But what a sight presented itself! The six apples, which had been so sound and smooth, were rotten, and spread a disagreeable smell through the room.

"O, papa," cried Robert, it is too bad! Did I not tell you that the decayed apple would spoil the good ones?"

"My beloved son," said the father, "have I not told you often that the company of bad children will make you bad. Why do you not listen to me? I want you to learn a lesson from these apples. Assuredly, if you keep company with wicked boys, you will soon be like them."

Robert did not forget this lesson. When any of his former, wicked playfellows asked him to join in their sports, he thought of the decayed apples; and was thus enabled to resist the temptation.

He became a great, a good, a learned and a useful man. Though he suffered most remarkably from disease for more than twenty years, he lived until he was aged, and died a childlike, humble, and Godly man. *Independent Third Reader 1887*

Granny Smith Most regions across the country, year-round . . .

. . . good for snacks, all-purpose cooking.

illustration: Julia Bresnahan

The Hill Orchard: Continuing A Family Tradition

by Gary Jones

T was a warm August afternoon when I followed Jean Hill's green pickup truck down to the Ray Nordeen place on Old Stage Road, just a quarter mile south of the Scandia intersection. My little compact reeled drunkenly over the rough trail that wound past the well-established rows of an old orchard, finally halting at a stately stand of Whitney crabs.

Mrs. Hill, dressed in casual slacks and a kerchief, slid out of the truck, handed me a paper grocery bag, and led me to one of the trees where together we picked ripe crab apples. I wanted only a few, I had told her, maybe a peck, to make apple pickles, the sort Granny Jones used to make. But the apples were so lovely and the picking so easy, that I filled two large paper bags before I could force myself to admit that I had picked enough.

Orchards have that effect on me. But who is immune to a landscape that is transformed in spring into a breathtaking display of colossal bridal bouquets, fields of pink and white that emit a fragrance which makers of perfumes only dream about. And who can pass an orchard in autumn that is heavy with lush fruit, and resist the urge to reach for it, much like Tantalus in the ancient Greek myth.

When one pops juicy scarlet tart cherries into his mouth, or sinks his teeth into a shiny red apple firm with sweet juices, he has the feeling of coming home. Like Odysseus' men who forgot their pasts with the first taste of lotus blossoms and were content to remain on the island forever, the cherry nibblers and apple eaters want nothing more than to forget the demands of nine-to-five jobs behind desks and smoggy commutes to sterile offices.

Ah, to own an orchard and sit back admiring the handiwork of nature, letting God do all of the work. Come autumn, you stretch from the indolence of summer, yawn, and begin plucking the bounty of the land, readying yourself for the onset of eager buyers of produce who will queue up before your door.

Where do I buy my orchard?

I posed that question to orchard growers Lyle and Jean Hill, and her uncle, Ray Nordeen, who has spent 66 years in the orchard business, as we sat around the kitchen table one winter evening sipping cider pressed from Hill Orchard apples.

They laughed politely. "If you're going into it for the money," Jean smiled, "don't." "You have to like it," Uncle Ray added, nodding his head. "It's a big investment," Lyle pointed out. "New trees cost from $5.00-$6.00 each, and will not reach peak production for six to ten years. In the meantime, spray that was $36.00 for a five gallon can six or seven years ago ran $115 last season." "And you go through a lot of cans," Uncle Ray added. Apples must be sprayed ten to fourteen times during the season; cherries, five or six times. (A cherry orchard dies in one year if it is not sprayed.) And an orchardman must be licensed to use many insecticides and fungacides.

"You'll need a tractor, sprayer, shaker — a new one can cost as much as $80,000.00 — a disk or a drag," Lyle continued. "And a hole digger for planting trees," Jean added. Uncle Ray noted that you can hire other orchard growers to perform these services for you, but then you make no profit. "You have to have a big outfit and do all the work yourself to make any money."

"And what people outside the orchard business can't understand," Jean laughed, "is that we sell cherries without knowing what we will be getting from the crop."

When you have a good crop. The mice, rabbits, and deer are foes of the orchard during the winter, according to Lyle, and the birds the bane of the cherries during the summer.

And don't forget the weather, mentioned Uncle Ray, recalling 1936 when Lake Michigan froze over and the orchard growers had to survive a severe winter kill. Every year there is the danger of frost during that critical water stage a week before the cherry blossoms open. A still, foggy spell during peak cherry bloom can mean poor pollination. Once the fruit has set on the trees, there is the worry of wind damage.

Together Lyle, Jean, and Uncle Ray listed the pestilences which plague orchards: yellow leaf, brown rot, lesser peach tree borer, June drop.

The three orchard authorities agreed laughingly that people who don't have cherries seem to know the most about the effect of a frost, the abundance of a crop, or the price which will be paid. The armchair cherry experts alternate between sending the cherry men to the poor house and to easy street.

In 1982 the price of cherries fell from the preceding season's forty-some cents a pound to thirteen and one-half cents. Lyle Hill blamed this

illustration: Jan Jablonski

phenomenon in part on the U.S. Department of Agriculture's prediction of a bumper cherry harvest. While the crop did not materialize, brokers responded as if it had with exceptionally low price offers. Unfortunately, the cherry grower has no choice but to stay with cherries. Farmers may plant corn the next year if soybeans do poorly. However, an orchardman has a multi-year investment in the trees he plants, and is always looking several seasons down the road.

A small crop, such as the 1983 harvest, brought fifty cents per pound. Conversely, last summer's bountiful picking only commanded a mid-twenties figure.

"During a good year, though," Uncle Ray pointed out, "orchard growers can spend the winter in Bermuda, unlike dairy farmers who have to work year around."

"We've never spent the winter in Bermuda, Uncle," Jean laughed.

"On a poor year, like 1982, we hope to at least get across the Brussels Hill," Lyle laughed with her.

"You have to like it," Uncle Ray repeated, "to be an orchard grower."

The Hills and Uncle Ray Nordeen obviously enjoy the orchard business. Jean proudly mentioned that she has never missed a cherry harvest since she was a little girl. She smiled when she remembered that her mother could pick 103 pails of cherries a day, after taking time off to fix three meals for the other pickers. Even after going away to college, where she met Lyle in the registration line on the first day of school and married him promptly after graduation four years later, she still came home summers to pick cherries.

However, Jean's life has not been entirely devoted to cherries. After her marriage she taught second grade in Michigan. Following her return to Northern Door, Jean worked as a teacher in the program for the children of migrant workers. Then during the 1970s, she was Director of the Peninsula Day Nursery.

Lyle, on the other hand, wasn't bitten by the orchard bug until he met Jean and came with her to the Door Peninsula during the summers. In the fall of 1968, they moved to Northern Door permanently, raising three children: Beth, a senior at the University of Wisconsin-Eau Claire; Jody, a sophomore at Bethel College, Minnesota; and Randy, a seventh grader at Gibraltar. The comfortable Hill household rests appropriately atop a hill on Scandia Road just outside of Sister Bay.

Until a year ago, Lyle worked as a teacher, and for a time as a principal, at a junior high at Sturgeon Bay. While he enjoyed education, commuting seventy miles round trip daily was a grind. But even more rigorous were the demands of two full-time jobs. Summers presented no problem, but the pruning, planting, and fertilizing of spring had to fall primarily on the shoulders of Jean, both as a supervisor of hired hands and as a chief worker herself. The fall harvest again conflicted with the start of school.

But the Hill Orchard consists predominantly of cherries with the August harvest occurring during summer vacation, Lyle was able to lead a double life for a decade and a half.

Presently, approximately seventy acres are planted to cherries. Another sixteen are devoted to apples, mostly McIntosh, Cortlands, and Delicious, although the Hills grow other varieties of apples in lesser amounts, along with apricots, plums, pears, and recently grapes.

The Hill children are a big help with the orchard, especially the eldest, Beth, who enjoys orchard work the most of all. She has helped with nearly every aspect of the work,

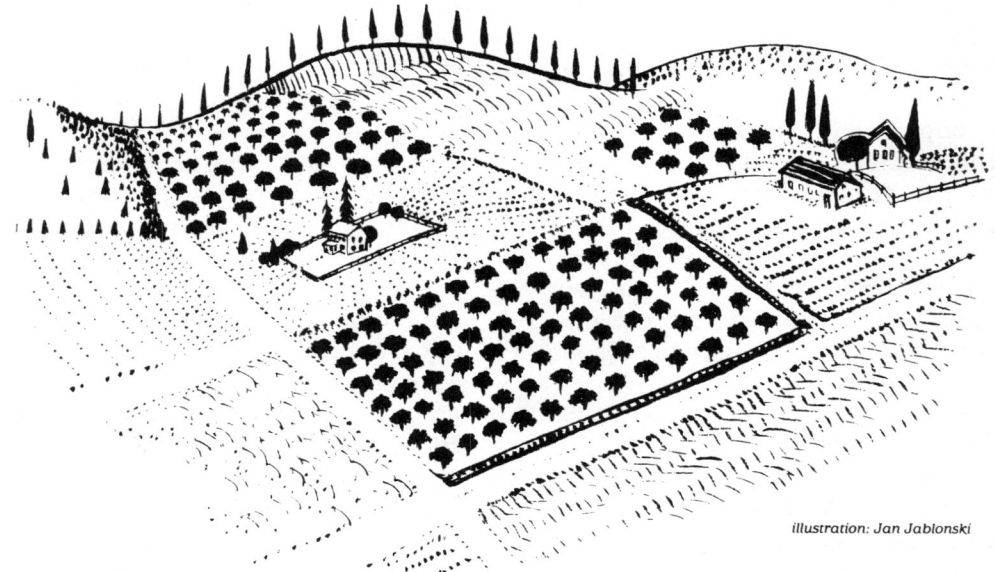

illustration: Jan Jablonski

including operating the forklift and shakers. Jody does not take as naturally to the orchard, but willingly does her share. Randy, while still young for orchard work, is learning to do his part. During the cherry season, for example, he is expected to pick a certain number of pails of cherries each day, and is beginning to drive tractor and forklift.

Jean Hill likes the family togetherness demanded by the orchard. The work is seasonal and intense. The times that are optimum for fertilizing or planting or harvesting are relatively short, and the hours that must be worked when the conditions are right are long. Subsequently, the kids are expected to pitch in.

Some college students, as well as friends and neighbors, have worked picking cherries season after season. In many ways, the harvest becomes a reunion. In fact, a couple of summers ago a picker from over four decades past returned with his family "To see if I was dead or not," Uncle Ray laughed, and to show his children where he had picked cherries as a young man.

Cherry picking, back in the days when there were movers rather than shakers in the orchards, was accomplished by migrant labor performing the tasks now completed by automation. The Hills and Uncle Ray recalled those times. Uncle Ray remembered Oneida Indians coming to pick cherries in the 1940s, pitching their tents in the orchards, and proudly displaying their bead work. One year during World War II, Jamaicans worked the orchards; only working age men came into this country, no families. Prisoners of war were available as workers at this time, too. In the 1950s and 1960s the pickers were primarily Mexicans and Southern Blacks.

During this later period, Ray Zimmerman served as a state funded coordinator for the utilization of migrant workers in the orchards. His agency functioned as a clearing house for orchard growers looking for labor and for the recruiters who brought buses of workers from the South.

Jean recalled the excitement of preparing for the arrival of the cherry pickers. When she was a child, it was her job to fill with straw the ticks which would serve as mattresses in workers' quarters. The buildings had to be thoroughly cleaned, the curtains and bedding laundered, and everything set in readiness for the arrival of the migrants.

Many of the same workers came back year after year, and quite naturally friendships developed between the orchard owner's families and the migrant workers. Lyle recalled fondly one worker who was also a cropland farmer in the South. He was called Blackie by owners and workers alike. "Blackie was considered to be really black, even by the other Blacks," Lyle offered by way of apology for what seems by modern sensibilities an insensitive nickname. Blackie picked a predictable six pails per hour, regardless of the time of day or season. Most good pickers filled only four or five pails per hour.

The secret to efficient picking, Jean explained, is to use fingers independently to pick cherries without raking them. The cherries cannot be mashed, but a rapid picker will let the cherries fall into the pail, rather than placing them one by one. She pantomimed the technique.

Lyle remembered the singing of the Black workers who began the work day at five or five-thirty in the morning. The clear voices penetrated the foggy peninsula dawn, working through endless improvisations based on familiar songs.

Cool summer days seemed frigid to the pickers from the Deep South.

illustration: Rosemary Utzinger

They bundled up, much as Northerners dress for winter, and sometimes even built fires for warmth in the orchard. Having never seen a Wisconsin winter, the workers were incredulous when told that Green Bay froze over each winter.

Now that the cherry picking days belong to the past, it is easy to romanticize that era. However, Ray Nordeen is quick to point out that those times were not golden in every respect. A recruiter might promise forty pickers, only to report to the grower later that the workers had left on a different bus and would not be available after all. Or the workers might be held up at another harvest and arrive too late for the cherries.

Although the six week season achieved through a balance of early Richmond and later Montmorency cherries was longer than the present two week harvest of Montmorencies alone, time was still of the essence. Not all workers were as industrious as the fabled Blackie. Some were reluctant to rise and begin the day's work. Others were sluggish once they were in the orchard. And a few practiced deceit, filling the bottoms of their pails with leaves or denting the pail bottoms upward to make them fill more quickly, or punching their own work cards to falsify the number of pails they had picked.

Several factors combined to end the era of the cherry picker. The most obvious was the introduction of mechanization to the harvest in the mid sixties. Government regulations concerning housing for migrant workers and minimum wages increased the cost of manual labor for the owners. "We almost had to build motels for the workers!" Uncle Ray exclaimed. Still another factor was the incompatibility of migrant workers and tourists.

But were things better in the good old days? "Not necessarily," said Lyle

Hill. "It's a tradeoff. There is a loss of the personal aspects of the harvest and a lot of the color surrounding the industry. But on the other hand, modern growers are financially better off. They don't have to worry about strikes or unreliable workers."

One local grower, Willard Kramer, whose orchard is located just outside of Sister Bay, still hand picks cherries, and occasionally employes a few migrant workers. But apart from his small operation, the only vestige of the bygone era of the cherry picker is the occasional appearance of a run-down row of bunkhouses lingering apart from the other buildings on a mechanized modern orchard. Many of these old buildings have become shabby with neglect, paint peeling, windows broken, spending their final years as storage sheds.

The cherry limb shaker was the first to nudge aside the pickers. The mechanism was attached to a major branch of the tree and the resulting vibrations shook the ripened cherries free to fall on the waiting canvases. Each tree had to be shaken three or four times, depending upon the number of major scaffold limbs.

Harvey Haen developed a limb shaker with two wrap around wings in his shop in Egg Harbor. About a dozen of the custom made shakers were completed, and in a sense have become collectors' items. Lyle Hill had one of the machines.

The shakers presently used are attached to the trunk of the cherry tree and complete the operation with only one shaking. These machines tend to be one of two different types. One sort is the double inclined plane shaker. Here, two machines are used: one is a slanted bed of canvas with a vibrating mechanism which fits under half of the tree; the complementary machine consists only of a canvas bed which fits under the other half.

The second type of shaker is the roll out sort. In this instance, a single machine has two wings which roll out, forming a giant canvas letter U, enfolding the tree trunk in the center. Again, the tree is vibrated and the falling cherries caught on canvas beds.

The one-man harvester represents the latest trend in mechanization for large growers. Several of these machines are in operation in the county, and, according to Lyle Hill, are the wave of the future.

The cherry orchard business has not only become mechanized, but it has truly become an industry. Nearly gone are the four to six acre orchards of the past, tucked away on some unproductive corner of the farm. With every year, the orchards become larger and fewer, an observable trend in every branch of agriculture.

And not only have the remaining orchards expanded, but they have formed corporations for processing their own cherries, rather than selling them to middlemen as in the past. The Hill Orchard joined with four other growers in 1980 to form the Northern Door Cherry Corporation, located not far from Baileys Harbor. In fact, all of the processing plants in Door County are now grower owned.

While in the past cherries were hot packed, much as vegetables are still processed in canning factories about

106

the state, most cherries today are pitted and then frozen, either sugared or unsugared, a much simpler procedure. Still, the Northern Door Cherry Corporation employs thirty workers per shift each season to man the factory. (Electronic cherry sorters will reduce the need for manpower in the future.)

The Northern Door Cherry Corporation in turn belongs to a marketing cooperative, Cherry Central. Located in Michigan, the cooperative services several processing plants and distributes fruit products under the Wilderness label, found on the shelves of most Midwestern grocery stores.

The Hills are also members of the Wisconsin Red Tart Cherry Institute, an organization which promotes consumer usage of cherry products, sponsors research and conducts legislative lobbying. The consumer tends to think of cherries only in terms of cherry pie, a confection avoided by weight conscious Americans. Non-fattening and non-dessert uses of cherries abound, if only the consumer were aware of them.

The Hill family has certainly done its part to promote the cherry industry. Jody Hill reigned as 1983-84 Wisconsin Cherry Princess. In addition to her parade appearances, Jody met the governor, introducing him to cherry products from Door County, and spoke to state legislature, thanking them for their support of a bill favorable to orchardmen.

Although the Hill Orchard has an ongoing expansion program that involves planting an additional 500 cherry trees each year, the operation is by no means an impersonal agribusiness enterprise. While the cherries are sold through a corporation, the other fruit is marketed traditionally. Many of the Hill apples are sold locally from the orchard, although the Hills do not maintain

Jody Hill, daughter of Lyle and Jean Hill, was the 1983 Wisconsin Cherry Princess

a salesroom as such, but rely on word of mouth and local newspaper advertising. In addition, the Hills retail apples in northeastern Wisconsin cities across the bay, selling them from a truck.

"Many people think fruit tastes better when it is grown here on the peninsula," Jean said. "Maybe because of the limestone," Uncle Ray explained. "It could be," Jean agreed. "But we let the apples ripen on the trees, and that makes a real difference. People say to me, 'Apples just don't taste as good when they come from a store.' "

Lyle pointed out that some large orchards, the ones that market to grocery chains, store their apples in refrigerated warehouses with carefully controlled atmospheres of carbon dioxide. While the apples may be stored for long periods of time, they don't go through the natural breaking down process which occurs after harvest, a mellowing that improves the taste of the apples. Hence, the grocery store apples tend to be very crisp, but appear to have less flavor.

The pears, plums and apricots are marketed primarily by subscription lists. "I'm at the top of the list for apricots," one acquaintance boasted to me, "because I've been on it for more than ten years." Once you have your name on the list, Jean calls you when your fruit is picked.

But the aspect of the Hill Orchard operation which makes it most unique, is it's personality. Uncle Ray Nordeen cautioned me not to go into the orchard business for the money, and money is not the prime motivating factor with the Hills. For them, orchard growing is a way of life, a lifestyle that for Jean extends back to her earliest memories. It is an operation that brings the family together to work with a common goal, the same spirit which bound pioneer farm families together. The children learn a sense of responsibility, the success of the orchard depends upon their contribution.

Jean's hand picking crews which follow the cherry shakers and harvest young trees are in the tradition of husking bees and threshing crews. Every year the same friends and neighbors come to help with the harvest resulting in a social occasion as well as an economic venture. The practice seems fitting considering the rich folklore surrounding cherries. Who can eat cherry pie without thinking of either George Washington or Billy Boy?

Above all, the Hills are sensitive to the beauty and the bounty of their orchards. "Every year we still take pictures," Jean said, spreading photos before me on the kitchen table of cherry trees in bloom, cherry trees loaded with fruit, family members working in the harvest. "Yes," Lyle laughed, "each year we herd grandparents, kids, everyone down into the orchard to have their pictures taken next to the cherry blossoms, standing on a carpet of yellow dandelion blooms." "I go out in the orchard and stand and stare and stare," Jean said. "Each year I marvel anew at God's creation."

"You have to like it to stay in the orchard business," said Uncle Ray again.

••••———◆———••••

Those who love Nature can never be dull. They may have other temptations; but at least they will run no risk of being beguiled, by ennui, idleness or want of occupation, "to buy the merry madness of an hour with the long penitence of after-time." The love of Nature, again, helps us greatly to keep ourselves free from those mean and petty cares which interfere so much with calm and peace of mind. It turns "every ordinary walk into a morning or evening sacrifice," and brightens life until it becomes almost like a fairy-tale.

— John Lubbock

photo: Advocate

Marie Henkel, Door County's first Cherry Blossom Queen.

Dressed in a gold gown Marie Henkel rode atop the Queen's Float in the 1929 Parade of Blossoms.

The First Cherry Blossom Queen

The county cherry industry's most spectacular promotional idea began in 1929 when the first Cherry Blossom Festival was held in Sturgeon Bay. The first Cherry Blossom Queen, picked from a field of fifteen contestants, was seventeen year old Marie Henkel of Institute. She was crowned at a coronation ball held the evening of May 24 at the Nightengale. She reigned over the Parade of Blossoms, riding an 18 foot float donated by the banks; a three day historical pageant, held at the city playground, where she was carried in on a sedan chair by four honor guards; and a bus tour of the state by the queen and her court, planned by Karl Reynolds. The first festival was a big success according to articles in the Advocate which said the "streets were jammed with people to see the principal parade that far eclipsed any ever held in Door County." The Advocate went on to state "The whole county was benefited by the wide publicity promoting the Cherry Blossom Festival, to say nothing of the favorable comments carried back home by visitors. The event was decidedly the most successful ever held on the peninsula."

The 1939 Cherry Blossom Queen, Goldie Krueger, with Gov. Heil.

WOULD USE THREE-LEGGED ORCHARD LADDERS TO HAND-PICK 9 to 10 LBS. of TART RED CHERRIES PER PAIL...IN DOOR COUNTY, WISC. DURING THE 1940's AROUND 10,000 SEASONAL WORKERS

K ZILISCH

photo provided by John Enigl

A History of the
Reynolds
Preserving Company

by John Enigl

book about the cherry indus-
try in Door County would not
be complete without men-
tion of the contributions of
the Reynolds family, and especially of
the work of Karl S. Reynolds.

One of the earliest canning companies in the state of Wisconsin was
the Reynolds Preserving Company,
which was organized in December of
1895, and operated for the first time
in 1896. The company was a closed
corporation, with family members
owning all the stock, the incorpora-
tion occuring in 1895.

Mrs. Eliza Reynolds and her sons
Edward S. Reynolds, Sr. and William
S. Reynolds had come from out East
and bought up a tomato canning's
equipment, moving it to Sturgeon
Bay. The machinery, by using addi-

tional equipment, was converted to
pea canning. Clarence Plummer, who
worked in the cannery of D.W. Archer
at Davenport, Iowa, was engaged, and
even though he had never packed
peas himself, he had a friend who had
given him a great deal of instruction
in that art.

When Plummer left the Reynolds
Preserving Company in 1897, Charles
"Bow" Augustine became plant superintendent. He remained with the Reynolds factory, and the Fruit Growers'
Cooperative for many years in the
same plant in Sturgeon Bay. In 1949,
he had served fifty three years there.

Karl S. Reynolds, brother of Donald
W. Reynolds, Fred "Fritz" Reynolds,
and Herb Reynolds, was the son of
William S. Reynolds. Shortly before
his death in an air crash while

Edward Reynolds

returning from a business trip to Beaver Dam on December 4, 1948, he wrote a history of the Reynolds Company. The following, except where noted are the words of Karl S. Reynolds:

The first (pea canning) season was quite a hectic experiment, with my father, William S., trying to make the rounds of the pea fields with a bicycle, with an attempt made to shell the peas by hand and many other evidences of lack of experience and adequate preparation. Luckily Tom Scott insisted on putting a viner in reserve to be used when and if it should become necessary. Needless to say, this viner went into operation almost immediately and was largely instrumental in saving the first season's pack.

The pea canning business continued with its ups and downs, until 1917, when the final pack was processed. During the latter years there was considerable grief with blight and other plagues that made pea canning quite unprofitable. Blight-proof seed was apparently unknown, and inasmuch as these difficulties had persisted for a number of years, plans were already being made to convert into some product other than peas.

As early as 1895, Professors Hatch and Goff, of the University of Wisconsin, had been experimenting with Door County as a fruit growing area.

(Here we must make a correction of Karl Reynolds' statement. A.L. Hatch was not a professor at the University of Wisconsin, but just very well experienced and intelligent commercial grower from Richland County, according to his grandson, Frank Ullsperger, another prominent figure in the cherry industry. Ullsperger still has a cherry orchard on the land once owned by his grandfather, the first cherry orchard in Door County.)

(Hatch is quoted in a 1915 brochure from the United Fruit Company, which sought investors for putting in a cherry orchard on what is now the Horseshoe Bay farms, owned by the Cowles of Green Bay, south of Egg Harbor:

"Plant six acres of your land to cherries, and you will some day have a little gold mine," Hatch said seventeen years before.)

To return to Karl Reynolds' history:

Certain orchards were planted at that time (1895) which had reached their prime by 1910 and 1911, to the extent that they gave quite evident proof that Door County had a rosy future as a fruit growing section. Accordingly, the Reynolds Preserving Company, in 1911, began its first commercial planting of cherry trees, and induced many other growers to follow suit. Much of the pea land and timber

William S. Reynolds

land (Reynolds logged in addition to raising crops) was converted to orchards.

By 1917 the cherry trees planted in 1911 and 1912 were ready to produce their first crops, and therefore, a fruit marketing and canning organization (The Fruit Growers' Union and Fruit Growers' Canning Company) were formed, to which the pea canning factory was sold. This sale took place in 1917 after the last pea crop was processed. 1918 was a very poor crop year for cherries, and the new organization did not put up a pack, and as a result the first cherry pack was put up in 1919, by the new co-operative organization. This organization was the forerunner of the present Fruit Growers' Cooperative, which today is one of the largest cherry packers in the country.

The Reynolds Preserving Company continued as members of the cooperative, and delivered the fruit produced from its orchards to the cooperative for processing and sale. By 1925, however, the production of the Reynolds Preserving Company orchards had reached a point where

an independent factory was justified.

Since 1925, the Reynolds Preserving Company has operated as an independent organization and has grown steadily to the point where it now handles approximately 35% of the cherries grown in this area and has some 250 growers contributing to the volume of output.

In 1942, a partnership was formed, known as Reynolds Brothers, and this partnership has continued to operate the orchards and factory, leasing physical assets from the Reynolds Preserving Company.

Products have been extended from the original canned cherries, to include frozen cherries, canned cherry juice, frozen cherry juice, and bottled and canned pasteurized apple juice. During the war, it was necessary to use glass in place of tin, and the results have been so satisfactory that doubtless some apple juice will continue to go into glass, even when more tin plate is available.

So ends the history of the Reynolds Preserving Company and Reynolds Brothers, as written by Karl S. Rey-

Reynolds fleet of orchard sprayers 1948

photo provided by John Enigl

nolds himself. Within a year, he would be dead in the crash of his Beechcraft Bonanza in fog, at the age of 49, along with his secretary, Erv Kossow, and the general manager and secretary treasurer of the Fruit Growers' Cooperative, Lougee Stedman. In the early 1960's the company would go out of business, with his brother, Donald W. Reynolds, serving as general manager of the company to the end.

The Story of Wisconsin's Great Canning Industry, from which this history is taken, was published in 1949 by the canning industry. This noteworthy work, long out of print, has more information about Reynolds Brothers:

In 1936 strawberries as well as cherries were packed, but whether this was only an experimental pack, or whether it became a regular part of operations is not known, but very likely it was discontinued. (The operation was discontinued. I was timekeeper for Reynolds Brothers in 1957, and the idea of packing anything else but cherries and apples was long forgotten by then.) The present factory is of four lines capacity and is able to handle about 12,000,000 pounds of cherries.

Don Reynolds has been general manager to date, and needless to say does not travel on a bicycle as did his father (Don drove a big Lincoln Turnpike Cruiser). Karl S. Reynolds was sales manager from 1925 until his death, and of recent years traveled mostly by air in his own plane. (Aaron Mildbrandt was plant superintendent from 1948 until the late 1950's when he moved over to the same position at the Fruit Grower's Cooperative.) E.L. Kossow was office manager from 1921 until his death.

A Green Bay Press Gazette article about Reynolds Brothers on June 15, 1948, gave the following information:

It is hard to visualize, the article said, that in a plant which began as a pea cannery (not at the Sevastopol location of the last plant, but in Sturgeon Bay along the canal) to later become a leader in the cherry processing field, something over four and a quarter million cherries being pitted every hour, but that's the speed pits will be flying around when production lines at Reynolds processing plants get rolling on the 1948 crop about mid July.

The company's orchards comprise about 600 acres of cherry trees and 200 of apples. Along the five mile stretch of road and for about a mile on each side, is the most concentrated population of cherry trees in the world. Here on 2000 acres, owned or controlled by Reynolds and two other independents, plus 1000 acres of neighboring orchards, are 300,000 trees with yield about 13 million pounds of cherries. In addition to canning and freezing the firm cold packs a large portion of its production.

Thus ends the exerpt from the Green Bay Press Gazette.

Reynolds work crew 1948

The Reynolds family is indeed a talented one. Donald W. Reynolds was mayor of Sturgeon Bay for a number of years around the time of World War II, a most difficult time, for, while the shipyards boomed, problems of urban expansion arose.

His uncle, Edward S. Reynolds, Sr., was an innovative inventor, having

Pickers camp ca. 1920, at Martin Orchard or Reynolds Bros.

developed several pieces of machinery for the handling of peas in canning factories, among them being the Reynolds thistle picker and conveyor. He died in 1919, at the age of 60.

William S. Reynolds, the father of Donald W., Karl S., Herbert, and Fred Reynolds (the youngest, and hale and hardy), died in October of 1926, as a result of injuries sustained in an automobile accident six miles north of Port Washington on his return from a business trip in Milwaukee.

His grandson, Tom Reynolds, son of Karl, to whom he bears a striking resemblance both in appearance and outgoing personality, says:

"There's an interesting story about my father and his father, Will Reynolds. There were about two years when they didn't get along very well, and didn't talk to one another.

"Then in October of 1926, they both went to Milwaukee, unknown to one another. They happened to go out to dinner at the same hotel, and spied one another.

"They must have thought it was a little silly not to eat together, so they did, and spent a most enjoyable evening together; they were friends again.

"They headed back to Sturgeon Bay in separate automobiles, Grandfather Will going first. About six miles north of Port Washington, my father, Karl, came upon the wreck of his father's car, but apparently Will had no injuries.

"But it soon became evident that Will did have serious internal injuries, so my father rushed him to a hospital in Sheboygan. It was too late, however. My grandfather died along the way, and my father, at age 23, and his brother Don, age 25, had to take over the operation of the Reynolds Preserving Company."

A bulletin dated December 6, 1948, from the Wisconsin Canners Association read as follows:

Three of the leading figures in the Wisconsin cherry canning industry were killed Saturday evening, December 4, when their plane crashed nine miles north of Sturgeon Bay in fog and bad weather. They were Karl S. Reynolds, Vice-president and Treasurer of the Reynolds Brothers, Inc.; Lougee Stedman, General Manager and Secretary-treasurer of Fruit Growers' Cooperative; and E.L. Kossow, Secretary of Reynolds Brothers, Inc.

Funeral services for Karl Reynolds will be held Tuesday at 1:30 P.M. at Sturgeon Bay; for Lougee Stedman, Tuesday at 3:30 P.M. at Sturgeon Bay; and for E.L. Kossow, Wednesday at

2:00 P.M. at Sturgeon Bay. (All were members of the same Congregational Church.)

The three men were returning from a conference on labor supply matters at Beaver Dam and took off from the Fond du Lac airport about 4:45 P.M. in the private plane piloted by Karl Reynolds. The crash occured about 6:00 o'clock Saturday evening but the bodies were not found until Sunday morning.

Karl S. Reynolds, who was 49, had long been active in industry and civic affairs. The son of a pioneer canner, William S. Reynolds, Karl was a member of the Old Guard Society and had served in various committees of the state and national canners associations, the National Red Cherry Institute and the Wisconsin State Horticultural Society. He had also served as executive vice-president of the Wisconsin State Chamber of Commerce and had been a director of that organization since 1929. He was active in aviation circles, having been appointed by the Governor to the State Aeronautics Commission and having headed the Wisconsin Flying Farmers and the Wisconsin Civil Air Patrol.

He is survived by his wife and four children, and by three brothers including Don who is President of Reynolds Brothers, Inc.

Ervin L. Kossow, who was 47, had been with the Reynolds firm for 29 years and was office manager in addition to being secretary. He is survived by his wife and one child.

Additional information about Stedman comes from the Door County Advocate:

Stedman, manager and secretary of the big Fruit Growers' Cooperative, was president of the National Red Cherry Institute and this spring was

Prisoners of War being taken to work in the orchards.

photo: Museum Collection

in charge of National Cherry Week. (Reynolds had been in charge of the first one.) He was a former member of the Sturgeon Bay Board of Education, and was a member of the Nicolet area council of the Boy Scouts of America. A former attorney, he was an honor graduate of the University of Wisconsin law school. He is survived by his wife and three children; a brother and sister also survive.

Many say to this day that if Karl Reynolds had survived, Reynolds Brothers would still be in business today. That would be impossible to prove; the company failed in the early 1960's, and by that time the Michigan orchards produced most of the cherries in the United States and controlled the market. Mechanical

photo: Museum Collection

Ahnapee and Western RR bringing POWs into Sturgeon Bay

picking had just begun to be used when the company folded (in fact I saw the only load of shaken cherries come into the plant.) The old Reynolds system of migrant labor for picking and factory would have had to be changed. Without a doubt, although no one seems to recall this, Karl S. Reynolds knew about the mechanical picking experiments in Michigan. Nine years after Karl's death, his brother Donald would be photographed with a prototype Gould cherry shaker.

photo provided by John Enigl

Reynolds north pickers camp

No doubt Karl S. Reynolds would have kept up with the times, so that, with his sales ability, he would have helped the company to get into good financial condition before his retirement, which would have been about 1965. But fate was not to have it that way.

The loss of Stedman, too, may have ultimately led to the demise of the Fruit Growers' Cooperative. We will never know.

Initials on Fruit

DID you ever see a name printed on a growing apple, peach or pear? Well, if you wish to have that pleasure, this is the way to obtain it. While the fruit yet hangs green upon the tree, make up your mind which is the very biggest and most promising specimen of all. Next, cut from thin tough paper the initials of your brother or sister, or chief friend, with round specks for the dots after the letters, and the letters themselves plain and thick. Then paste these letters and dots on that side of the apple which is most turned to the sun, taking care not to loosen the fruit's hold upon its stem. As soon as the apple is ripe, take off the paper cuttings, which, having shut out the reddening rays of the sun, have kept the fruit green just beneath them, so that the name or initials now show plainly. *from Chatterbox 1882*

page from Reynolds Bros. recruitment brochure

118

CHERRYLAND IS CALLING

"Come Cherry Picking—A Working Vacation—Good Wages"

REYNOLDS' CHERRYLAND ORCHARDS

STURGEON BAY, WISCONSIN

Snaps from CHERRYLAND

SMILES from Cherryland!

Cherries—UM!

Four Graces

HELLO!

The Office

Direct from Cherryland

Picnicing

R.A.K.
2/T N/2010RD
CHICAGO

Companion-
ship

Get a Tan

Wear
Old Clothes

Out of Doors

page from Reynolds Bros. recruitment brochure.

Wanted!—500 Pickers—July 7th to Aug. 5th

NO EMPLOYMENT SHORTAGE HERE!

Help Pick 30,000 Cherry Trees---Pleasant Outdoor Work
Modern Camp for Workers---Home Cooked Meals---Auto Camp Site Too
RECREATION, WORK, HEALTH, MONEY

Earn Money

Working Vacation

Good Crop

Low Expenses

page from Reynolds Bros. recruitment brochure

⊸⊰ "A Beautiful Life" ⊱⊶

DOOR COUNTY PIONEERS, HOMESTEADERS AND WOODSMEN TO HIGH-TECH ORCHARDS

A conversation with Dale and Gloria Seaquist and their son, Jim at Orchard Hill Farm, Sister Bay, in November 1982.
by Bev Njaa

By 1860 the entire Western world was either at war or preparing for war with itself in every area of life. Individuals were becoming aware of the many possibilities of freedom; freedom not only from slaveholders, but from the tyranny of oppressive ideological, religious, political and social systems. In that year Anton Chekhov was born. In the years between 1880 and 1890, Chekhov's writing focused on the decline of the Russian social and political system. Chekhov said he wanted his play "to make people look at themselves, to see how bad and dreary their lives are, and thus make them want to create another and a better world.

The children of Anders and Sophia Sjoquist were born in Sweden in the same chaotic period as Anton Chekhov. It fell to Chekhov to write about old country injustices and blindness, and it fell to the children and grandchildren of Anders and Sophia Sjoquist "to create another and a better world" in theirs.

Congress and the American public, preoccupied with the Civil War, largely ignored the immigrants who fled to the United States in the early 1860's. Among them was Anders Sjoquist, eager to leave behind the oppressiveness of the Swedish state religion, and to take advantage of the Homestead Act passed in 1862 — America's promise to reward hard work and individual effort, in a climate of religious freedom.

Anders made his way to the new state of Wisconsin, where he found work in one of the sawmills in "Menominee". After working for two years to provide The Union with lumber, he managed to accumulate enough money to send for the rest of his family. Anders' wife, Sophia, and ther sons Frank and Carl, crossed the Atlantic as uncomfortable passengers in an immigrant hold. Sophia's brother, August Kellstrom, his wife

Karin and their daughters, Anna and Tena, also immigrated with the Sjoquists to "Menominee".

There they worked until Anders and August each decided to buy a forty of land across the bay in Ephraim "from an Ephraim storekeeper". "Although their home was unpretentious and their means very limited, they valued the freedom they enjoyed. They felt free to carve out their own future in the land of their adoption — 'Landet i Vester' (The Land in the West). Not only did they feel this land to be the land of opportunity, but here they could enjoy religious freedom. They were free from the stifling restraints of the State Church of Sweden, and their hearts expanded in thankfulness to God . . . " so writes Anders' grandson, John, in a collection of reminiscences he called "Pioneer Experiences in Door County", printed in Sister Bay in 1954.

The Cherry Orchard, written in 1903, became Anton Chekhov's best-known symbol of the decay of the Russian aristocracy, and of Old Country decline in general. In the final act of the play, a former peasant buys the estate, and cuts down the cherry trees to make room for summer cottages.

To Anders Sjoquist, if he'd had time to think about it, an orchard would have been a symbol of pie, jelly, jam, apple butter and apple sauce. It would have represented just another aspect of a pioneer family's total self-sufficiency. But Anders and Sophia didn't have time for literary symbolism. They were totally involved, as were the children, in the activities of basic survival — cutting two cords of wood a day to pay off the Ephraim homestead.

When Anders and Sophia thought about anything beyond the necessities of life, they dreamed of establishing a church where memories of the oppressive state religion of Sweden could be erased in the freedom of America. Soon after they settled in Ephraim and long before they held formal title to their own homestead, Anders and Sophia began a Sunday School for their own and their neighbor's children. As more and more pioneer families gathered to worship, the congregation evolved into the Swedish Baptist Church of Sister Bay. The Church was formally organized in 1887 at Norwegian pioneer Hans Gunderson's log cabin in Sister Bay. The First Baptist Church of Sister Bay continues an active ministry today, with the Sjoquist descendants active members of the congregation.

illustration: Rosemary Utzinger

Six years after the church was founded, the family moved to land that included a mile of shore frontage in Sister Bay ... land purchased from Hans Gunderson. The family of homesteader/pioneer Anders Sjoquist depended heavily on the lake for food, water and travel. They collected driftwood for firewood, fished and ice fished the waters of Green Bay, and watered their stock at its shores.

The contemporary American family moves five times between the birth of the first child, and the day the last child leaves home. But the Seaquist families (the name was changed by Anders' children) living along Seaquist road at the northern end of Sister Bay, defy modern statistics and are quietly raising the fifth generation of Seaquists on the same land that was homesteaded by Anders and Sophia Sjoquist.

At the end of Seaquist road, on a ridge near the lake, a hulking shell is all that remains of the house that belonged to Anders and Sophia. The house was partially destroyed by fire in the summer of 1982. Dale Seaquist, great-grandson of Anders, discovered Anders' 16 x 18' log cabin within the walls of the larger home, and plans to work toward restoring the small structure, which contains many innovative features, including an early form of rock insulation.

Dale guides me along the leafy edges of a steep road that is slick with ice this early November morning, to the family-owned dock where Anders' descendants moor their boats, thus continuing the family's tradition on the water and on the ice. Dale points out his own tiny sailboat, pulled up high on the rocky shore and half covered with fallen leaves.

A steep incline of "perhaps 200 feet" runs from the ruined house to the bay. Not far from the house is one of the homestead's original log barns, still standing, and still in use on what is now David Seaquist's farm. This is where Anders built the "water railroad" described in the family history: "He laid wooden rails on cross arms attached to posts dug into the ground. On the rails ran a wooden car — a tight box with a self-shutting valve near the bottom. A rope was attached to the "car" which rolled down the incline into the water of the Bay. A windlass near the house pulled the box, now full of water, up to the house where a valve was opened, and the water released into the tank."

The inventive and hard-working Anders, pious churchman and powerful woodsman and fisherman, never did get around to planting an orchard of any kind. That step in the Seaquist Saga was left for his son, Carl Robert Seaquist. Carl Robert and his son, John, planted the first Seaquist orchard behind Carl Robert's home. In 1911, in the same decade that Chekhov wrote **The Cherry Orchard**, Carl Robert set out the first Seaquist cherry trees. He also planted McIntosh — a favorite apple variety of the period. "Only a half-dozen acres were planted at Grandpa's below the hill, east of the present farm," said Dale Seaquist, son of John, and great-grandson of Anders. "After John married, he planted 5 or 6 acres more in the spring of 1912." Since that first small orchard was planted for family use, Dale Seaquist, and now his son, Jim, have increased the Seaquist orchards far beyond Anders' and Sophia's wildest immigrant hopes.

Today, Seaquist Orchards boasts "somewhere between 175-80 acres of cherries and 60 acres of apples (70 acres if you count the young trees). There are a couple of acres of pears, plums, just as a curiosity, just for fun. Altogether, we have maybe 20,000 trees," said Jim.

If Chekhov's cherry orchard

symbolized the decay of Russian aristocracy, the trees of Seaquist Orchards are living evidence of the constant adaptation of each American generation of Seaquists to new methods, new technology, and finally to the newest in agribusiness techniques. This is the "other and better world" that Chekhov envisioned.

Today, only the winter months remain essentially unchanged for the orchardman who follows in his father's, grandfather's and great-grandfather's footsteps.

"The pruning is never done," says Jim. "You're supposed to prune every year. But apple trees . . . sometimes you should prune them two or three times a year . . . cherries need less work."

"And when it's too cold to prune, you do the shopwork and maintenance," said Dale. "It's always been like that. But now we have more bookwork to do in the winter. Much time is tied up in billing and paperwork."

An image comes to mind of Dale working on an old-fashioned ledger in front of the fireplace he built in his home, as the snow whirls between their living room and the lake a quarter-mile down the hill, but that image is a generation out of date.

"We're tied into the Agrifax computer record now. The secretary feeds the sheets to Agrifax, and they are all sent to Forestville. There's a big computer in Minnesota that handles farm records in winter from all over the midwest," said Dale. There was not even regular mail service, and the roads were just trails through the trees when Dale's great-grandfather and great-grandmother raised their family in the house at the end of what is now Seaquist Road.

In the winter, Dale, Jim and the Seaquist's all-around hired man, Leonard Leyendecker, are able to handle the bulk of the pruning and maintenance chores among the three of them. In 1982, Francois Raviore, born in France near the Swiss border, worked with the Seaquists until Christmas — a participant in an international farm exchange program. "He and Jim are the same age and have the same interests — Increased Production," said Dale. "They talk and talk about irrigation systems and spraying programs and hedging . . . They're two of a kind."

A musical remnant of Swedish intonation lies in Dale's speech, a constant reminder of the family's immigrant past, when English was a second language in the home and in the church; an alien tongue used only in schools and in business (sometimes).

Dale might never have become an orchardman. He might have been a professional musician instead. As a trumpet student of Melvin Kasen at Gibraltar, Dale won many honors for his trumpet playing, then performed in the university symphony and the First Army Band. As a freshman at the University of Wisconsin, Dale was forced to return to Door County because his father was not well that year. Then Dale also fell ill, and couldn't go back to school.

"So the decision was made for me," Dale said. Instead of going back to the University of Wisconsin, Dale stayed on the farm and went into partnership with his father in 1952. Although Gloria was planning to study nursing that fall, she too changed her plans, and Dale and Gloria were married.

Although he had to stop his formal studies in music, Dale's interest continues. His father played the organ for the church, and organized the first church choir. Dale sang in the choir, and now directs the male chorus "The Singing Men." Dale also sings with The Spectrum Choral Ensemble, travelling "at least once a month", to sing in concerts throughout the midwest.

Like his father and his grandfather before him, Dale's life has been one of long involvement in community and church affairs. There have been three generation of Seaquists who served as Town Clerk of Liberty Grove. Dale's father served on the County Board and as Sunday School Superintendant. Dale served on the Gibraltar School Board, and is the music director for the church. With his son, Jim, Dale has developed a new interest — flying. Both are taking pilot lessons from their former pastor, James Campbell, now at a congregation in Janesville. "It's one of the advantages of not being tied to a time clock," said Dale. "Orcharding can be very intense at times, but it does leave you time to pursue your other interests, and to grow new ones."

Gloria, Jim and Dale in front of the trees that were planted just before (in 1960) Jim came to them (Jim is adopted) in 1962.

"My father now, he was very studious all his life. He took a correspondence course and became a civil engineer."

"There's this thing about Seaquists . . . they're all inventive and innovative," said Gloria, and they recall the water railroad built by Anders.

Jim's mind too is innovative, and swings along high tech lines, planning Increased Production through every scientific orcharding technique that he learned in Michigan. Jim is the energy, physical strength and new ideas that a mature man recalls, but doesn't stress much any more, being tied up with paperwork, taxes and theological, ecclesiastical and civic policies and politics. Jim is youth's vitality undimmed by red tape.

Jim is a product of the Gibraltar School System, where a former teacher described him as a "goof-off, mainly interested in basketball." Gibraltar prepares its product for export, explained another teacher, at another time. Gibraltar exported Jim in 1980 to Michigan State, where high school goof-off Jim graduated at the top of his class in a two year (plus the summer) program that awards an Associate Degree in fruit production.

At Michigan State, Jim developed an interest in trickle irrigation and growth regulators. He designed an irrigation plan to be installed in one of the Sister Bay orchards. Fertilizer (nitrogen or potassium) is run through the irrigation system, "and some herbicides for grass control." Jim's current responsibilities include the orchard spraying schedule. "Apples are sprayed 8 to 12 times a season, cherries four or five times."

"Cherries. I always liked cherries," said Jim. "All my friends grew them. Apples — those are more drawn out. Cherries are exciting. There are a few weeks of very intense work, and then you're off for a while. But you're never done with apples. We have somewhere between four or five thousand bushels of apples still to process since August. With cherries, you pick them, freeze them, and you're done. And cherries are mechanically harvested, where with apples, you hire pickers."

"Yes," Dale continued, "when Spring comes, things break loose. As soon as the ground is thawed, we

Dale and Jim in orchard planted in 1969, where new "Hedging" technique is being used to produce a larger cherry crop.

begin planting. We usually plant some new trees each year, even just to stay the same. Right now 65 per cent of the cherries are still non-bearing."

"Then it's time to spray herbicides and to fertilize. In April we begin to hire student help part time. That's when the other two Seaquists pitch in." (Daughter, Ann and son, Mike). "From April on, it seems we spend three or four days a week spraying. Seems as though you have to spray for everything . . . for weeds, to make the trees grow, then to spread fungicide and insecticide. The final cherry spray is "alar" a growth regulator applied 10 to 14 days before harvest. It makes the cherries shake more easily," said Dale.

"Alar firms the cherries so they won't bruise so easily. The fruit holds its shape better," explained Jim. "The growth regulator helps to increase production. You get more pounds per acres."

There is increased production too, in "Hedging." A hedger is a giant mechanical tree pruner "built on the lines of a sickle mower, with the blades cutting through the trees as if they were hedges. This gives you a high density cherry tree. About 45

days after the tree is in full bloom, you cut off half the new growth," said Dale.

"We have about fifty acres of hedged trees, cut in Christmas tree shapes. It's a different idea that works. It takes somebody with new ideas to keep in step with the times. Jim took me to visit the Michigan State experimental blocks where hedging was done, and he showed me how it works. There are other growers in the county that are trying this process too," said Dale.

A tidy 14-year old block of cherry trees out on Highland Road is pruned by this method. "We got 326,147 pounds of cherries out of here last year," said Jim who was both proud and embarrassed to have the exact production figure in his mind. "Maybe you better just say 330,000 . . . round it off, sort of."

Both Dale and Jim believe that Door County is great orchard country. "It's a good place for orchards, although there's not all that much soil. The people who put Door County down . . . you have to realize that many orchards were planted by dairymen who took marginal land with very little soil, and put it into orchard. But if you select your sites, and treat it like a business, Door County is a good place to raise fruit," said Dale.

"Door is a bigger gamble though, than Michigan," said Jim. "It's a high risk venture. Michigan can diversify into sweet cherries, berries and peaches, so a Michigan grower has six crops to our two."

Jim said he would like to expand into small fruit crops. "I think there's a future in small fruit. You let go a lot of employees in the dead period between the cherry harvest and the apples. Then you have to hire them all back. Small fruit could keep us busy right through."

In May and June the pace picks up at Seaquist Orchards. "We keep mowing. We mow all the orchards at least three times a season. We keep spraying, fertilizing, applying insecticide, fungicide. Cherries are just easier to take care of. There aren't so many problems. Apples, you have to be more scientific. You might have three separate insect programs going on at the same time" said Jim.

"Then the last week of July and the first two weeks of August, we begin the cherry harvesting process. We use two shakers, and hire 19 people for the orchards and 30 for the processing plant."

"When we had the migrant workers it was much more human, much more civilized," said Gloria.

"It wasn't until '64 or '65 that we got into shaking and catching the cherries. It used to be there were 75 or so handpickers. I liked it better. It was more relaxed. It was more educational too, with all of those different cultures to live and work with. I loved being out with the crews. We had Hispanics. Jim Lawrence's Missouri crew was an all-Black crew. We had Indians ... Oneida and Ottowa ... and during the war we had the German POW's. There would always be a guard with a rifle leaning against a tree. The guards got to be a joke, almost. Once when it was time to stop for the day, they were missing one of the POW's. It turned out he had run off thru the woods and gone swimming down at the lake! Once a Jamaican government program sent us a crew that spoke the most beautiful British English ... it put us all to shame ... Do you remember any of the migrants?" she asked Jim. Jim couldn't remember. He remembered only Lawrence and his crew. "Well, Jim came to us in '62, and we got the first shakers a while after that."

Jim also remembers the boys from

World War II Prisoner of War working in a Door County orchard.

photo: Museum Collection

Rawhide. Until twelve years ago, disadvantaged and/or delinquent boys from Rawhide lived with the Seaquists, and like the Seaquist's own children, provided some part-time help in the orchards. After providing foster care for a total of 30 boys over a span of several years, Dale and Gloria planned and built a huge addition onto their home so they could care for as many as eight boys at once. But bureaucratic red tape — ("The state didn't want to send a social worker once a month all the way out here from Green Bay. They said it was too expensive.") — closed their "satellite" Rawhide before the addition was finished. It stands ready today, except for the finishing work. Built to state codes, it has four bedrooms, a workshop, a tower overlooking the lake. "We thought we might set up a radio station here, but . . . " Dale's voice trails off. All that space, ready for a new idea, ready to be finished and put to use. Now it is a huge storehouse for the overflow from the main house, "another and a better" way that was never used.

(On February 2, 1985, the Seaquist house, including the addition, were completely destroyed by fire.)

I liked having the boys come. It was fun, and we had a good time together," recalled Jim. "I was really sorry when they stopped coming."

Neither Dale nor Gloria welcomed the advent of the mechanical harvest, and Gloria especially regrets that Ann and Mike didn't have the experience of sharing their lives with so many different kinds of people.

"Once you've heard the sound of a crew working in an orchard, heard the singing, all the different conversations going on, you would never forget it," said Dale, "It's all lost now."

The cherry shaker and the mechanical cherry harvest has come to mean a time of intense, around the clock activity for the cherry grower.

In the summer of 1982, the Seaquists began processing their own cherry crop. They went into partnership with Mitch Larson, and bought the old Larson processing plant. "Only a small amount of the crop is stored here for retail sales," said Dale. "Most is stored in Green Bay. As soon as the truck is filled, the fruit is sent to the freezer."

"After the shaking and the trucking, we clean up the machinery, and store it away. For a few days we just fall in a heap, all tired out, and the pressure is off for a while."

Then it's time for the apples.

"At the end of August to the first of November, we harvest apples. Some are packed for wholesale sales, and others are sold locally."

"Meanwhile, we are pressing cider, freezing it all through October and November. We process several thousand gallons, then steam clean and close up," said Jim, stacking the filled gallon bottles of cider in the freezer.

"The cooler apples will sell out by mid-winter and several thousand bushels will be sent to Krier for processing."

Together we drive through the orchards. The day is Door County bright. November and chilly. We drive through the orchard nearest the house, past the Starkrimsons, Northwestern Greenings, Idareds, Spartans, McIntosh and Cortlands. Jim pointed out the plums that froze out this year. We see apple trees that were planted in 1912, and find the trees that Dale planted when he went into partnership with his father. Dale, Gloria and Jim pose for a photograph in front of the trees they planted near the time Jim came to them in 1962.

We view the young orchard planted by Jim last spring, where the trickle irrigation system he designed will be used. There are toothpicks stuck in

Dale and Jim Seaquist and a young cherry tree, planted the summer of '82. Note toothpick in between branches to form a better angle for lateral branch.

photo: Bev Njaa

between the branches, holding them apart. "That's to give the lateral branches a better angle — to make them stronger," said Dale. "Jim and Francois stuck all these in the trees last spring, and some are still in place, six months later."

Father and son look at the young tree together. There is a strong feeling in them for the trees; the same feeling that exists between father and son . . . between mother and son.

There is a holiday feeling in the car, a delight in touring the orchards instead of working them. It's a chance to say sentimental things and to voice deep feelings about the land, the trees and the past.

"Door County is a good place to be. I think it's a great place to live, and I wouldn't want to live anywhere else. Look, people work all year just so they can come up here and live here for two weeks. I live here all year!"

"There are so many ways in which our lives parallel the lives of our ancestors. The hard work, the faith, the community activities. I like the feeling of following the footsteps of my ancestors, of following patterns established by them. We are blessed with modern technology that makes the work less difficult, but we have to admire what they accomplished with very little in the way of material resources."

"The farm, the orchard, is a place to develop. It's not just a matter of taking over from your father. It's a matter of being able to use your ability, your ideas, to put in hard work and to take pride in it. I take great pride in looking at the result of my hard work. Jim brings in the new practices, new ideas. As we use more and more of them, the place becomes more and more Jim's place . . . and his responsibility if it doesn't go," Dale grinned.

illustration: Mike Judy

Chekhov said that a man with a hammer in his hand ought to stand behind the door of every happy man and knock to remind him that others are unhappy and that some day he too will feel life's sharp claws. The Seaquists don't need a man with a hammer. The know "the sharp claws of life," but they chose to remember and to talk about the good times.

"The area, the life comes to rescue us when things seem to go badly. The beauty rescues us and refreshes us. It is a beautiful life," concluded Gloria.

(Gloria Seaquist, 51, passed away August 2, 1984, after a long illness.)

A CHERRY JUICE WEDDING

In the 1930's, during the depression, Mitch LaPlant, the editor of the Door County News, came up with a unique promotional idea for the county's cherry industry: a wedding in cherry juice. Sturgeon Bay businessmen donated prizes for the wedding couple, and a large canvas tank surrounded by a platform was set up in the street at the corner of 4th and Louisiana in Sturgeon Bay. There wasn't enough cherry juice available to fill the tank so it was diluted with colored water. Although some religious groups protested the idea, the event took place and must still rate as one of the most unique weddings, and cherry promotions.

Fruit Grower's Cooperative
A Magnificent Experiment

····—◆——·····

by John Enigl

THE Fruit Growers' Cooperative played an important part in the Door County cherry industry from June 10, 1933, until the early 1970's, when it faded from the scene almost unnoticed and unmourned. (There are still many of its former members who will debate the last word in that statement.) Yet when the Sturgeon Bay plant was sold and all operations were consolidated at the new Sister Bay plant, observers knew it was the beginning of the end of a noble experiment. When a company elects to grow smaller, the next thing is to go out of business.

For those that may not know how a cooperative is organized, a few brief words of explanation are in order. A true cooperative is like a corporation in some but not all respects. Stock is issued, for which money is paid by the members, and the money is used to buy equipment to get the company going. Profits, if any, are shared by the members in proportion to the amount of stock they hold. A member is considered to be an owner of the cooperative, much more so than in a corporation, and expected to take an active part in the decisions of the company.

To encourage wide participation of members in the running of the company, one member has only one vote, regardless of how much stock he holds in the cooperative. This allows for a more democratic operation than in a corporation, in which if one stockholder corners 51% of the stock, he can control the company. That is the main difference between a cooperative and a corporation.

Growers were pledged to ship cherries only to the cooperative of which they were a member, but they didn't always follow that rule, as we shall see.

The Cooperative had its predecessors, first the Fruit Growers' Exchange, and then the Fruit Grower's Union. These companies may be considered, for all intents and purposes, one continuous company from 1918 on.

The late Lougee Stedman, killed in a plan crash on December 4, 1948 with two other greats of the cherry industry, Karl S. Reynolds and Ervin Kossow, was manager of the Fruit Growers' Cooperative at the time of his death. The year before, with the help of the president of the Cooperative, Kurt Stock, Stedman wrote a history of the company for a book, **The Story of Wisconsin's Great Canning Industry**. The following story is his, except for parenthetical remarks:

The Fruit Grower's Canning Company was organized by a group of cherry growers in January 1918, and purchased the pea cannery of the Reynolds Preserving Company. At the same time there existed the Door County Fruit Grower's Union which actually controlled the disposition of raw cherries. The Canning Company was organized for the purpose of creating another outlet (in addition to fresh fruit sales) which would be in the hands of cherry growers themselves.

The first president of the Fruit Growers' Canning Company was A.W. (Gussie) Lawrence (who was also president of the Fruit Grower's Union.) Edward S. Reynolds, Sr. was the first manager of the Canning Company, (which was a stock company, not a cooperative.)

After two terms as president, Gussie Lawrence was succeeded by Herman W. Ullsperger. E.S. Reynolds, Sr., died in 1919, and for a few months, his brother, Will Reynolds, acted as manager.

In April 1919, after being called home from occupation duty after World War I, Capt. Edward S. Rey-

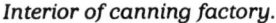

Interior of canning factory.

nolds, Jr. became manager, and occupied that position until February, 1924, at which time Herman W. Ullsperger became manager. Ullsperger served one term as president of the Canning Company until in January of 1921, James G. Martin was elected president. He, in turn, served until April, 1924, when there was a reorganization effected for the bringing of the Canning Company and the Door County Fruit Grower's Union under the control of a joint board consisting of directors from both the Canning Company and the Union.

A.W. Lawrence was again made president of the Canning Company, and Dr. A.J. Gordon of the Union, with the latter acting as chairman of the joint board. Dr. Gordon served in both offices until 1929, when Moulton B. Goff was made president of the Union on Dr. Gordon's death, and Will Marshall served as chairman of the joint boards.

The many changes in managers indicates the severe strain on men in executive positions. (Especially on those who grew up as farmers and not trained as executives. One must admire their courage in setting about such a venture into the world of business. Stedman had a degree in law from the University of Wisconsin, and Edward S. Reynolds, Jr. also attended the U.W. as did his cousins Karl S. and Donald W. Reynolds. — Enigl) It is a killing pace, and grower-member relationships in a co-operative enterprise contribute their share of grief. On the other hand, we have found it of advantage to introduce new methods and ideas through such changes. It is hard on men, but good for the association.

In June, 1922, a news item stated that manager E.S. Reynolds, Jr. "has the big plant all tuned up ready for the start on red sour cherries. The capacity of the factory has been increased from 250,000 cases of fresh fruit to 425,000 cases. Twelve additional pitters have been installed, making thirty three pitters in all." A later report in August, 1922, said, "The Fruit Grower's Canning Company this season just completed August 1st, canned a total of 9,280,000 pounds of cherries."

As of March 29, 1924, appeared the following: "If plans now under consideration at Sturgeon Bay, Wis., the center of the largest red sour cherry producing district in the United States are carried out, the cherry and apple growers of Door County, and the canning interests there, will be united into one organization. At present the Door County Fruit Grower's Union does the marketing for most of the cherry and apple growers, but there are a few apple growers not represented in the union. The Fruit Growers' Canning Company is made up of stockholders, all of whom belong to the grower's union. While both the Union and the Canning Company are separate corporations, the same men are directors of each. It is proposed to unite the two organizations as well as the unaffiliated apple growers. Secretary E.L. Johnson of the growers' union says that several hundred acres of new fruit will probably be set out next year. At present there are about 1500 acres of apples, 3,500 acres of cherries, and 50 acres of strawberries under cultivation in Door County."

Picking out bruised and cull cherries.

A movement to effect a merger with Michigan cherry growers had been under consideration and in January, 1930, the following item appeared: "At the annual meeting of the Door County Fruit Grower's Union and the Fruit Growers' Canning Company, Sturgeon Bay, Wis., resolutions were passed authorizing the proposed merger with the Michigan cherry growers and providing for the acceptance of the much talked of $720,000 loan by the Federal Farm Board. Directors of the Fruit Growers' Canning Company elected were Dr. H.F. Schroeder, Marinette; H.E. Stedman; and T.A. Sanderson, both of Sturgeon Bay. The directors of the Fruit Grower's Union elected were: A.W. Lawrence, John Boler, and John H. Miles, all of Sturgeon Bay. Officers elected by the directors of the Union board are: Moulton H. Goff, president; Kurt Stock, Fish Creek, vice-president; John Boler, secretary, and H.W. Ullsperger, treasurer. Canning Company officers are: A.W. Lawrence,

president; P.W. Donahue, Milwaukee, vice-president; H.W. Ullsperger, secretary and treasurer."

Not all of the grower members were favorable to the plan and a fight to prevent the merger and loan was begun and carried to the Supreme Court a short time ago to prevent the company from borrowing $720,000 from the Federal Farm Board. The action was started by the Martin Orchard Company, which contended that the Canning Company, of which it is a member, was violating its rights in contracting for the loan to attempt stabilization of the price and marketing of packed cherries. The funds for financing the program are to be obtained by a loan from the Federal Farm Board not in excess of $720,000 for the repayment of which the fixed assets of the Canning Company are to be mortgaged."

William Kinnaird became associated in the sales department under Mr. Ullsperger in May, 1930, and the "Cherry Sales Corporation Cooperative" was organized in 1931, to handle all sales of the Sturgeon Bay group, the "Cherry Growers' Packing Company" in Traverse City, Michigan, and the "Great Lakes Fruit Industries" in Benton Harbor, Michigan. Mr. Kinnaird functioned as sales manager until the end of the 1933 packing season, when the deal was called off and each of the three participating became independent, disposing of their own pack in 1934, and thereafter.

Mr. Kinnaird remained with the Fruit Growers' Cooperative until November, 1935, resigned his position and left Sturgeon Bay, going to Traverse City, Michigan, where he has been in business ever since.

The Fruit Growers' Cooperative handles tremendous quantities of cherries, fresh, cold pack and canned, having seven lines for canning operations, with factories at Egg Harbor and Sister Bay, as well as the main plant at Sturgeon Bay. They are also shippers of fresh apples and strawberries.

So concludes Lougee Stedman's history of the Fruit Growers' Cooperative, up until 1948. The writer questions one statement, that about a factory being at Egg Harbor. He is aware that the Fruit Growers' had a cherry receiving station at both Egg Harbor and Sister Bay, but he thinks that the Sister Bay plant was built later than 1948, and he is not aware there was a Cooperative factory at Egg Harbor, although he has lived there for many years. There may be an error here in transcribing of Stedman's report.

An August 7, 1958, article in the Door County Advocate featured the modernization efforts of the Fruit Growers' Cooperative.

The article tells of the machinery and methods that replaced 35 men. The American Can Company (to which Edward S. Reynolds went when he left Sturgeon Bay in 1924) had installed a new palletized system of handling cherries. An elevator on the outside of the factory was installed to lift both cans and sugar on pallets to be filled in the factory with cherries. New labeling and boxing equipment was also installed.

The pallet system was used to deliver cans to Sturgeon Bay from Canco in Milwaukee, and also used to ship the canned cherries from the Fruit Growers' plant to the buyer. The wooden pallets required the use of fork lift trucks, but the amount of hand labor, and damage to the product, was greatly reduced. Now all cherry factories, and most businesses, make use of the fork lift trucks to move just about any kind of product from one place to another in a plant and into trucks and around warehouses.

On Tuesday, February 28, 1961, the Door County Advocate produced a special tabloid section about the cherry industry. In his editorial, Robertson, a cherry grower himself, said:

"As a processor, and many Door County growers are processors, whether independently or as members of the Fruit Growers' Cooperative, he must meet entirely new concepts and ideas in packaging, marketing, and merchandising from what they were only a few years ago."

The Fruit Growers' Cooperative was addressing itself to this challenge, and to an old problem, member disloyalty, at the same time. One article in the tabloid stated:

"Without a question, recent years at

the Fruit Growers' Cooperative have been lean years, but then they simply reflect the position of the cherry industry in general which low production and rising costs are putting an ever-tightening squeeze on the cherry grower."

"And when it comes to the Co-op member, the squeeze catches him in two ways. As the owner of his own processing plant, he not only must meet the problems on the farm but in the plant as well."

"R.V. Jacks, who took over the reins of the cooperative in January, 1960, as general manager, recognizes that many of the cooperative's problems have resulted from high overhead and low volume, but feels that they also reflect a loss of the original meaning of the cooperative."

"In this respect, Jacks explains that with membership in the cooperative, growers actually process and market their own cherries. And as owners of their own processing

facilities, they must continue to re-invest and improve on those facilities through the annual purchase of stock."

"However, every co-op has members who actually are not co-op members in the true sense and look on their organization as simply a buyer for their product. At the far extreme are those members who will even violate terms of their contract and sell to private individuals or concerns, especially when the price makes it profitable to do so."

(Co-op members signed a contract to sell all their cherries to the cooperative. But in some years when the price was high and cherries were in demand they would take a large amount of their crop to Mike Miller, a processor in Sturgeon Bay, or out to Reynolds Brothers, where they got their payment in a shorter time than from the co-op, and did not have to take stock as part of the payment. To try to stop this, Fruit Growers'

No. 2 cans entering hot water exhaust box.

officials would sometimes walk down the row of trucks in line for the other factories and check to see if they carried any Fruit Growers' boxes.)

"And so it is no secret in Door County's cherry industry that co-op contracts have been violated by split deliveries, some cherries going to the independent processors, the rest to the Cooperative."

"No secret either is the fact that contract violations have been more apt to happen in lean years. When the Cooperative needed cherries, it got fewer from the violating members who found a ready market and cash price on the open market. Of course this situation was reversed in the big crop years when the co-op proved a ready dumping place for the surplus."

"However, under the new policy of the board of directors enacted under Jacks, this will change. A rebuilding program currently underway at the co-op is concerned not only with plant operation, but with membership as well. Instead of continuing futile attempts at gaining volume, the board has decided to concentrate on acquiring a hard core of growers and gearing plant facilities only to the demand of those growers."

"Adopting the policy of other successful cooperatives such as Lake to Lake Dairy in their building programs, the Fruit Growers' Cooperative will now adhere to rigid enforcement of contracts in its building program."

"Thus the accent on cherry volume is being taken off but is being replaced by a diversified operation in which other products will keep plant facilities busy as long as possible instead of just a few weeks at cherry harvest. After assessing present contract membership and its crop potential, the board decided to convert the cold pack plant into a diversified production plant. Ten

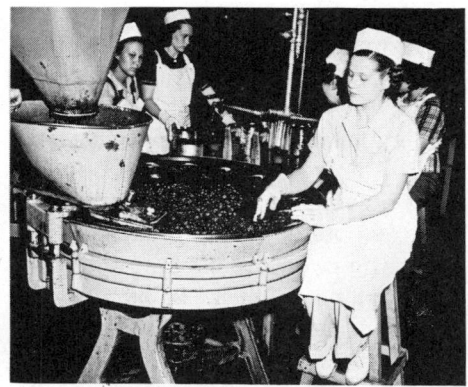

Filling No. 10 cans

pitters have been removed from the Sturgeon Bay plant and more could be on their way out as board and management continue their analysis of whether the 'britches' are too big for the membership."

"The new diversified look was reflected this past apple season when about a million more pounds of apples than cherries were processed at the co-op's plants at Sister Bay and Sturgeon Bay. At the present time, potatoes are being processed in the diversified plant where once only frozen cherries were handled."

"The diversified plant was also used during the months of fall and winter to make caramel apples, apple cider, and jellied cherry sauce — all products introduced this year. Jellied cherry sauce is catching on so fast that some are beginning to think it might actually be the salvation of the cherry industry. The co-op started out with 12 ounce cans of the jellied cherry sauce, but will introduce a 40 ounce can to the institutional trade at the Wisconsin Restaurant Show."

"Diversification at the Cooperative started in 1958 with apple processing at the Sister Bay and Sturgeon Bay plants. Sauce and sliced apples were processed at Sister Bay and canned apple juice and crab apples at Sturgeon Bay. This year the apple operation was expanded to caramel apples and apple cider in glass jugs at Sturgeon Bay to a higher grade apple sauce in addition to standard juice at Sister Bay."

"The new year found the Cooperative moving into still other products, such as potatoes. The initial operation finds the co-op peeling and canning medium potatoes in 16 ounce cans for the consumer trade."

"Jacks is also asking his growers to move into products which can be processed by the co-op, garden and tree crops alike. He says members have indicated that they will plant some 100 acres of plum trees this spring. More thinking is being done by members on strawberries and other garden crops. They can be sold either fresh or processed, depending on the market."

"With diversification, Jacks envisions the day when the total sales of these other products will actually exceed that of cherries, long the only product processed by the co-op. When that happens, he feels the investment and sacrifice now being made by the hard core of cherry growers will start paying off."

Good ideas, but by the late 60's the Sturgeon Bay plant grounds would be sold to Peterson Builders shipyard, and later the Sister Bay plant would be sold to Red Cheek to run a few more years as a cherry processing plant and then close.

Moulton B. Goff

Moulton B. Goff, actively connected with horticultural interests in Door County, gives his time and attention to the development and care of a large orchard at Sturgeon Bay, in addition to which he maintains stock raising interests. Indeed he is one of the most progressive agriculturists of this section of the state and took up his present line of business well equipped by thorough scientific training for the work which claims his thought and energies. He was born in Madison, Wisconsin, June 15, 1889, and is a son of Professor E.S. and Antoinette (Carr) Goff, both of whom were natives of Elmira, New York. In the year 1888 they arrived in Madison. For seven years the father had been horticulturist at the Geneva (New York) experiment station and he held the same position at the State University of Madison up to the time of his death, which occurred in 1902. His wife passed away the previous year. It was in 1894 that Mr. Goff purchased land in Door County in connection with A.L. Hatch and D.E. Bingham, the three becoming pioneers in the development of cherry orchards for commercial purposes. Few, if any, have done so much for the progress of the state along horticultural lines as Professor E.S. Goff, whose study and experiments have demonstrated the possibilities of Wisconsin in fruit production. He has indeed given an impetus to fruit raising the value of which is immeasurable, and his name should long be honored in this connection.

Moulton B. Goff was the younger of two sons but his brother, Charles E. died in childhood. At the usual age he became a pupil in the public schools of Madison and after completing his high school course there spent a year in the State University. He then went east to Cornell University, where in 1913 he completed the agricultural course. He had previously been connected with the fruit business at Sturgeon Bay and following his graduation he returned to take charge of the business at this point. He now has seventy acres devoted to fruit, thirty acres being planted to cherries, thirty acres to apples, five acres to plums and five acres to small fruit. In addition he has one hundred and thirty acres of land which he farms, and upon his place he has a herd of pure bred Guernsey cattle.

On the 20th of August, 1913, Moulton B. Goff was married to Miss Agnes Davis, of Madison, a daughter of R.W. and Helen (Hopkins) Davis, and they now have two sons, Charles D. and Robert W. In politics Mr. Goff is a progressive republican and fraternally is connected with the Independent Order of Odd Fellows. He is one of the county's most progressive farmers, acquainted with every phase of the work and continually studying, so that he keeps in touch with the latest researches, discoveries and improvements in methods of fruit and crop production. His ideals are high and he grasps eagerly every opportunity for raising himself to their level.

Professor E.S. Goff

Moulton B. Goff

In Door County cherry orchards you will find single branches with five and six feet of lucious fruit thickly growing along their length.

"With sunshine and running water,
Snowfall and Summer's rain,
The orchards and quiet meadows
Are filled with fruit and standing grain."

Fruit Growing
from H.R. Holand's History of Door County - 1917

The earliest attempt at commercial horticulture in Door County was made by Dr. E.M. Thorpe on Strawberry Island near Fish Creek. In 1865 Dr. Thorpe cleared the island and planted most of it - more than twentyacres - to grapes. For a few years the grapes did moderately well but when the doctor moved away the whole island relapsed into a wilderness.

The earliest farm orchards of which there are any records are those of Joseph Zettel and Robert Laurie. Zettel began setting out trees in 1862. Laurie must have begun just as early. At the first county fair, held in the courthouse, October 20, 1869, Robert Laurie exhibited thirteen varieties of apples, for which he received much praise.

In 1866 several commercial orchards were started in the county. J.J. Pinney at this time traded a tract of land in Ohio which he had never seen for a large quantity of fruit trees. These were shipped to Sturgeon Bay and sold to the farmers. The biggest investor in these trees was Joseph Zettel who by this time had become an enthusiastic fruitgrower. After a few years Mr. Zettel had forty-five acres planted to apples, this being the largest apple orchard in the state for many years. In 1892 he harvested 3,000 bushels of apples. The next year he had a big exhibit of more than twenty varieties at the world's fair in Chicago.

Unfortunately, notwithstanding

this demonstration of successful conditions, fruit growing was as yet a side line and the care of the trees was indifferent. The varieties were largely unsuited to the markets. Nevertheless Mr. Joseph Zettel is entitled to great credit for having by persistent and abudant planting demonstrated Door County's fitness for growing fruit.

About this time Door County's favorable conditions for fruit growing as successfully demonstrated by Joseph Zettel and others began to attract the attention of certain men who were soon to make Door County famous as a fruit growing region. In 1891 Door County was visited by Mr. A.L. Hatch and Prof. E.S. Goff. Mr. Hatch was a large commercial fruit grower of Richland County and Professor Goff was professor in horticulture at the University of Wisconsin. They were pleased with the evidences of unusually favorable climatic conditions for growing fruit,

as shown by several small plantings of plums, apples and cherries in different parts of the county and were particularly impressed with Mr. Zettel's testimony that for forty years he had never suffered injury from a spring frost. They, therefore, bought eighty acres of land, about a mile north of the city. This land was on a stony ridge of land stretching northward from the city, a pine slashing, which up to that time had not been considered valuable for farming purposes. But Mr. Hatch with his indomitable energy immediately proceeded to grub up the stumps, bury the stones and soon converted the wilderness into the highest priced lands in Door County.

In 1983 they set out six acres of plums of European and Japanese varieties, some mixed cherries and pears and 50,000 apple grafts. In 1894 and 1895 they added ten acres of plums, set out more apple grafts and many strawberry plants. In 1896

Small vegetables and fruit planted in young orchards in Door County have demonstrated their ability to produce from $500 to $800 an acre.

"For plenty and peace and playtime,
The homely goods of earth,
And for rare immaterial treasures
Accounted of little worth."

they began to plant the sour cherries which was to become such a famous factor in Door County's industries and publicity. They set out three acres of cherries this year. They also set out eight acres of apples, one variety of which, then new to the county, later became the most popular. This was the Wealthy.

illustration: Mike Judy

W.I. Lawrence also began to plant cherries, one-half acre, in 1896. In 1897 A.W. Lawrence planted five acres of cherries. It was this orchard which after some years of neglect became the most profitable and famous orchard in Door County. D.E. Bingham who had for some years worked for Mr. Hatch, became his partner in 1895, and later, as successful fruitgrower and public speaker at farmer's institutes, became the most widely known orchardist of the state. Professor Goff withdrew from the partnership in 1898. Messrs Hatch and Bingham, however, continued to plant trees and operate the nursery from which most of the important orchards in the county got their first plantings. Mr. Hatch did not become a permanent resident in the county until 1898.

Up to this time and for several years afterward the plantings had been confined to the immediate vicinity of Sturgeon Bay. The first commercial planting in the northern part of the county was made in 1894 by L.D. Thorp at Egg Harbor. His trees were nearly all summer apples, for which there was but little demand. The next planter was H.R. Holand at Ephraim. In 1899 he set out six acres of winter apples, which was followed three or four years later by a much larger acreage of the same fruit trees. In 1903 Dr. Eames of Egg Harbor began his plantings which shortly became very extensive. About this time William Marshall, D.E. Bingham, N.C. Jacobs and Geo. Christianson, all large growers near Sturgeon Bay, set out their large orchards.

For a few years this work of setting out orchards continued in a quiet way by a small number of men who had faith in Door County's special fitness for growing fruit. Their enterprise did not attract much attention, however, because horticulture is a waiting game. Eventually the orchards of A.L. Hatch, W.I. Lawrence and A.W. Lawrence, for many years the big three in Door County horticulture, began to yield crops. In 1908, 1909 and 1910 these crops became fabulously great and Door County received national attention. This peninsula, formerly supposed to be a land of pine forests and icebergs, began to produce luscious cherries by the carloads, with such returns per acre as to be quite unbelievable. Below is a statement copied from a pamphlet entitled "The Truth About Fruitgrowing in Wisconsin," published by the Wisconsin Horticultural Society in 1914:

"Seventeen years ago a man planted 600 cherry trees. He lacked faith. The trees were neglected for seven years. The neighbors of the man took care of their trees and waxed rich. The man was wise and sought counsel of his neighbors who said: 'Spray, cultivate, prune, cultivate, spray and prune.'

"The man sprayed, cultivated and pruned, cultivated, pruned, and sprayed as exhorted.

"Fifty of the trees had already died but the remaining 550 in nine years yielded 343,792 quarts of cherries which brought the man a net revenue of $21,218.30. One year the trees bore 48,144 quarts, which sold for $4,724.13. It cost the man $1,373.28 to cultivate, prune, spray and to pick and market the fruit, leaving $3,350.85 net profit, an average net return of $609.24 an acre.

"In 1911 the average net return was $388.82 an acre and in 1910 $338.90 an acre.

"Here is the story for nine years:

1905	1,931 crates
1906	1,972 crates
1907	2,121 crates
1908	2,060 crates
1909	3,447 crates
1910	2,745 crates
1911	2,194 crates
1912	3,009 crates
1913	2,008 crates

"The man is A.W. Lawrence of Sturgeon Bay, the orchard is just back of his house. Other orchards nearby yielded nearly as much."

As a result of this success, which was practically equalled by Bingham, Hatch and W.I. Lawrence, there now, in 1909, began a boom in fruit growing which lasted for several years. Huge wagon loads of two-year-old fruit trees were to be seen in springtime on every cross road. They were sometimes planted with dynamite rending the rock in fragments and sometimes they were rammed into the soil with a crowbar. Vast areas of wild land were feverishly conquered by every human and mechanical device and set out to cherry trees. Others had not the patience to plant new orchards but bought other orchards set out a few years, paying from five hundred to one thousand dollars per acre for them. Every back yard and stone pile had its bunch of cherry trees.

Chief among these plantations were a number of large corporations which set out hundreds of acres of cherry trees. The first was the Sturgeon Bay Orchard and Nursery Co., which in 1910 set out forty acres in cherries. They now have 160 acres of cherries and apples. In 1911 the Co-operative Orchard Co. planted 200 acres of cherries. They now have about seven hundred acres of cherries in one body, being the biggest cherry orchard in the world. The Reynolds Preserving Co. planted sixty acres in 1911. They soon had about three hundred fifty acres but now only about 2 hundred acres in cherries. The Ellison Bay Orchard Co. planted fifty-six acres in 1911. They now have 210 acres in fruit, mostly in apples. The Peninsula Fruit Farm Co. planted 110 acres in 1912. They now have 210 acres in cherry and apples. The Sturgeon Bay Fruit Co. have about eighty acres in cherries and apples and so has the Cady Land Co. Many other growers have more than forty acres in orchards.

There is now in Door County a total of 5,460 acres planted to fruit. Of these we have 3,270 acres in cherries, 1,900 acres in apples and about three hundred acres in small berries, particularly strawberries.

The cherry acreage is distributed as follows:

	Acres
Sturgeon Bay & Sevastopol	2,262
Sawyer and vicinity	344
Egg Harbor	253
Gibraltar	180
Liberty Grove and Sister Bay	136
Washington Island	49
Baileys Harbor	31
Jacksonport	15
Total	3,270

The cherries are about equally divided between Early Richmond and Montmorency.

Early spray rig ca. 1890.

There is at present (1917) a total of 95,000 apple trees growing in the country. Of these there are 27,000 Wealthy, 18,000 McIntosh. 12,000 N.W. Greening, 5,200 Fameuse, 4,000 Duchess, 3,600 Dudley, 3,400 McMahan, 3,000 Wolf River, 1,300 Windsor, 17,500 in other varieties.

In 1917 there was shipped through the fruit exchange 103,000 crates of cherries. Private shippers disposed of about twelve thousand crates. This required no less than two hundred and thirty railroad cars to haul it away, and the value of this cherry crop was about one hundred eighty-five thousand dollars. The fruit exchange also shipped 8,514 crates of strawberries, 2,675 crates of currants and 1,186 crates of gooseberries. Private shippers would increase these figures by at least 5 per cent. The small fruit brought in about twenty-five thousand dollars. No statistics are available for the value or extent of the apple crop, but it may safely be put at thirty thousand dollars. The total value of Door County's fruit crop in 1917 is therefore not less than two hundred fifty thousand dollars. As most of the orchards are only in the infancy of their fruitfulness it will not be long before the fruit production of the county will pass the million dollar mark.

The boom has now ceased. A few of the smaller orchards which were planted in unsuitable locations or which have been neglected will be cut down. The biggest orchards will no doubt be divided into smaller tracts as it is too much of an undertaking for any one manager to handle such huge plantations. Nearly all the orchards of Door County are in the immediate vicinity of Sturgeon Bay, Egg Harbor, Fish Creek, Ephraim and Ellison Bay. The southern part of the county, with its heavy clay soil, has been found less adapted to fruit growing.

The chief reason why Door County possesses such marked advantages over the rest of the state for producing fruit is its peculiar climatic conditions caused by its insular locations. The modifying influence of the waters and ice of Lake Michigan and Green Bay gives the peninsula a cold, backward spring. It is generally considered that this retards bloom until the frosts are over. The fact is, rather, that it prevents a rapid, tender growth that would not be sufficiently hardy to endure subsequent frosts. Further south there is too little steady cold; fruit trees burst quickly into bloom with the advent of warm days, and the tender growth succumbs to subsequent frosts. In Door County the buds come on very slowly; often it is several weeks from the time they first swell until full bloom. During that time they strengthen and become hardy. Further south what we consider hardy vegetables like the cabbage, the onion or beet are sometimes destroyed by frost on account of their rapid, tender growth. In the fall of the year we have another effect of the waters which so modify the temperature that there is a long time when frosts are not severe enough to destroy the leaves, but allows them to do their work to the fullest extent, ripening the twigs, storing surplus food for spring use, hardening and perfecting the buds. Thus our climate helps at both ends of the season. Fruits of this region are fine keepers and good shippers on account of the climate, and this is a valuable factor in commercial fruit culture.

Fruit growing has now become an established industry in Door County. Not only is the climate remarkably favorable but the cherry trees are also more immune to insect pests here than elsewhere. The cherry curculio and other causes of wormy cherries, for instance, are unknown here. Similarly apple trees do better here than anywhere else in the Middle West. While we can grow almost any variety the most successful in a commercial sense have been found to be N.W. Greening, wealthy, McIntosh Snow, Duchess and Dudley.

Door County has also been fortunate in having had excellent teachers in fruit growing. Due to the intelligent and thorough example of A.L. Hatch, D.E. Bingham, A.W. Lawrence and W.I. Lawrence, the fruit growers of the county have learned that it pays to cultivate and spray. The result is that nowhere can be found better orchard treatment. More than one-half of all the spraying outfits in the state are in Door County.

Apple Time at Uncle Jerry's

from Harper's Weekly Oct. 9, 1858

I wonder who doesn't love to be in the country in apple-time, when the boughs bend down under the weight of the ripe, juicy fruit!

Uncle Jerry has apple orchards on the hill, and under the hill, and behind the barn, and even the great red farm-house stands in an apple-orchard.

Every autumn I like to go to "Sunny Meadow" and pass a week at Uncle Jerry's, and help gather apples with his boys and girls.

Early in the morning I am wakened by his jolly voice shouting to Billy, and Robby, and Liddy, and Polly, and half a dozen others, to "come along with the ladders and baskets and poles to put into the cart." Then I know the merry work is to begin. I spring out of bed and dress myself as quickly as you could say "Jack Robinson," and run downstairs to be with them and help enjoy the sport.

Aunt Debby won't let me go a step till I have eaten some of her fresh brown bread and milk. She says she can't come yet, because she must make some September butter, and Polly must "tidy up" the house; but they will follow by-and-by, with the other wagon and the one-eyed mare.

In we all scramble, and sit on the bottom of the cart. Uncle Jerry takes the whip, and marching alongside of the oxen, commences a long strip of outlandish words, such as "Whish!" "Whop!" "Kerbrike!" "Bake!" "Whop wa ho!" and a great deal more, of which I never clearly comprehended the meaning, and between you and me, I don't believe the oxen did either; I know they would have walked on just as sedately if Uncle Jerry had said, "Come, 'White Face' - come 'Whisker,' we are going to gather apples on the hill."

Oh, how full the trees hang! How large and tempting the rosy apples look! They make my mouth water so that I must eat one before I begin to pick. Sitting on a bushel basket, I am just in the act of meeting my teeth in a juicy "Seek-no-farther," when I hear a shout over my head.

"Look out, Cousin Letty; you'll get pelted!"

Up I spring again, knocking the great basket over in my hurry, and just escape a shower of apples on my head. That little rascal of a Robby is up in the tree, looking like his bird namesake, with his red calico apron on, shaking the boughs till his hat flies off, and his white hair dances over his little round head like a wick-yarn mop, when Aunt Debby shakes it out the back window.

Down come the apples by the hundreds; sounding in their quick fall like a troop of wild horses galloping over the field.

After a few minutes of this violent exercise Robby sits back upon a branch to rest, and eat the big apple which he cabbaged and pocketed when he first climbed up. All the rest of us dart down at the fruit, like bees upon clover. Baskets are filled quickly, and Uncle Jerry hoists them upon his broad shoulders and upsets them in the cart.

The whole orchard is delicious with fragrance! I think an apple smells as good as it tastes. I know peaches are rich flavored and plums are luscious, grapes are tempting and pears are "kill'n," as they say in the "Bowery;" but give me a ripe, juicy, crispy **apple** and I am willing to forego all the others. I heartily join with Mary Howitt in her song of

 "The apple-tree,
The bright, rosy apple-tree!"

When the tree has been shaked until it looks **breathless** there are still a dozen or so of kingly great fellows, standing by their fortress while life remains. Then pitiless Uncle Jerry takes the long pole and comes on to the attack. After a few determined pokes he fetches them rolling to the ground, and tosses them in, with their red brothers, ready for market.

So we go from one tree to another, stripping them of their "recruits" until they are left naked and forlorn to brave old Winter's blasts, and shake their bare arms in defiance at the wind.

There comes Aunt Debby, jogging along with the horse and wagon. The old mare is continually turning to the left; because she has no eye on that side, and she is dying of curiosity to see what lies on the **blind half** of the road. This keeps poor Aunt Debby pulling at the other rein, until, out of patience, she gives them a great jerk, and calls the mare a **"pesky old critter!"** The astonished animal holds her head up in the air and stretches open her mouth, thinking she is desired to stop. Then Aunt Debby, with determined severity, gathers up the reins and lays them soundly over the mare's back, assuring her that if she don't "git along" she'll find a way to **make** her!

Uncle Jerry stands in the orchard laughing; and says, "Mother's a good 'un; she fetches 'em up to the mark!" and Aunt Debby drives victoriously in at the bars.

When both cart and wagon are filled we take leave of the orchard under the hill. Next day we sweep clean of apples the orchard **on** the hill; then the one behind the barn; and last of all, the orchard where the house stands. This contains the rarest and most delicious fruit of all. Here grow the "pumpkin sweetings," and the "blueberry-mains," and one tree of golden, pear-shaped apples, which Uncle Jerry calls "rattle-boxes," because the brown seeds shake loosely about in the core.

When I bid good-by to the good folks my pocket and carpet-bags are stuffed well with the fairest apples to be found, by dear Aunt Debby and the children, and they send me off with cordial invitations to repeat my visit "next apple-time."

Peninsular
Experiment Station

1922-1985

by Richard Weidman

OCATED on the geographical thumb of Wisconsin, the University of Wisconsin Peninsular Experimental Station began its research work in 1922. At that time, most of the early research at the station involved the dairy farming industry and small grain and pea breeding programs. Dr. E.J. Delwiche, superintendent of the station from 1922 to 1945, conducted a very active plant breeding program that yielded several significantly new grain and pea varieties. Most significant of Delwiche's achievements was the development of wilt resistant pea varieties which helped save Wisconsin's pea industry. By 1942, approximately 70 per-

cent of Wisconsin's pea varieties were derived from Dr. Delwiche's program.

Even though several new grain and pea varieties were released through the plant breeding program during the early history of the station, fruit research at that time was also receiving attention. C.L. Fluke, entomologist; R.H. Roberts, horticulturist; and G.W. Keitt, plant pathologist; comprised the original fruit research team on the Peninsular Station. Many insect, disease and cultural problems associated with fruit growing were severely limiting the fruit industry from developing in the Door County area. At this time, both Fluke and Keitt made considerable progress in determining the life cycles of several fruit diseases and insects. This basic research was critical at this time if the fruit industry was going to survive in Door County.

Fluke initiated early insecticide programs that aimed at controlling insect pests during the most vulnerable stage of the insect's life cycle. This early research enabled growers to actually develop spray programs based on insect activity rather than a continuous spraying schedule throughout the course of the growing season. G.W. Keitt, at this same time, was beginning to develop spray programs to combat the spread and detrimental effects of two very important fruit diseases, apple scab and cherry leaf spot. He studied the effects of two major chemicals found in early fungicides used on cherries that not only affected fruit quality but also caused the fruit to be more susceptable to rot infections. Sulfur, the major fungicide at that time, was found by Keitt to decrease sugar content of cherries and at the same time caused the fruit to be softer than normal, causing the increased incidence of fruit rot. He also at this time found that sour cherry yellows was not a symptom of a nutrient deficiency as previously believed by fruit specialists during the 1930's, but rather caused by a virus infection.

While Keitt and Fluke were working with disease and insect problems, R.H. Roberts was researching cultural practices relating to the production of tart cherries. From a 1922 bulletin that Roberts produced on growing cherries, he related the pruning practices of the time to decreased yields and tree vigor. Instead of allowing the cherry tree to develop naturally with light pruning cuts, he advocated making significant pruning cuts to head back and thin out excessive growth in the tree to allow for better light penetration.

As more people became aware of the ideal climate that Door County offered for fruit production, the industry began to expand greatly. Along with the expansion of the fruit industry in Door County, came also the need to expand the research programs at the Peninsular Station. In 1946 the main research emphasis at the station was shifted to fruit research; and facilities, equipment and staff were expanded. At that time, Dr. F.A. Gilbert, a horticulture graduate of Rutgers University, was named superintendent of the station and fruit plantings at the station were expanded greatly. Nutritional studies conducted by Dr. Gilbert on cherries revealed that previous leaf curling symptoms were a result of potassium deficiency and not a disease problem. Dr. J.D. Moore, plant pathologist, began an extensive study to identify virus problems present in cherry trees. Although some of these viruses never appeared through external symptoms on the tree, they greatly attributed to gradual decline and shortened life of the tree. New fungicides and insecticides were constantly being evaluated for effectiveness and possible detrimental effects upon fruit quality.

The cherry industry was expanding tremendously in Door County with over 10,000 acres devoted to production. With that much acreage to harvest by hand, maintaining a work force that large presented its problems. It was during this time that agricultural engineers began designing prototype mechanical cherry harvesters. The Peninsular Station during this time initiated an active program with the University of Wisconsin Ag. Engineering Department to test and develop an early prototype model. Damage to tree and fruit during the mechanical harvest were measured and it was from this early research that the basic principles involved in present day mechanical harvesters were evolved. Concepts such as the use of large holding vats of water for harvested cherries not only helped preserve the quality of the fruit but also helped to eliminate unwanted dirt and debris.

Along with an active program in fruit research at this time, the Peninsular Station was also involved in establishing a germplasm or seed bank for wild or non-cultivated potato species. Since many of the species collected from plant expeditions to Central and South America were often lost soon after collection, the need for a central collection point to maintain these species became a necessity. Therefore in 1950, the Potato Introduction Center became

an important part of the research program at the Peninsular Station. The project distributes to potato breeders world-wide seed and tubers of wild potato species that in turn are grown and used in potato breeding programs. The genetic traits of these wild species, whether it be increased disease and insect resistance or increased drought and frost tolerance, can be incorporated to new potato varieties. The project also has through the years sponsored expeditions to Central America and Mexico to discover and bring back for the collection new species of potato which in turn has offered new sources of genetic material for potato breeders.

Variety of cultivar evaluation as well as development of new fruit cultivars has always been an important part of the research program at the Peninsular Station. Dr. Gilbert, through his strawberry breeding program, released three new strawberry cultivars. 'Badgerbelle', 'Badgerglo' and 'Gilbert' were accomplishments of the strawberry breeding program. The strawberry breeding program is no longer being carried out at the station since Dr. Gilbert's retirement in 1982, but cultivar evaluation of new and older

strawberry cultivars is being presently maintained. Another fruit introduction by Dr. Gilbert included the 'Viking' apple. Selected from a block of seedling apples, the 'Viking' apple is an early summer apple with red skin, fine textured flesh and good quality that enables growers to begin marketing apples four to five weeks before the fall apple crop is ready. As with small fruit cultivar evaluation, apple cultivar evaluation has also been conducted at the station. Since 1951, almost 200 cultivars, selections, redsports and spur-type apples have been or are presently being evaluated.

Present day research at the Peninsular Station includes continuation of many of the initial research programs in insect and disease control on cherries and apples that were initiated some fifty-sixty years ago. This research takes on a new perspective though as insects become immune to commonly used insecticides and disease organisms build-up resistance to fungicides. Integrated pest management, utilizing and protecting natural predator insect species, has become a very important aspect of insect control studies at the station. New fungicides being tested and released for use at the station today are no longer simply protectant in action but now have the ability to attack and eliminate disease organisms.

Clonal rootstock evaluation on apples and cherries has and will become a very important part of the research program at the station. Since almost all apple cultivars today are grated onto clonal or size-controlling rootstocks, performance evaluation of these rootstocks under varying climatic conditions is of much concern by apple growers. This is especially true in the upper midwest where winter conditions often time are quite severe. By being a cooper-

ating member in the North Central Rootstock Research Project, along with twenty other cooperating state members, the researchers at the Peninsular Station are able to evaluate various apple rootstocks and their effects upon the cultivar that is grafted onto them. In 1986 a new cherry rootstock planting will be initiated at the station in an effort to find a more size-controlling and earlier fruiting rootstock.

Other projects at the station presently include pea variety trials to assist area canning factories to select those varieties that perform best under local weather condition. Home or backyard gardeners can find many demonstrational areas of special interest. Grape cultivar trials, annual flower trials, vegetable variety trials and woody ornamental trials are some of the items of interest to home gardeners that can be found on the station grounds. The station also sponsors various special events and field days throughout the course of the year. As the case with all experimental stations maintained by the University of Wisconsin, visitors are always welcome.

Some Wisconsin Seedlings Were Named

Whenever anyone walked across uncultivated land eating an apple — or any other fruit — the seed, dropped in a favorable spot, might produce a seedling tree. There were thousands of seedlings growing all over the state in the early days and no doubt there are still a great many.

Early settlers cherished their best seedlings and some were quite popular for a time. There was, and still is, the hope of finding a fruit superior to any we now have.

The Northwestern Greening

The Northwestern Greening, of all the seedlings, became the most popular and most widely grown in Wisconsin. It is still favored by processors because it is of good uniform size and has adaptability for freezing and canning. It originated near Iola in Waupaca County and was introduced by E.W. Daniels of Waushara County in 1872.

The Wolf River

The Wolf River apple was found near the Wolf River and the Village of Freemont, Wis., and introduced by W.A. Springer of Freemont.

The variety was first mentioned in the Annual Report of the Society for 1875 when Mr. Springer exhibited a box of seedlings which included the Wolf River. It was favorably described as "large, red, tender and of good flavor." It had already been named in 1875.

The McMahan

The McMahan apple became one of our popular varieties for a number of years. The seed was planted by Mrs. Isaac McMahan of Richland County in her garden in 1860, and came from a large red apple received from Ohio, thought to be the Alexander. The McMahans lived near what was then the West Branch P.O. In 1870, the Richland Horticulture Society named the seedling McMahan's White, to distinguish it from a red seedling they named McMahan's Bloom, which proved undesirable because it was subject to Fire Blight.

The Newell

The Newell apple was first known as the Orange Winter. At the 1909 convention, Mr. Wm. Toole of Baraboo reported that it originated from a seed planted by Mr. Orange Newell on a farm about four miles north of Baraboo in the 1950's. It was a good cooking apple, late in season, at its best at about Thanksgiving time. It did not become popular with commercial growers and soon disappeared from nursery lists.

A Great Seedling Is Saved
The McIntosh

Allan McIntosh of Dundas County, Ontario, Canada, was clearing land one day in 1811 on his homestead. He found three young apple trees and decided to save them. They were planted near his home and had a precarious existence for a time.

Mr. McIntosh recognized the value of one of the trees and tried to tell folks about it, but 59 years would pass before his son, in 1870, began to propagate it, and named it the McIntosh. By 1907 it was widely grown in New York State, but only then did it become known in Wisconsin. We find R.J. Coe, nurseryman of Ft. Atkinson, and D.M. Bingham, fruit grower of Sturgeon Bay, recommending it to Wisconsin fruit growers at the Annual Convention of the Society.

One may well ponder why it took almost 100 years for this now most popular variety to become recognized and recommended.

The Pewaukee

The Pewaukee apple was originated by George P. Peffer, Pewaukee, Wis., by crossing the Duchess with the Northern Spy. It was first brought to the attention of fruit growers about 1870. It proved to be hardy but in quality it was only fair. It never became very popular.

The Windsor Chief

The Windsor Chief is reported to have originated in Wisconsin, but we have been unable to find any record of its origin. It was quite popular for many years although not of high quality.

The Connell Red

To Thomas W. Connell and his father William F. Connell of Sun Ridge Orchards, Menomonie, Wis., goes the credit for discovering and introducing a new apple variety, the **Connell Red**. It is the first "color sport" or mutation of value named in Wisconsin and was found in 1949 by Thomas Connell in a block of **Fireside** apple trees planted in 1943.

A mutation is a sudden departure from the parent type: a differing in one or more characteristics caused by a change in a gene or chromosome. Such changes in character, in this case a solid red color, are retained when the plant is propagated.

The Fireside is a "striped and splashed red over yellow" apple developed at the University of Minnesota Fruit Breeding Farm. It was one of several thousand seedlings planted in a test orchard in 1917. This seedling, Minn. No. 993, proved very winter hardy and productive. The fruits were "large, highly flavored and kept well in common storage."

The Connell Red has all the good characters of Fireside plus its attractive all-red color.

It takes many years to evaluate the qualities of an apple variety. The tree and fruit of the Connell Red were observed from 1949 to 1952, during which time several authorities identified it as a red strain of Fireside. When William Connell was satisfied that he had a new variety he secured a plant patent on the Connell Red and arranged for propagation of nursery stock. The first trees were budded in 1952 and planted at Sunridge in 1955.

In 1957 the new variety was named at a meeting and special ceremony at Sunridge Orchard at which Prof. W.H. Alderman, Former Chief of the Department of Horticulture at the University of Minnesota, acted as Master of Ceremonies.

The Connell Red is now being grown and sold from coast to coast. Wm. Connell reported that in 1960 alone nurseries had 37,000 trees available. Twelve hundred trees were planted at Sunridge Orchard as soon as they were available.

Prof. W.H. Alderman in his comments at the meeting to name the variety said: "While the perfect variety of fruit may never be produced, it is true that modern varieties are step by step approaching that goal. The Connell Red has achieved one such step."

Published in One Hundred Years
The Wisconsin State Horticultural
Society 1968

Typical Pickers Group

photo: Museum Collection

In Search of
Appleport

by Richard Carter

I stood at the foot of Apple-port Road where it ends abruptly at the shore in a ridge of stones not quite right for skipping. In my hands was a century old map of Liberty Grove Township showing large capital letters APPLEPORT strung out from this point into the lake, like something important was once here. All I could see now was a model "T"-sized garage and a few big boulders just under Lake Michigan's surface.

After a dozen years of kicking around the trails and shore line, being curious about the suggestive name and seeing signs of another "civilization", I decided to find out just what this place called "Appleport" was. I had rescued an abandoned cottage from ruin, chased out the bats and red squirrels and declared myself a resident of a quiet road named South Appleport Lane. Now I

wanted to know who had lived here? What were their lives like? What was the history and links to the living present which I shared. Was it once a brisk little port shipping local apples to Chicago or Milwaukee for apple pies, apple cobblers, apple bobbing? Appleport, naturally.

Of course I knew a little about the fishing business that once operated right across the road from me. There remains the tumble of rocks and timbers known as "Larson's dock", now just a low ridge being reclaimed by Lake Michigan. And, the cottage next to it was remodeled from an old fish house just a couple of decades ago when the last of the commercial fishermen gave up. Then, there are the paths that zig zag like lightening strikes through the wild wetlands and go nowhere. Buffalo berry and red dogwood throw up their many arms to block any view of the scars and hold back trespassers from the old logging trails. I had heard stories about Appleport, the haunted village. A stranger I met at a Ridges Sanctuary meeting told me he had slides of all the old buildings which once clustered there. "A ghost town," he said.

Hints and rumors. Nothing concrete, no records. Even the place itself is hard to find and there's nothing distinct to define its borders. Some local folks know where it is, more or less. "Oh yeah, Appleport. It's over east of Sister Bay along the Michigan shore." That's about it.

photo: Fred Johnson

First, to find Appleport, the traveler should back all the way to Sister Bay and take a good running start across the peninsula. Driving east on County ZZ, the road dips and rises in gentle undulations noticeable only to the biker or jogger. Each ridge is crowned with large, old maples, the kind of tree line that, in the fall, makes me stop the car and reach for my camera. There are both new orchards and mature ones along the way, apple and cherry. No resorts. No condos. Just your basic interior Door County agriculture: orchards, pastures, a few black angus and some jersey cows. Apple trees march up the slopes in perfect military order. In the spring they look like the Continental Army all freshly wigged and awaiting Washington's command.

Once over the last crest at Gisar's Apple Barn, the land pitches downward toward Lake Michigan. The first hint of the place is a small green placard with white lettering pro-

claiming, "Grief Erickson, Founder of Appleport". It's an unlikely setting for a pioneer with its well kept lawn and modern home well back from the road. Just Erickson's little joke, but it's followed immediately by three perfectly restored log cabins grouped as though it were a small settlement. Makes you wonder if this is "it"? Well, it's not.

Oh, the cabins are authentic enough, but they didn't grow there. They were salvaged from abandonment and decay, hauled out of the woods from remote locations and restored. A provocative wooden plaque on one reads, "Accuse not nature. She hath done her part. Do thou but thine." Milton. The cabins are at the intersection of Old Stage Road and County ZZ. Across the road to the east is a one room school house and a boarded up cheese factory. The 1960 edition of the U.S. Geologic Survey's map of the area identifies "Appleport School" at the intersection, but the daisies stand tall in the yard, unmowed, untrampled. The swings hang straight on rusty chains. It's someone's vacation home now.

Other symbols sprinkled along County ZZ on the old topographic map tell much of the physical story: orderly green dots for orchards; crossed picks and shovels for gravel pits; and blue tufts of grass for wet lands. Tiny black squares indicating homes are few and widely scattered.

From this point the rises and dips in the road are more subtle. The swales tend to be wet. Off on the right a pair of tire ruts in the gravel lead deep into the distance and disappear. At the end of the ruts is the site of one of the early settler's homes, the Seaquist family. It's in a swampy area known as Three Springs. These springs send damp green fingers poking into fields and through culverts under the road. This simple

geography shows the marks of the last great influence on the land, the retreat of the glacier. It left its signature on the ridges where it paused and the swales in between.

There's one last rise just as the highway starts its big bend to the north. County ZZ curves around a field of new cherry trees standing on skinny burgundy legs wrapped with white stockings. It's like a bend of a river taking the main current away from the quiet backwaters.

If you're not paying attention it would be easy to be carried right past the small road headed east, a tributary called Appleport Road. Navigation is uninvited by a "Dead End" sign. Just past Hazel Larson's hand-painted mail box, a few grey ghosts of dead cherry trees can be seen. A line of shacks, the color of old bones, hide among the maples along the low ridge. Over the past couple of years they have been disappearing one by one. At the abandoned gravel quarry on the left, thick rows of Christmas trees hide deer. After that, there is no attempt at enterprise, just wild fields and woods. Old pasture land grows spotted knapp week whose lavender blooms swim with Monarch wings in the fall. A few surviving, but unattended, apple trees stand out among the fields as stragglers from another time. Sprigs of Juneberry blossoms break up the green on green of cedar, spruce and balsam fir in spring. Here and there a fresh gravel drive to a new vacation home interrupts a landscape left alone, returning home.

At last, the road snakes around a little "S" curve to reveal a sometimes blue, sometimes grey band stretching across the horizon; Lake Michigan in one mood or another. Next there's a one room cabin with boarded up windows at a crossroad: South Appleport Lane and North Appleport Lane. On the southeast corner of the road stands a big 1920's home on a stretch of grass the size of a football field leading all the way to the lake. Appleport Road runs right to the water's edge, ends abruptly at the shore and looks out at the vast lake expectantly. We are back where we started, having glimpsed Appleport, but not quite seen it.

I look out there to see what the road sees. To the southeast is Marshall's Point, the site of an Indian village. The Indians lived lightly on the land and left little mark except for their bones, some pot shards and a few arrow heads which still turn up. Out ahead is Spider Island, a thin shelf of rock and trees uninhabited except by herring gulls. Northeast is the curving shore of Newport State Park where the little logging town of Newport once thrived. It disappeared decades ago along with the timber.

There are vague stories about the loggers who came to cut the cedar, the white pine, the red pine and the hemlock. They were gone in just a few years. Only a few stands of virgin timber can be found, salvaged by luck or unusual vision.

There were no descendants of the early loggers left behind that I could find to talk to and my neighbors are mostly like me, summer residents without history. So, I began with Hazel Larson, whose family I heard, had been around for a long time. We bought raspberries and beans from her garden when we first camped out and started restoring our cabin in 1972. The land had been in her family for many years and I purchased it from her son, "Wink". In asking about the history of the area, I was directed to her sister-in-law, Grace Landstrom. "She was born there, right down on the shore." Hazel told me, "1904. She can answer your questions a lot better than me. I've only been here sine '33."

When I met Grace at Hazel's place she greeted me with a warm grandmotherly smile that seemed so at home on her smooth face. She sat with hands folded in her lap, her eyes often showing delight as she recalled experiences in response to my questions. Her dad had come to Appleport just about 1900 she told me. He was a fisherman just like his father before him. Started his own fishing business right down at the end of Appleport Road.

I asked about the big dock that was supposed to have been there.

Someone said it went a quarter of a mile out into the lake. That mules hauled wagon loads of timber and cord wood out to be loaded onto sailing schooners bound for Milwaukee and Chicago.

Her dad had taken over a big timber and stone dock for his fishing business. Before that, she thought shallow draft vessels used it. Logs were also rafted out from there to larger ships waiting in deep water. In turn, sailing vessels had brought food and supplies to a general store located at the foot of the dock. The "store" was actually their 1860 vintage Victorian home.

"And what about the name 'Appleport'? Did they once ship local apples out of that dock?"

"Oh no, that's not where the name came from at all. My dad bought the store from two gentlemen. One was named Mr. Apple and the other Mr. Port."

I felt the story was ending before it began. I had been so sure, but pressed on with my questions.

My wanderings along the edge of the boreal forest near the shore led me to old timbers and pieces of iron being stitched into the ground by twin flower. The remnants of a saw mill? Grace nodded. Her father did operate his own mill which he used to cut lumber for the twine shanties for his fishing business and the packing cases for his catch.

"What about the village of Appleport", I asked her. "People told me there was a town there that had been abandoned, a haunted village. One man said he had pictures of it."

Grace looked perplexed. "No, there was never any village. I would have known about that. There was just our place and one other family that fished, too."

"But what about all the buildings that were once there, the pictures, the kids who said they used to scare

Appleport School

themselves coming over to the haunted village?" What they had seen was nothing more than the half-dozen or so twine shanties and working buildings of the fishing operations of John Larson, abandoned after his death. They were the same small buildings that now line the dirt lane up at Hazel's. They had been moved inland along the edge of the cherry orchard. They looked like forlorn migrants displaced from their homeland, some with old fishing sets still rotting on the floor. They belong clustered at some shore waiting for fishing boats to return, not gazing at a dead orchard. Years ago, a few were used to house other migrants, back when there was still a cherry orchard.

Hoping for some deeper history of settlement, I asked about the fallen remnants of a small shack back in the woods off the rough trail.

"Why that was just a hideout my brothers built when they were kids. They took a horse and hauled logs out of the forest. Put it all together themselves. Oh, it was real nice. Had a stove and some school desks. One night my dad went down there to look for them. They had taken the cream separated from the milk and

the ice cream freezer. He found one of them making ice cream and the other was cooking candy by lantern light."

"You know, we had no electricity, just lamps and gas lights. Later, after the fire, when my dad built the new house, he put in one of those plants that generated its own electricity. That's what we had until the current came down, you know, the high volt."

"What about school? Was the one at County ZZ and Old Stage the same one you attended?"

It was, except she also went to the old one before they tore it down to build a bigger school on the same site. Forty to fifty children were taught in the peak years.

"We were a bunch of kids for one teacher, but we learned just as much as they do now. We walked the two miles winter or summer. The only time my dad would come for us was in the winter if there was a storm. Then he would hitch up the horses and come with a sleigh. We had friends from the farms all around and there was a big stone along where the road to North Bay comes in; and we used to put our own stones on top of it so you could tell who had come by that morning on the way to school.

Down where the stream from Three Springs came in there was a crook in the road and an old bridge. The boys would catch frogs and cook up the legs. Now the road's been straightened out, the bridge is gone and the stream's in a culvert."

We went back to talk about her father's fishing. Each morning the first sound she heard was that of the big Collumberg engine starting up and the chugging off into the darkness of predawn. The boats were called pond boats. They were wide of beam and open in contrast to the fully enclosed types which we usually see today. "There are just a few families still fishing around here now, very few," she offered. "In those days, they didn't use the gill nets, they

photo: Fred Johnson

used pond nets, like a big cage. They drove long poles with a pile driver into the bottom of the lake and hung the nets around them. You should have seen the fish they brought back each day. The boats were full right up to the gunnels, almost spilling over. It was herring mostly, but whitefish, too. The best seasons were spring and fall, summer wasn't much."

"The day's catch was dressed flat along the back, salted and packed in wooden crates. We cut the wood from the forest at our own saw mill and made the crates ourselves. I nailed a lot of them together starting when I was eight or ten. The Dormer Fish Company would send its big boat down from Marinette and anchor off the shoals. Dad would have to go out in his boat to load the catch because

it was too shallow for the big boat to come in."

Grace only went out with her father in his boat a couple of times. In her own words she was "never much for the water", even though she lived at its edge and they drew their living from it, she never learned to swim.

As intrigued as I was, Grace seemed to attach no special significance to her way of life. She just lived it, that's all. A typical day to her was of little importance. Their days were filled with hard work, she would recall, "But, we had good times, I can tell you that."

"In the morning, we had to get ourselves up and get 'goin', pack our lunches in a tin pail. We had a good time in school with spell'n bees on Fridays, our Christmas program and our big picnic the day school was out, all the games, ice cream, and lemonade, you know how that went. They don't have that anymore. At night we had our work, get the wood, carry in the water and plenty of barn chores. I was eleven when my mother died and my oldest sister didn't stay long, so I had lots to do. When my dad went on the lake in the morning, he'd call me to milk the cows. Then I'd make breakfast for them when they would come back. Once in a while, I'd wait in bed, but when I heard that old motor chugging, I got up! We had a strict dad, he was, but he kept us together."

"Later, when I was in my twenties, we had the cherry orchard. I hauled plenty of cherries in our old Model "T" truck down to the dock in Sister Bay by Anchor Sam's. After I was married, they built that plant up here at Old Stage and County ZZ across from Appleport School. That's when you should have been here to see all those trucks lined up for miles waiting to get in. The orchard business isn't the same anymore. There's no money in it so people gave up, just quit and let the orchards die."

The orchards were first planted in the twenties, probably peaked in the forties and the Larson family finally abandoned their Appleport orchard in 1960. You can still see a few dead trees, last remnants of several thousand. There is still a Larson orchard in Ellison Bay, however.

Like his father before him, Grace's dad fished all his life. When he died in 1952, her brother Everett took over and fished until 1966. The catches had declined and there just wasn't a living to be made anymore. Her father's death marked the end of one era and the beginning of another. John Larson's lands were divided among the children and slowly they turned to other ways of earning a living.

Just as the wood cutters came and went in the late eighteen hundreds followed by the fishermen and farmers, now the land moved towards another wave of change.

The hemlock has been cut to extinction, the last herring netted, the cherry orchards abandoned, and the pastures turned to weed and the gravel quarried from the land. The old dock is being reclaimed by November storms, the fish shanties rot in woods, the clapboard peels on the boarded cheese factory, the school has been sold for a vacation home and the cherry plant houses a few pleasure boats for the winter. All that remains is the land. Now that final resource is being sold as the last generation of pioneers takes its

photo: Fred Johnson

due before passing from the scene. The land has been divided and sold and divided again for homes with a view of the lake or a piece of wild roadside. Summer residents who now settle the land bring a love for Door County and a desire to be part of it, but they bring no sense of history nor will they leave any.

The Scandinavian names will be replaced by the polyglot of midwestern heritage. Our children won't attend school together and we won't be trying to win a living from the land nor the lake. Hopefully, we will remember why we came to this place, respect it, will not hastily recreate the city and suburban environment we just left behind.

I like to stand at the shore in the early morning and watch for the few remaining fishing boats to chug out of Sand Bay as they have for decades. There is something about being witness to this tradition that moves me. And, it troubles me to know their sound will be replaced by that of my neighbors' power mowers.

I have told you of the man who always put on his spectacles when about to eat cherries, in order that the fruit might look larger and more tempting. In like manner I always make the most of my enjoyments, and, though I do not cast my eyes from troubles, I pack them into as small a compass as I can for myself, and never let them annoy others.

— Robert Southey

photo: Fred Johnson

A PIG JOKE

illustration: John Sieger

While driving on a back road through the middle of the peninsula one day I happened to glance into an orchard. There was a farmer holding a pig up to an apple tree and the pig was biting an apple off the tree. Strange way to feed a pig I thought, and drove on. About an hour later I drove back the same way. As I neared the orchard I remembered the pig, and again looked into the trees. To my surprise once more I saw the same farmer lifting a pig up to the apples. I slowed down and saw the farmer carry the pig, apple in its mouth, over to a stack of apple crates, where the pig dropped the apple into a crate. This seemed strange. My curiosity aroused I turned the car around and parked along side the road, watching as the farmer and his pig circled the tree moving from branch to branch. The farmer holding the pig up to an apple, the pig picking it from the tree with his mouth, the farmer carrying the pig over to the apple crates, the pig dropping the apple into a crate, and the pair returning to the tree and repeating the whole process. Fascinated, I watched this action repeated over and over. Finally not being able to stand it any longer I had to go ask the farmer what in the world he was doing. His curt reply, "Picking apples." "With a pig?" I asked in bewilderment. "Sure," was the farmer's only answer. "But why," I questioned, "its taking so long, isn't that a waste of time?" "Aw shucks," the farmer replied, "time don't mean a thing to pigs."

illustration: Julia Bresnahan

The Art of Winemaking in Door County

by Mike Nelson

HE history of winemaking has not been a long standing tradition in Door County, however the growing of fruit in Door County began as early as the 1860's. It was not until the 1890's, though, that the commercial production of apples and cherries began in the county. In 1891 Professor E.S. Goff of the University of Wisconsin visited Door County, he found that the county had the ideal characteristics for winemaking with its protracted autumn, its limestone soil and its relatively cool springtimes. With the results of professor Goff's findings numerous orchards were established throughout the county. Apples were at first the most popular, but cherry orchards soon rivaled them in popularity.

The Door Peninsula Winery located in the former Carlsville elementary school was created to fill a need for a top quality, moderately priced wine made from Door County fruits. The schoolhouse was renovated in 1974, but the actual launching of the Door Peninsula Winery was on May 1, 1975. The founders of the winery were Julius Alberts and Mark Feld. Today the winery's owners and principal winemakers are Tom Alberts and Mark Feld. The Door Peninsula Winery is located in Carlsville, 8 miles north of Sturgeon Bay, on highway 42.

The winery processes a wide variety of wines from Door County fruits, including: Montmorency cherries, McIntosh and Red Delicious apples, Stanley plums and Bartlett and Flemish Beauty pears.

The story of the Door Peninsula winery winemaking process begins in the springtime with the arrival of the blossoming of cherries, the apples, plums and pears follow soon. Contracts are maintained with several local orchards in the area which supply the winery with the necessary fruit needed to produce their Door Peninsula Fruit wines, which are available in both dry and sweet versions from cherries, apples, plums and pears.

The entire winemaking process is performed at the winery. Before the fruits are made into wine the following steps are carried out:

Pressing — After reaching the winery all fruits are pressed into juice. All the cherries and plums are pressed whole, while the apples and pears are first cut, then pressed into pulp. The pulp is placed by the winemakers on wooden pallets, which are placed under a hydraulic press to squeeze out the juice.

Fermenting — When the fruit is pressed, the juice is pumped into the wine cellar via a plastic tube, where it is alloted into stainless steel vats. After the winemakers add yeast and sugar to the juice, the fermenting process takes place. As the yeast

converts the sugar into alcohol a vigorous reaction occurs in the vats that causes large bubbles of carbon dioxide to form. The fermentation of the juices takes about two weeks.

Aging — After the fermentation is completed, the new wine in the vats becomes still. The winemakers then seal the wine off from the air by covering the vats with a sheet of plastic. The aging of the wine now

Winery photo

occurs which takes from six to eight months. The aging process gives the wine its mellow flavor.

Filtering — After the aging of the wine, with the use of a filtering machine, the wine is filtered through a series of pads, thus removing all the impurities. The result is a clear wine.

Bottling — When the wine has been filtered it is then bottled through the use of a siphon flow bottling machine. Immediately after bottling the dark green bottles are corked, closures placed over the bottle's top, and the bottles put into cases. Approximately

150 cases are bottled during a season.

Labeling — After the wine is bottled, the wine cases are ready to be labeled. The label of the bottles, designed by Mary Ellen Sisulak, bears a facade of the old Carlsville schoolhouse.

The winery is open year around. There are guided tours offered 7 days a week from May 1st to June 1st, 9:00 A.M. to 5:00 P.M., from July 1st to August 31st, 9:00 A.M. to 7:00 P.M., and from September 1st to December 31st, 9:00 A.M. to 5:00 P.M. A 50¢ admission fee is charged for persons 12 and over, under 12 is free. Winery tours, which last about twenty minutes, begin with a brief description of the winery's history and the background of the schoolhouse. Next visitors tour the wine cellar, where a slide-tape presentation is given to explain the winemaking process. The tours end with a visit to the salon area of the winery for wine tasting, giving visitors the opportunity to sample the full-line of fruit wines and cherry wine cheese.

The winery was originally named the Old School Winery. In 1979 the name was changed to the Door Peninsula Winery and an addition was erected on the winery's north side. This addition houses two large vats and the fruit press, and is also used as the bottling area. In 1984 the building was again enlarged to provide more work and storage area.

A tour through the Door Peninsula Winery provides you with an excellent opportunity to learn how wine is made, and is an educational experience for the entire family.

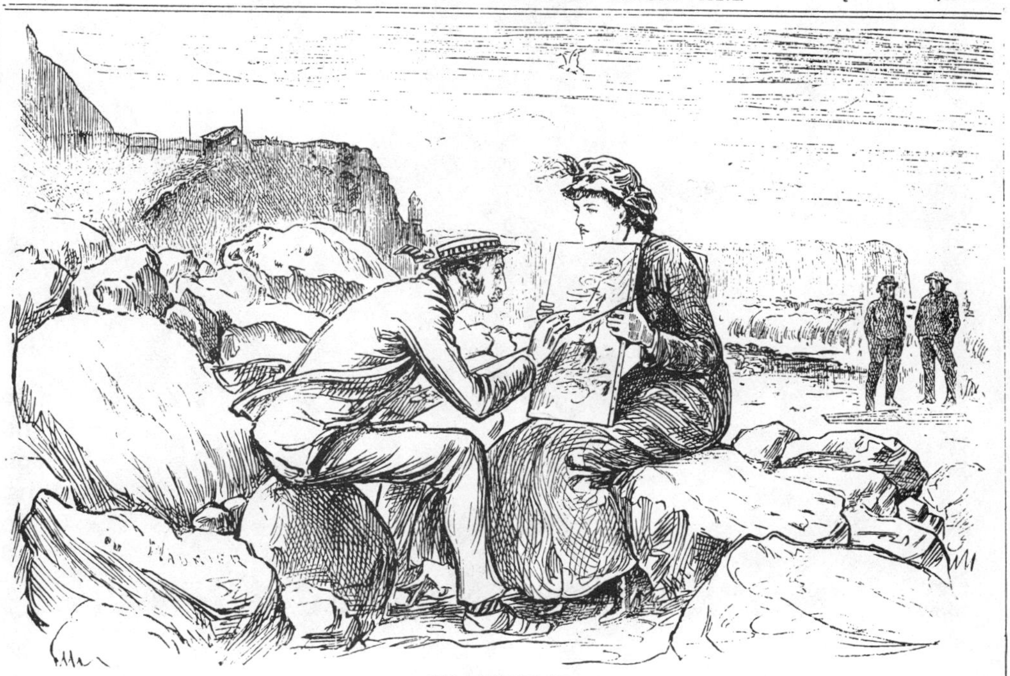

TO ARTISTS.

The best kind of Easel in a High Wind.

Artist Profiles

So Art has become foolishly confounded with education that all should be equally qualified.

Whereas, while polish, refinement, culture and breeding are in no way arguments for artistic results, it is also no reproach to the most finished scholar or greatest gentleman in the land that he be absolutely without eye for painting or ear for music - that in his heart he prefer the popular print to the scratch of Rembrant's needle, or the songs of the hall to Beethoven's C minor symphony.

Let him have but the wit to say so, and not feel the admission a proof of inferiority.

Art happens - no hovel is safe from it, no Price may depend upon it; the vastest intelligence can not bring it about, and puny efforts to make it universal end in quaint comedy, and coarse farce.

This is as it should be - and all attempts to make it otherwise are due to the eloquence of the ignorant, the zeal of the conceited.

— *Whistler*

photo: Fred Johnson

Jim Ingwersen
Portrait Painter

by Liz Maltman

HE light faded gently through the huge studio windows as we talked comfortably, warmed by the wood stove on this bright-cold January afternoon. Jim Ingwersen had just finished painting for the day and was glad to sit and relax. A partially finished portrait rested on the huge easel. "Empathy is the most important quality a portrait painter can have", commented the artist. "One must have the ability to know something of who they are and what they are like and the portrait will come across." I glanced around the spacious studio while reflecting on his words. Portraits hung everywhere. They were portraits of people young and old, rich and poor, friendly and serious. They were of people I knew and

people I somehow felt I knew, although I had never met them. Each portrait had a certain humaness, a life about it. I thought about this quality, empathy, and began to understand Jim's amazing sense of portraiture. It was more than his ability to render an exact likeness, more than his talent as a painter, more than his knowledge or experience as a portraitist. The essence of this man's art clearly comes from within: the ability to empathize.

This ability seems to have been worthwhile for Jim regarding the "business" of painting portraits as well. One would expect conflicts to develop between artist and subject in such a business, due to the immense personal involvement of each in the work. Yet in 30 years or so

of painting portraits, Jim has had only a handful of subjects with whom he simply could not work.

A quiet man, not given easily to words, Jim knew early in his life what he wanted and worked to get it. His interest and talent developed as a young boy. His father, dissatisfied with his own career as a commercial artist, encouraged his son to become a fine artist. After serving in World War II, Jim attended the American Academy of Fine Art in Chicago, his home, regularly recommending the art school experience to aspiring young artists today because of the necessary discipline it teaches. Discipline and hard work, though, came easily for Jim. He simply lives and loves to paint. After graduation the young artist worked briefly as an illustrator, but the economic climate after the war and Jim's own motivations did not inspire the artist toward a career in illustration. Thus, encouraged by his father and new wife, Phyllis, he decided to focus primarily on portrait painting. His career started out slowly, but word of mouth led him to become well known as a portrait painter fairly quickly. His first love, after all, was painting interesting faces.

The portraits are rendered in different styles — some with loose, broad strokes and others more intricate and detailed, some in which the light plays an essential part in creating a mood, others the posture of the subject or the facial expression. The composition of the portrait is also extremely important in creating the overall effect. To accomplish what he needs to, the artist takes a series of photographs of his subject. After careful study he selects two or three that will work best with the composition of the painting, and works from those. While it is possible for him to work only from photos, Jim much prefers to have the subject sit once or twice for him to prepare sketches, color samples, etc., which enable him to create the most realistic effect. Always the likeness is close to exact and the humaness of the sitter comes across to the viewer.

The artist works in oils and pastels and enjoys both equally, although they have very different characters as a medium. Oils are in a constant state of flux: they dry slightly different colors than when they are put on, their consistency varies, and they take a long time to dry. Pastels on the other hand are very precise and definite. The colors remain the same and they are fast to work with. Interestingly, Jim's portraits of women and children are most often requested in pastel. The artist expects the reason is cost. Oil is an appreciably more expensive medium in terms of both cost of material and time.

While commissioned portraits comprise the major income-producing source of his work, Jim enjoys

painting landscapes and still-lifes for diversion and enjoyment. He will often experiment, painting the same still-life once in a very loose, fluid style and again in a painstaking, deliberate style, rendering every detail exactly. He enjoys the still-lifes. "They don't move, object, or talk back", he confesses.

As Jim's career progressed in Chicago, he and Phyllis found their way occasionally to Door County for weekend visits and began to consider a move. Phyllis initially had reservations about the seeming isolation of the area, but was encouraged by the abundance of cultural activities during the summer months. The couple purchased a farm outside Sister Bay in 1970 and have lived there since, satisfied with the move. When one visits the picturesque setting where Jim lives and works, he can see why: the log home, the

weathered sheds, the barns that house Jim's studio and galleries, are in themselves a landscape worth viewing. The artist reflects with a smile that the whole set-up would be perfect if only the house and buildings could be moved to the center of the 40 acre property.

But everything has not gone quite perfectly for the Ingwersens. A barn fire in 1980 destroyed the studio, taking with it many portraits and all the artist's work from his college years. He suffered the significant loss of several major, recently completed commissioned portraits. A new studio/gallery was constructed, though, which remains in character and feel much like the old barn. Weathered, rough-hewn beams and cedar shakes give it a feeling of age. The huge windows give a wonderful feeling of space, let in an abundance of natural light, and create a sense of being outdoors. There is a small solarium attached, lit by windows salvaged from an old school and filled with plants in the summer. In this way an atmosphere enjoyed by the artist for his work environment was preserved. An added advantage of the new studio in a Door County winter is its greatly increased energy-efficiency.

A visit to the Ingwersen Studio/ Gallery will be fascinating, tranquil, and well worth your time. The gallery is open to the public Wednesdays and Saturdays from 2 p.m. until 5 p.m. and is located 1½ miles east on Old Stage Road, off Highway 57 south of Sister Bay.

Jonathan
Mid-Western and Eastern states. Sept. thru June . . .

. . . good for snacks, fruit cups, sauces, all-purpose cooking.

Participate In The Door County Almanak

We invite you, one and all, to submit work for future issues of the Door County Almanak. If you have an interesting idea, whether on an issue's major theme or not, we'd like to hear it. We are looking for articles on interesting people, historical facts and events, Door County's ancestors, settlers and visitors; basically anything concerned with the history and events of Door County. Also recipes, poetry, fiction (short stories), recorded oral histories, artwork and photographs. We especially would appreciate the use of old photographs of the Door County area. Everyone is encouraged to participate in the Almanak, residents and visitors alike. The Almanak is here to present the works of both professionals and amateurs alike, please do not be afraid to submit work. If you would like to contribute send a #10 SASE for our writers/artists guidelines.

Pangaea Gallery:
The Wathalls

by Henry F. Shea

T is not often that an artist is called upon to design, render and otherwise produce the finished work that appears as an attractive poster which gives him personal publicity and serves as a promotional device for a printer, in this case, the Independent Printing Co. of DePere. Such is the experience of Lionel Wathall, who with his wife, Betty Becker Wathall, own and operate the Pangaea Gallery, on Juddville Road, east of highway 42, between Fish Creek and Egg Harbor. The poster in question is the third in a series sponsored by the DePere firm. The subjects are not limited to artists but are of general interest and depict some unique personalities.

The first of the series, in photographic form by Glenn Sanderson, is a portrait of Wally Kacor, owner and operator of a Kewaunee feed and grain mill, a local landmark, which has been in the families possession since 1871. A second is a portrait, by painter Bridget Austin, of Catherine Grassl of Menominee. Her distinction, in addition to B.A. and Masters degrees in art and library science from the University of Chicago, is her collection of advertising illustrations by famous practitioners of that applied art. She is 74 and expects that her collection will eventually go to the Smithsonian Institution in Washington, D.C.

The Wathalls came to Door County in 1969 after purchasing their present farm property, with barn, which was converted to a gallery. Actually, Mrs. Wathall got her first taste of the county on their honeymoon here in 1945, just after Lionel had been released from the Army. His first experience of the area was in 1936-37 when he was the summer guest of artist/instructor F. DeForest Schook of Baileys Harbor. While this was basically a holiday, it turned out to be a very formative influence on Wathall. Artistically it was the ending of an era, the impressionist view of painting was being replaced in the U.S. by a new realism, typified by John Stewart Curry, and Thomas Hart Benton in Missouri. Viewers who looked for "pretty" pictures were apt to characterize some of the emerging American artists as members of the "Ashcan" school. Wathall learned much from Schook who in turn had gained knowledge from a black painter, H.O. Tanner, who because of racial prejudice, had little recognition in America.

"ETERNAL CYCLE" — LIONEL WATHALL

Lionel Wathall was schooled basically at the Chicago Art Institute plus, just after his marriage to Betty, the Art Student's League of New York. In addition other schools added to his art education. He opened his own commercial art studio on Michigan Ave. in Chicago, close to the major advertising agencies which were his bread and butter. Here he developed a special skill which not all artists can master, that of the air brush. Essentially an air brush is a tiny spray gun which must be handled with the utmost delicacy. Some readers may remember Esquire magazine of the late 30's and early 40's which featured the work of George Petty, actually cartoons in color, usually of voluptuous blondes, all limned with consumate technique. In commercial art air brushing is generally used to enhance photos by smoothing rough edges, placing highlights and deepening shadows.

One of the more interesting experiences for Lionel took place in World War II. Because of his art training he was assigned to Army Engineers. Two years were spent in New Guinea, building roads, air strips and similar projects. Then an opportunity occurred to join the staff of Yank, "Down Under" the G.I. written and edited Army newspaper. As staff artist he did not achieve the fame of Bill Mauldin but nevertheless did creditable work in describing the daily rou-

tines, frustrations, and very occasional enjoyments of the American soldier in the Pacific. Though Wathall still furnishes, from time to time, a piece of commercial art for old customers like Revlon, International Harvester or Maybelline, he concentrates now on local watercolor scenes. His heritage has been of the arts, his father was a successful professional cellist, one uncle was also a musician and another was an artist in a New York advertising agency.

Trying to condense Lionel Wathall's philosophy of art is not easy. He seems to feel that, basically, it is a desire to communicate his pleasure and perceptions of the world around him to others, so they may see, at least in part, the special joy he has in recording his own reactions to field, sky, character of persons and understand, as he puts it, that art is a "lifetime occupation with the reward always just a little out of reach". No doubt many writers and musicians would define their pursuits in much the same way, perfection is always

somewhere ahead, beckoning the artist to follow.

Betty Becker Wathall is another who has a long felt feeling for the art of the graphic person. Hers is perhaps a more abstract approach than her husband's, perhaps because she has spent relatively less time in purely commerical work than he and has given more time to the "fine arts". Her scholastic background included graduation from the University of Illinois and further study at the Chicago Art Institute and New York's Art Student's League. It was during those years that she met and married Lionel.

172

Among her more or less commercial work have been decorative drawings for the book sections of the New York Times, the Chicago Tribune and the Saturday Review of Literature. Her experience has also included teaching art classes at the Clearing, and she has been well represented in many private and corporate collections. Among the awards of which she is most proud is the golden "European Banner of Arts", an Italian honor not frequently given to artists other than European. She is the daughter of Maude Becker, a musician who became skilled in arts and crafts, and moved on to writing of poetry and short stories. Betty has inherited some of this talent in the form of creating Japanese style poetry, called "Haiku"; brief lyric snatches in words that evoke a fleeting instant's view of nature, an emotion or a view of life. Her feeling for this craft seems to go along with her feeling that there exists between an artist and his or her materials a form of communication in which the material speaks out to be used in a certain way. The view of a semi-mystic, perhaps, an expression of an inner vision not noted by all of us.

Betty can be credited with suggesting the name of their gallery. The word Pangaea derives from geology where it is used to describe the form-

less mass that gradually formed into the island continents as we know them and that are to a certain extent still shaping themselves into new shorelines, new environments, but in a manner so slow that we are hardly aware of it unless we are scientists used to recording these subtle changes. As Betty sees it, there is one primal, creative urge which as we experience it, gradually divides itself, like some primitive organism, into several branches of art, whether painting, literature, music, sculpture or drama.

The Wathall's gallery brochure extends an invitation to look beyond villages and highways and enjoy, along with the gallery, a world of wild flowers, fragrant grasses, and birdsong. It is another way of capturing that inner vision, which Betty says, we all possess, but which needs cultivation.

KEN ZILISCH

by Liz Maltman

"To be creative, an artist must be aware, even if he doesn't want to be . . . always looking, learning, seeing. One has to not only like art but live it."

LEXIBLE and imaginative artist Ken Zilisch sees everywhere, constantly recording ideas from his travels about the world and about town in sketches, notes, and slides. Ken is an unusually versatile artist, expressive in watercolor, pastel, woodcuts, serigraphy, pen and ink, and photography. "I could live two lifetimes and still not have enough time to do all the art I want to do", he says enthusiastically. Even as we talked, the artist's awareness of the changing afternoon light, the volume of music in the small studio, the way I was sitting pervaded the conversation. Ken feels the more he sees and becomes aware of, the more he knows. The more he knows, the

better able he is to add to and subtract from a work to make it more expressive of himself, giving the work a greater sense of life, a greater pull. Ken is influenced in this philosophy by mime/artist, Marcell Marceaux, who said, "Paint what you know, not what you see."

Ken is as versatile with his subject matter as he is with his media. Some of his works are meant to be a preservation of something beautiful or meaningful. Others are very personal statements. Some works are recordings of dream images, while others are simply ideas. Ken's interests go from people to history and events, from thoughts and ideas to nature and architecture. Ken is involved in life, portraying how he feels about his subject, wanting to get across what is alive about the person, thing, or event. This empathy, or feeling for people or things, is especially visable in his portraits. "George", for example, displays a tremendous enthusiasm, but, Ken explains, "**I'm** only doing what's there ...what **I'm getting** from the person." The essence of the subject, what is alive about the subject for Ken comes across in his work, whether it be the historical significance, the warmth of a person, or the beauty of an object. The artist may add words of explanation to express something he knows and wants the viewer to know too, or he may include, for example, a light left on or a curtain fluttering through an open window to make evident the life that is present but not always apparent.

Ken's talent and interest in art began as a child in Milwaukee where he would draw for hours from comic books, then published only in black and white. This experience may well have influenced his art: the black and white work is very strong. Ken attended the local Famous Artist's School as a young boy and later the Leyton School of Art in Milwaukee, majoring in graphic design. Money was tight for Ken and he worked at a variety of jobs from sign-painter to salesman to put himself through school. He met and married his wife, Diane, during this time and the couple worked summers in Door County where Diane had grown up. Especially worthwhile was his experience in the job-shop at the Door County Advocate where he learned to be "fast and accurate" in his work.

Ken's school/work experience and knowing Diane significantly influenced his attitude and his art. Because he needed a scholarship, Ken had been working for grades in school. Consequently, he did not enjoy what he was doing and did not do well. He tended to blame his poor performance in school on lack of money to buy materials. With Diane's encouragement and insight, Ken began to see more positively, to forget about the grades and do the best he could with what he had. He began to realize he could do better with only two colors than the students who had five colors. He began to get the A's. "I finally realized," explained the artist, "that it's not what you have, but how you use it that makes the difference."

With this understanding, one can see a reason for Ken's unusual versatility as an artist. He **has** pen and ink, so he does many drawings; he **has** wood scraps saved for him by a local lumber yard, so he does woodcuts. The time Ken has to work on his art is limited and often available only late at night or early in the morning. He uses pastels, which require natural light, when he is able to work in the daytime. When night time hours are free, woodcuts or pen and ink drawings can be produced because they do not require natural light. Photography is something the artist enjoys all the

time because the camera is easily portable. Having a variety of media which he enjoys working in and is good at clearly makes more options available.

Ken's own experience of having little money has influenced his art from the point of view of the public as well. He can easily relate to the frustration of being unable to afford something he wants. In response, Ken produces some art that is affordable to anyone. He makes woodcuts, for example, that sell for under $10.00. (The process of wood block printing allows for numerous prints to be made from one block.) On the other hand, a large pastel or original pen and ink drawing takes days to complete and is costly to frame, thus raising the selling price substantially. The artist though has had reproductions made of some of his more popular pen and ink drawings ("Kaap's" and "Vita Park") and plans printings of some of his other drawings so more people can afford them.

Ken's dream is to become a full-time artist. He works continually in his spare time toward that end. To support their family Ken and Diane run a resort and an advertising agency. Those committments don't leave him with a lot of extra time. "It can be very frustrating to have the ideas but only a limited amount of time to work on them", he explains. Ken finds it difficult at times, too, to remain motivated and disciplined, to maintain continuity. But with the encouragement of his family and many successful Door County artists, Ken has pushed harder in the last few years and is confident. "I **can** do it", he says, "It's just a matter of time and hard work". Ken is getting closer to his dream.

PARK. THE PAVILION WAS BUILT BY S. CARROLL of BEAVER DAM. PARK GROUNDS DESIGNED BY Mr BENSON SUPERINTENDENT of LINCOLN PARK, CHICAGO DR. G.E. SWAN, MAYOR of BEAVER DAM, WISCONSIN ESTABLISHED ACKERMAN'S SPRING AS VITA SPRING PARK WITH A PAVILION IN 1880. NOW SWAN CITY

Like many fine artists, Ken is up against a formidable barrier in these days of instantaneous communication, mass production, and technology, not to mention difficult economic times. Society thinks, "It's just a painting". Few stop to consider what is involved in producing an artwork of merit. Ken explains:

"An artwork is a little piece of the artist. It took their mind, coordination, feelings, and experiences up until that moment to produce the work. An artwork is confidence in one's own ability. It's dexterity. It's knowledge. There hasn't been another like it."

But people do not typically understand that idea. "Oh, it's just a painting", they say. "Oh, that's nice", they say. Few stop to consider it took the artist 40 years and a day to produce the work.

As Ken talked I began to have a deeper understanding of what it **really means** to be an artist:

"An artist is not 'just an artist'. An artist needs to know about mechanical things, the inner workings of things: plants and animals, nature, weather, business, communication, marketing techniques. He needs to be flexible, versatile, imaginative, disciplined, and motivated. He needs to work and work and work."

Ken himself is only now beginning to realize the full meaning of his words. He is beginning to know if he keeps working it will come back for him in the end. The writer strongly encourages his efforts and looks forward to viewing the results.

Ken Zilisch has exhibited in a variety of galleries and juried shows including the Hardy Gallery in Ephraim, The Brown County Library Show in Green Bay, The 1981 New York Pastel Society Exhibition, and the Miller Art Center in Sturgeon Bay. He has won a number of awards for artistic merit. A visit to Ken's Sturgeon Bay studio can be arranged by appointment. (743-9247).

David Hatch — David Aurelius

Tilewood

A Collaboration

by Shirley Nelson

OOKING for something that will bring a touch of Door County class into your home?

Two young Davids of Northern Door are local artisans joining their creative talents to make distinctive home furnishings and accessories that reflect Door County's natural settings. They are Dave Aurelius, ceramist, and Dave Hatch, woodworker.

At a time when the county's creeping commercialism gathers increasing numbers of tourists into a wide variety of shops in expanding numbers of mini and maxi malls, the two young craftsmen prefer their individuality. The home base for for each artist is rural and includes display and workshop space close at hand. Wares are tastefully exhibited in Aurelius' Clay Bay Pottery and Hatch's Interfibers.

It's a natural for these two to enjoy working together, since they feel deeply about nature and the environment and the best possible growth for Door County. Their goal is to create quality pieces of both beauty and util-ity that will spell "Door County" to the purchaser: a blend of nature, simplicity, and contemporary function, something to contemplate and enjoy day by day.

"We spark one another," says woodworker Hatch, in noting advantages of joint design and decision-making sessions, when the two explore possibilities of tile and wood combinations, which they have named "Tilewood".

Often Door County woods are combined with tiles abstractly designed in soft colors. Or Aurelius' tiles may feature a favorite flower, tree, or pictorial symbolic of the county. Samples of "Tilewood" include a buffet table with a "dancing doll" tile insert, a formal coffee table with a floral tile insert, occasional maple tables with abstract tiles, and an ash serving-table with folding stand.

Such samples may be seen in either artisan's shop. Driving north on Highway 42 one finds Interfibers near the north end of Ephraim. Dave shares this complex with weaver wife Wendy, who was born in Duluth. It is set back from the road on the edge of a field still farmed by father, Don Hatch. Dave's Interfibers is a part of the original Arthur Anderson farm, where his mother was born.

The young Hatches came back to Door County four years ago after studying their crafts in the West.

Wendy's weavings, sometimes attractively combined with David's woods on chairs and stools, are in evidence. Though Dave has used principally Door County woods, which he has logged or bought locally, he is planning future use of mahogany, rosewood, and teak which he has collected.

About two miles north of Sister Bay Aurelius' Clay Bay Pottery sits close to Highway 42 in the shadow of a TV tower and looks across at fruit orchards which have been there many years. Wife Jeanne shares Dave's enthusiasm and skill for creating ceramic art. Together they have filled thier attractive showrooms with a wide variety of home accessories . . . mugs, pitchers, dinnerware, lamps, wall hangings, to name a few. Now their shop includes samples of "Tilewood".

They opened their shop here in 1976, moving from Decorah, Iowa, where they had their own "pottery place" for a few years after studying at Luther College and with Marguerite

Wildenhain in Northern California. Dave came from St. Paul, and Jeanne from Wauwatosa and years of summer sailing in Door County.

With common philosophies of what is good about and for Door County, Aurelius and Hatch work within a framework which combines beauty and utility in their home furnishings. Their woods and tiles are a happy combination and complement one another. They find their customers are interchangeable.

Custom orders have accounted for one-third of their "Tilewood" sales. Wendy's weavings-under-glass or Jeanne's special pictorial or floral tiles may be requested on these special orders.

Plans for a third annual show of their work is planned now for early fall 1985. A stop at Clay Bay Pottery or Interfibers this spring or summer may give visitors a preview of "Tilewood's" latest ideas.

County Books

and

Authors Update

by Harold M. Grutzmacher

HE first edition of the **Almanak** gave me the opportunity to write an overview article on the state of writing in and about Door County. In that essay, the re-issue of H.R. Holand's **Old Peninsula Days** in 1972 was picked as the beginning of the "modern era," since, after that successful re-printing, new books and a reprint or two began to appear with regularity, to the point that there is now a respectably long Door County bibliography, with additions occurring frequently.

One irony should be noted: **Old Peninsula Days** has been out of print since October, 1983. Stanton & Lee, successors to Wisconsin House, have promised to bring the book out again, but it won't be this year. Meanwhile, requests for the book continue, and frustration mounts. "Out of print" is

the status of a number of successful books. June, 1983, was the date when "Journeys to Door County" became unavailable. Buyers searched the county, and the publisher, Voyageur Press, found a few more copies in their storeroom, but the book is now long gone. Voyageur promised a successor volume, as yet untitled, for June, 1984, but the book did not appear. Perhaps this season will see the new picture book.

Voyageur Press has other titles that have been put on hold and should be forthcoming, Pauline Wanderer's Door County cookbook and Grace Samuelson's collection of essays and reminiscences notable among them. But Ellis Press, which decided to hold Norbert Blei's **Door to Door**, the third volume in Blei's Door books, will issue the book in early summer. **Door Steps**, the second book, appeared in October, 1983; it and **Door Way**, the first, continue to sell well.

The range of books being published is impressive. Pat Spielman has continued his successes with Sterling

182

Publishing, New York, with **The Router Handbook** and **Realistic Decoys**; the latter is co-authored with Keith Bridenhagen, who is the author of the **Decoy Pattern Book**, also by Sterling. Esther Lind's **Songs from My Mother's Diary** is a charming and well-done art book, as is Millie Armato's **Sojourn to Sicily**. Three poetry collections have been published since the first edition of the **Almanak; Crowlady Letters**, Maggie Perry; **Tell Me about the People**, Frances May; and **Generations**, Harold and Stephen Grutzmacher. Reprints include **Faith Builds a Chapel**, Winifred Boynton, and **Mask, the Door County Coon** by Earl Sherwan. Biography is represented by **I Seen A Million Sparrows**, Jocelyn Reichel, and **Thor Johnson, American Conductor** by Lewis Nicholas.

The list goes on, and what has been noted above is not exhaustive. There is work underway on a number of projects, and, as mentioned, there should be some new books during the summer and fall of 1985.

Does this continued production mean that Door County is some sort of writer's paradise? Probably not, and some would say decidedly not. There is no widespread writers' network, although the Sturgeon Bay writers who are organized as the Door County Writers Club, provides a structure for some. The county does have numerous outlets for books, and, since distribution and resulting sales are necessary to support production, this has helped. Until 1978 there was no bookstore in northern Door County.

Now there are two, and two in Sturgeon Bay do a brisk business in Door County books as well.

There has been an increased interest in books in general, and one can play chicken-and-egg with books creating interest or interest creating books. In any event, a writer can depend on an audience of some size; publishers can as well. The tremendous increase in tourism has also helped; the greater the number of people the greater the potential for sales.

Obviously, there are many factors, but I think the greatest is one not previously mentioned. The county is, for most, a good place to work. I doubt that output is standard throughout the year, but the winter, especially one that does not have a great deal of snow to be moved around in order to survive, is a good time to write. Solitariness is a support to production, and there is no longer the problem of really being cut off from civilization that there once was. In theory a writer can work anywhere, but some places are better than others, and the county seems to be one of those good places.

So the books keep coming, even as some disappear. Treasure your **Once Around the Sun**; it's gone. Think about picking up **Out on a Limb**; there aren't many left. But also take heart from the continued production of Door County authors and watch for new books.

Wildwood School in Liberty Grove

School Names
In Door County's Past

by Conan Bryant Eaton

**HERRY School** — What a lusciously appropriate name for a rural schoolhouse nestled among the burgeoning orchards of Door County's Sevastopol township in the days following the first World War! Looking back two-thirds of a century to recapture the flavor of those simpler times one finds in the name the taste of utter rightness, of being as completely appropriate to its situation as a glossy maraschino topping an ice cream sundae. One might be tempted to assume that this school name, bestowed upon the landscape by an intelligence above mankind's muddled gropings, had been there forever. One would be wrong.

The waning years of the nineteenth century saw in Wisconsin and Door County a New England-style educa-tional system based on a profusion of independent rural school districts, each identified within its township by a dual system: A strict numerical list-ing gave, for example, **Clay Banks District No. 2, Gibraltar No. 3, Nase-waupee No. 4**; in addition, some human need for identification beyond mere numbers demanded a **name** for most school districts as well. And so, Clay Banks No. 2 chose to cele-brate the proximity of the settlement of **Cheeseville**, Gibraltar No. 3 took note of nearby **Blossomburg,** and Nas-ewaupee No. 4 honored the landowner named **May** on whose property its educational edifice was erected. Thus it went throughout the County, from Town of Washington in northern waters to the solid base in the town-ships of Clay Banks, Forestville, Brus-sels and Union.

A few districts satisfied themselves with forthright but prosaic information: **Primary Dep't., Southern, Middle, Central, New School**. A big handful honored that vital functionary of any school system, the district clerk; **Fetzer, Bassford, Schaefer, Pinney** and **Haines** were among them. Others commemorated the local landowner who had given a half-acre or more on which to build a temple of enlightenment in his neighborhood. At least now and then, a school's name took prideful notice of an extended family — **Carmody** might be an example — which by its own generational accomplishments filled many of the seats in the one-room institution. But the greatest number of districts were named for the nearby settlement they served (**Juddville, Newport, Tornado**), for a local natural feature (**Kangaroo Lake, Stony Creek**), or even for a monument to man's ingenuity and industry (**Canal School**). And inescapable in that period of immigration from Europe were such culturally enriching school names as **German, Norwegian, Poland,** and **German Settlement**.

On the eve of the twentieth century the 1899 **Illustrated Atlas of Door County** published by Randall and Williams showed the names and locations of more than sixty rural schools, most of which still followed the naming patterns of the past several decades. But at least three school names foreshadowed changes to come. Nasewaupee's relatively new District No. 7 bore the revered name **Lincoln**, and No. 1 in Brussels township had turned from honoring a local worthy named **Mizier** to saluting a national hero named Theodore **Roosevelt**, who had led the charge up San Juan Hill in 1898, was already governor of New York, and was soon to become the nation's vice-president, then president. Above these understandable patriotic namings stood out a change of another sort: One district had dropped the name of a local clerk, **Schaefer**, and had reached far beyond this earth for a name blending inspiration and poetry. Nasewaupee's District No. 1 now enlightened its pupils in **Morning Star School.**

Through the early 1900s most established school names lay peacefully on Door County's landscape; then, from 1916 onward, two outside forces intruded upon the scene. Wisconsin adopted a statute requiring **all** rural schools to be named; and the United States was drawn into World War I. While most County schools had long been at least informally named, there could now be no exceptions. Responsibility for naming was laid by statute upon each school district's electors; failing their timely action, the district's school board was required to act. With the naming process thus brought to public notice, some changes were inevitable. And the War, as wars invariably do, added to the ferment.

By 1922, the conflict's influence on school name changes was clear: Liberty Grove township had replaced **German Settlement** with the inspirational and doubly appropriate **Liberty School; Pershing School** had defeated **Poland** in Gibraltar; **Victory School** had gained the field from **Fetzer** in Forestville; **Thrift School** (harking back to wartime Thrift Stamps?) appeared in Nasewaupee, which had elected **Wilson School** in place of **Myers**; and, somewhat puzzlingly, the Prussian-rooted name **Kolberg** had been substituted for **German School** in Brussels.

Meanwhile, proliferation of Early Richmond and Montmorency trees in Door County had brought forth **Cherry School** to supplant the locational name **Bay Shore** in Sevastopol. And Jacksonport's **New School**, so-called for more than a third of a century, now looked back to the Father of his Country to become **Washington School**. (Distant **Washington Harbor School** on Washington Island had clearly been baptized in about 1850, not for the first president, but for its location near the harbor and for the surrounding settlement.

Beyond these easily explainable changes, a crop of new school names had appeared which fall loosely into three categories — with distinctions among them often blurred. "Descriptive or locational" would seem to embrace Sevastopol's **Hilltop** and **Lakeside** schools, and may well include Sturgeon Bay township's **Evergreen**, Forestville's **Plainview**, Gibraltar's **Maple Grove**, and **Sugar Creek** in Gardner.

"Subjectively descriptive" seems to describe the names of **Pleasant View School** in Liberty Grove, **Pleasant Grove** and **Sunny Point** in Egg Harbor, and **Pleasant Ridge** in Union. We can only guess at the degree of poetic license in such names as **Rocky Glen** in Union; **Silverdale** in Sturgeon Bay township (did a grove of silver-barked beeches, birches or aspens glow nearby?); **Woodland** in

Baileys Harbor town and **Wildwood** in Liberty Grove; Sevastopol's **Fairmont**; and Jacksonport's **Farview** and **Groveland. Fairland School** in Union may well have blended subjective description with a touch of the inspirational; and symbolism and inspiration were still offered up in Nasewaupee's **Morning Star School**, with its suggestion of earliness and guidance. Each of us is free to cherish or to deplore these names from the county's past. One scholar widely known in the field of place names condemns as "savorless" and "regrettably vapid" those names which lack any flavor of local history.

The 1937-38 school year saw the number of Wisconsin school districts (and school names) reach its peak; from then on, consolidation of small districts, which had been proposed some eighty years earlier, went on at an increasing pace — and with it went the names of Door County's rural schools. (For better or worse, their place has been amply filled by the names of real estate developments.) In any case, we should take note of what remains of that once-rich endowment of non-prosaic school names: The City of Sturgeon Bay offers **Sunrise** and **Sunset Schools**; two high schools — **Sevastopol** and **Gibraltar** — reach back by way of their township names to Old World roots; and the School District of **Washington** Island still enshrines in its name one national hero.

One is tempted to speculate concerning our possible response were we to be ordered today to meet in small neighborhood groups and to choose names for Door County's sixty-some rural schools. **Cherry** might again seem appropriate to at least one school district, and **Apple** would seem equally apt. Any school in or near a rural settlement might adopt, as readily as in time past, the settlement's name; and schools within view or even earshot of surf or lapping waters might well be named for bays, inlets or harbors.

Vistas might still strike us as **pleasant;** dales, groves and glens would quite probably still appear to some of us as **sunny,** or **shady,** or **silver,** or **green;** a few national heroes (probably from the distant past) might still command our respect and remembrance. Some local patrons of education might again seem deserving of seeing their names attached to a school.

One suspects it would be the intangible, more visionary concepts which might fail to earn general agreement. In the world of the 1920s such words as **Liberty** held a simpler, more understandable range of meanings, closer, perhaps, to the purposes of the Constitution's framers, less cluttered with self-indulgent demands for personal license. **Vic-**

tory implied then a certain, happy, and well-deserved outcome to any national problem or contest, unclouded by the possibility of compromise or defeat. **Thrift,** a widely-accepted virtue at the time, might today be subject to ridicule, in view of present-day attitudes and actions of consumers and their government.

At least one citizen who long ago walked miles to a rural Wisconsin school hears an echo from Door County's past and has made his choice. More deeply today than in boyhood he knows the human need for inspiration and guidance, and, metaphorical as they may be, they shine upon him most brightly from the name of **Morning Star School.**

GUARANTEED

Winona Knits — MADE IN U.S.A.

We offer sweaters and sportswear at factory direct prices, and we fully guarantee them. We guarantee that every item we sell will give complete satisfaction or you may return it and we will replace the item or refund your money, whichever you prefer.

We're proud of our American made sweaters, our factory direct prices and our straight forward guarantee.

Winona Knits

OUR GUARANTEE

We guarantee that every item we sell will give complete satisfaction or you may return it and we will replace the item or refund your money, whichever you prefer.

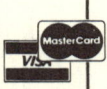

Open Daily - 10 to 5

COUNTRY WALK SHOPS — SISTER BAY — 854-4743

Poetry

CHERRY ORCHARD AT ITS PRAYERS

The cherry orchard
Stood in faithful rows
At devout attention
Facing west
As I passed
On my way home.
They were lifting myriad delicate fingers,
Purple gloved in the sunset —
Grateful devotions for the bit of sun
Brightening momentarily an otherwise gloomy December day.

— Gary Jones

The End of Winter

He said it like a man who has lost
a lover he was beginning to know.
Perhaps her skin reflected moonlight,
once or twice. Perhaps he felt
its texture articulate in a shiver,
wind exploring the cracks around the
   windows,
she insisting the drapes be spread, stars
   and moon
routing the dark. There was no talk
of permanence, only the dangerous
   exchange
of intimacy deforming the silence.

Of course, he was not that man.
His concern was with the snow. Rain
would soon distort the landscape, colors
   intruding
on the simple scheme of winter. And
   what remained
would be the preoccupied earth.

— Tom Davis

At The Pond: June

Dawn.
Silent as a gray-
edge knife
slicing into day

Sudden start
crow fight; raucous, wrangling
black feathered fruit peddlers

Black duck dives
through bluing sky

Pond throws back
misty blanket
   lover moon

          slinks away.

— Susan Peterson

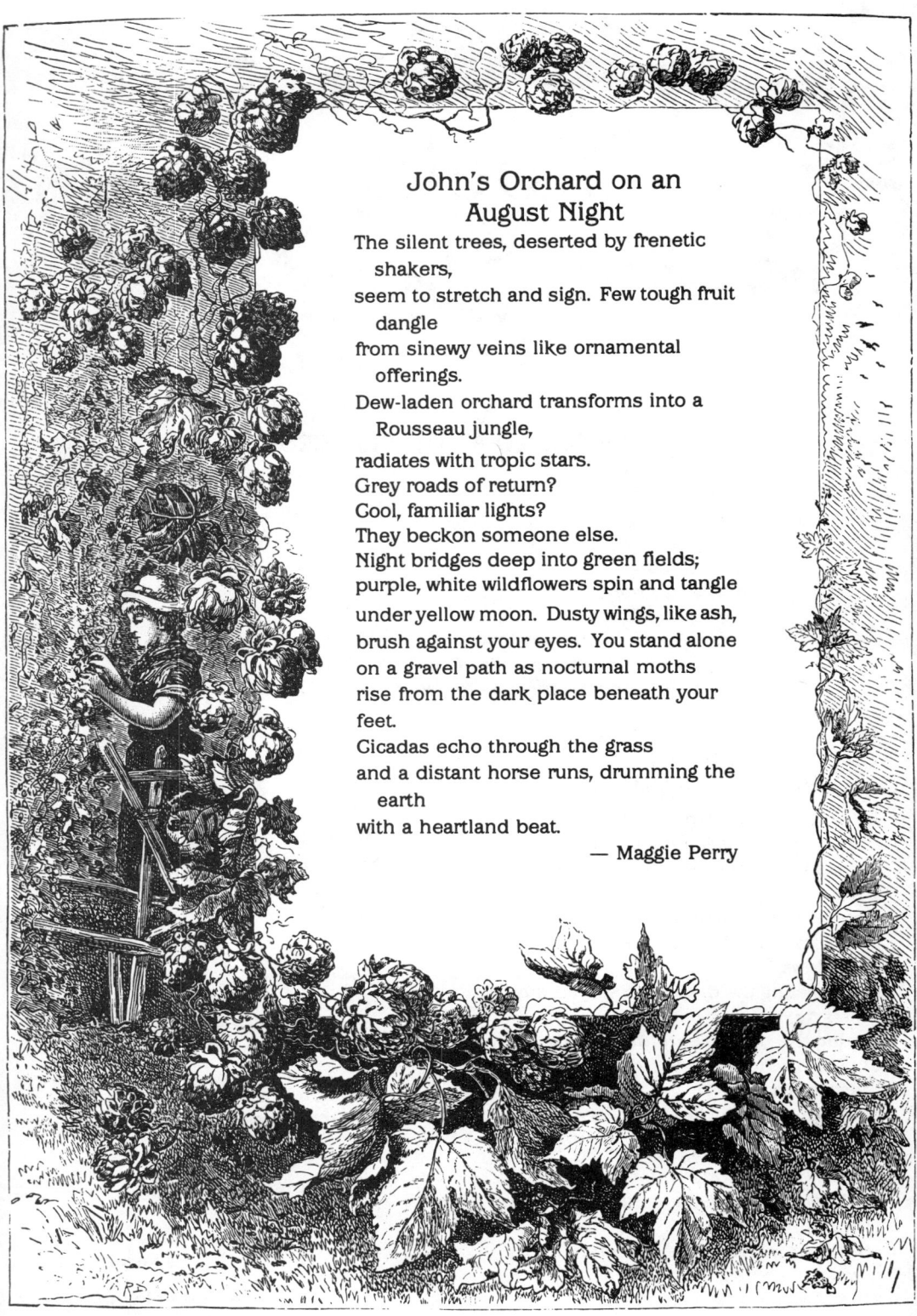

John's Orchard on an August Night

The silent trees, deserted by frenetic
   shakers,
seem to stretch and sign. Few tough fruit
   dangle
from sinewy veins like ornamental
   offerings.
Dew-laden orchard transforms into a
   Rousseau jungle,

radiates with tropic stars.
Grey roads of return?
Cool, familiar lights?
They beckon someone else.
Night bridges deep into green fields;
purple, white wildflowers spin and tangle

under yellow moon. Dusty wings, like ash,
brush against your eyes. You stand alone
on a gravel path as nocturnal moths
rise from the dark place beneath your
   feet.
Cicadas echo through the grass
and a distant horse runs, drumming the
   earth
with a heartland beat.

— Maggie Perry

HORSESHOE BAY

1.

Sunset.
And the afterglow becomes
embers slowly warming our affections.

2.

The trees behind
take the darkness into its branches
its leaves shimmer a new night's
   approach.

> Where do the gulls go in evening?
> Will this particular wave ever return to
> shore?

3.

I place the camera atop the car roof
setting aperature, shutter, time exposure;
run back, embrace and kiss;
click, flash.
With luck we'll become
a memory within a box, on paper
of chemicals and special elements.
A picture to be stored in an attic
to be viewed by someone
whose star just sparsely lit over the
   Bay
its glint like the sparkle in your eyes.

4.

The wind snuffs out the last
fragmented bits of twilight.
Night persuades.

> Now to find where the gulls have gone
> and wait for that one special wave
> to return to us there
> and wish upon that first faint
> shining together.

                — John Gease.

ABANDONED ORCHARD

The old Swede
gave up on the place
maybe thirty years ago.
Was it frost
that got the orchard,
some damn worm
or just time?

Rotten cedar planks
crack beneath my feet.
The last tenant uncoils,
winds into the grass.
Purple weed buries barbed wire
and chunks of old farm iron.
A stone fence stained with sweat,
recalls bent backs,
sinks into the land.

In returning wilderness
hoary old survivors
who never got the word,
unpruned, unsprayed, unloved,
keep bearing fruit.

We picked their apples,
made a pie,
and thanked
old Swede what's-his-name.

            — Richard E. Garter

APPLE CORPS

The apple corps
Lining country roads,
From cast-off cores
Recycled this May
As phoenix bouquets —
Princes from toads.

            — Gary Jones

illustration: Linda Silvasi-Kelly

Thoughts of Tamarack

I can see you standing there
 on that pile of rocks,
Your brown and black curly hair
 gleaming in the sun,
Your head held high,
 nose searching the air for scents
 unfamiliar,
 eyes scanning the out-of-place,
I reach out to cup your soft head in my
 hands,
 but my hands only grasp air
Your soft brown eyes are filled with
 looks for take-me-home
                    Why?
Every day I go back
I try to put the puzzle together right,
 but the pieces don't fit
I try to solve the mystery,
 but can't find any clues
I try to make all the right decisions,
 but they're always wrong
One day I will go back and I will do
 everything right
I will cup your soft head in my hands
 and I will take you home.

— Linda Silvasi-Kelly

ELLISON BAY

No telling
from the trees
stilled in a sepia haze
or Tuesday's bruised weather
heating thunder into the hills
of Ellison Bay
the rain sopping so it bleeds away
what's left of September.

That this is October now
and Summer is over
ending in a quiet barely noticed
a ritual certain and complete.

Pleasure boats have disappeared
from their moorings
sunk into sheds for winter storage
clearance sales stalk
empty gift shops' shortened hours
all fruit has gone to preserves
and the odors of fallen apples
burning leaves and the damp
smoke of logs lighting stiffly
anoint the air
the woods and a season
memorialized as they lie
in each other's lengthening shadows.

A sharp breeze empties trees
and its cold snaps into place like
some missing piece of a game;
frost tightens the earth solid
rain falls freezing and
October ends lame in the last
of a destitute season.

All the while patiently winter waits
at the otherside of the wind.

— John Gease

illustration: Jave Hughes

6 AM
From my window I watched
The black-gloved February fingers of the orchard
Pluck furtively at the dim hem
Of a cool lilac dawn.

— Gary Jones

The day tips down
as earth turns
to bring us light:
each hour earns
a touch of sun
before the night.

— J.K. Woitesek

EPHRAIM

The weather
most unusual
as if it were three months ago
now the last day of the year.
Winter has been that slow in coming.

At Ephraim
the whole of Eagle Harbor
was silence
save metallic chimings
of translucent ice breaking on ice
and the woolen noise
of the wind feeling and
wrapping round our faces
as we sat on shore rocks
in the warmth of each other's smiles.

I spotted an old Whitefish
grey, mottled and worn
hugging the thin shore in search
for specks of sunlight to warm itself
and slowly, back and forth
it lurched alone.
Occasionally he would glance up
"eyeballing us" you said
as he passed perhaps
in envy that we had each other
or lonely that he was so alone.

As we walked hand in hand
along the shoulder of 42
the old fish curiously followed us
and you wished outloud
the best of the new year
to that broken creature.

And as we were about to leave
reaching the car
we looked once more to the water's edge
and with the play of the waves
or perhaps it was the ice and reflections of
    sun
it appeared there were, not one
but two fish now
first circling, winding then
with a splash they broke path
and began to head out into open water.

We ran back to the shoreline searching,
no signs of life.
Our eyes saw nothing but
the best of wishes coming together
into the new year
and the beauty of dancing light.

— John Gease

illustration: Stern

DORMANT ORCHARD

The gnarled fists of the apple orchard
Unclenched, grasping, clutching
Upward
Toward the unrelenting grey spring sky.

— Gary Jones

Remember

Silence is an overture
                    of sound,
Limited to Angel's ears,
And precious few who reach
                    to listen;
When roses speak of love,
Or clouds whisper all
                    that is.
For a moment we know all.
Til man's sounds come
                    crashing in.
Later, later I will listen . . .
        and remember.

—Amy McKenzie

III.

51. OUR ALMANAC.

ROBINS in the tree-tops,
  Blossoms in the gràss;
Green things ă-grōwing
  Everywhere you pàss;
Sudden little breezes;
  Showers of silver dew;
Black bough and bent twig
  Budding out anew!
Pine-tree and willōw-tree,
  Fringèd elm, and lärch,[1]
Dōn't you thi̲nk that Māy-time's
  Pleasanter than March?

2. Apples in the orchard,
  Mĕllōwing one by one;
Strawberries uptûrning
  Sŏft cheeks to the sun;

Roṣeṣ, faint with swēetnèss;
  Lilies, fâir of face;
Drowṣy scents and mûrmûrs
  Häunting every place;
Lengths of golden sunshine;
  Moonlight bright as dāy—
Dōn't you thi̲nk that Summer's
  Pleasanter than Māy?

3. Roger in the corn-patch,
  Whistling negro-sŏngs;
Pussy by the heärth-side,
  Rŏmping with the tŏngs;
Chestnuts in the ashes,
  Bûrsting through the rind;
Red-leaf and gold-leaf,
  Rustling down the wind;
Mŏther "doin' peaches"
  All the àfternoon—
Dōn't you thi̲nk that Autumn's
  Pleasanter than June?

4. Little fâiry snow-flakes,
  Dáncing in the flue:
Old Mr. Sänta Claus,
  What is keeping you?
Twilight and firelight;
  Shădōws come and go;
Mĕrry chime of sleigh-bells,
  Ti̲nkling through the snow;
Mother knitting stockings,
  (Pussy has the ball!)—
Dōn't you thi̲nk that Winter's
  Pleasanter than all?

INDEPENDENT THIRD READER.
1877

illustration: Stern

Time Warp

August: 4:06 P.M.

Somewhere
a woman is full of bliss
holding the first red sweet
sun-hot garden tomato
in her soft palm.
        And at the same time
on the beach, alone,
a bikini-buttocked woman
is bitterly realizing
once again his betrayal.
        In someone's backyard
a solemn girlchild
gently arranges hollyhock dolls
on an old stone wall.
        While further up the road
a farm woman muffles sobs
over yet another swelling
of her prolific belly.
        In town
the old bookkeeper thinks of nothing
as she deftly balances the day's debits
against the credits.

— Susan Peterson

COASTER WAGON

1.

Well beyond
the gravel of Garrett Bay Road
back of Ellison Bay
and deep within a stand of birch
behind a rented cottage
laid a child's wagon
broken and abandoned to
the poor care of weather.

2.

It sat as some sort of
archeological find
a relic beneath years
of leaf clutterings mounded over it
and spider's webs well occupied
that now the wagon was half-digested
back to the ground
resolving some childhood
these woods could only know and tell.

3.

As I sat on a nearby tree
I reminisced about my very own
personal "Radio Flyer" I owned
gleeming a red that rivaled any hot color
a fire could shed
the black lacquered handle that
broke between two many tugs and yanks
the axles that bent from the weight
of too much attention.

4.

Where is that old coaster wagon now?
This should be it here
where all wagons could come
like elephants when no longer
needed or noticed
and too sick to care
to this secret spot
to bare open souls and circumscribe
memories long since worn
a lovely place to die away.

— John Cease

Cinquain

The cat sleeps at my feet
aware that night passes
and a new day
full of wonder
will come.

— J.K. Woitesek

Fisherman's Daughter
for Russell

Only one week since ice moved out
from the bay. Two fishermen stoop on
   shore,
up to their ankles in water. The sunset,
an absence of heat on their backs
as they clean fish.

I remember my father, twenty-five years
   ago;
quick as a magician he chopped heads
from sunfish, blue gills, thin silver perch.
Then slit straight down the belly,
pulled guts dumped into a bucket at his
   feet.
Fish bodies curled like autumn leaves
in a blue ceramic bowl.

I was five and laughed as headless fish
hop-scotched upon the wood bench.
Large pines circled us, filled the air
with sweetness. Everything was food.
Our talk always mean; we were best
   togeher
when fishing, weeding gardens, picking
   beans.

Tonight, I wait through the last light.
Peach and lavender clouds feather across
a pale sky. The first stars appear.
Gulls, like crazed saints at confession,
fall from the sky devouring entrails.
I'm spell bound by the sound
of open water, my father's wet hands,
and the shapes of fish beneath.

              —Maggie Perry

March 21st

Spring:
yet blizzards of cold
thicken our every impatient gesture

lilac bush, still icy brown
a sad twist of dry sticks
   its greening passion
   waits waits
to unfurl flowers
into a hot noon

in the garden
Grandfather patiently digs
the hard plainess of parsnips

I hunger
for a fierce and frantic light;
   the sky serves up
   cold stone soup
   from the dull and obtuse
   winter-blanketed sun

           — Susan Peterson

A View From Across The Bay

I always knew you were there. I could see
your hazy shore across the bay.

Door County. Around home, people
spoke your name like an incantation. My
thoughts were driftwood in the moonlit
bay, spellbound by you, washed ashore.

Now, my family tree was rooted deep in
the backyard. High in its branches I could
see you there, waiting.

Down below, my cousin called, "Would
you like to come along? Pick cherries in
Door County?"

No sooner said than gone.

Hills and forests, stores and orchards;
Door County. I picked the fruit and knew
for certain, "This must be the Garden of
Eden!"

Forever in my memory, this vision I will
treasure: a childhood glimpse at paradise,
still in view across the bay.

— Karen Stillman

Back to the Source

One of many fallen leaves
I picked up along the lake:
curled, yellow and brown,
tells me more of autumn,
solitude and change
than I have read (and written)
in many poems.

— Gregory Vidas

Nordheim Quarry

Precision of the perpendicular:

a steep of limestone,
shoreline sheared clean at the bay's edge,
the island planing back
to where thick trees form a wall.

It is a place without kindness,
a steeled harbor of quiet closing.
An altitude of ache rises
where our words climb the air.

What intent could bring us here,
or what measured passage take us out?
So much of the world,
sealed as a life,
will not receive us.

And we learn
to enter every port discreetly,
to leave some waters behind us wide.

We carry our language in pockets of
 longing.

When we speak,
words carefully cut and shaped
glide out weightless.
They are only bright stones skimming
the cold, inpenetrable bays
of silence.
— Judy von der Nuell

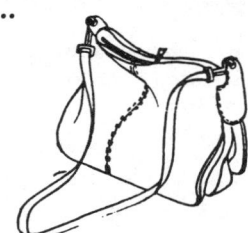

The Doe

Headlights tunneling the narrow night.

We chose the dark road
knowing we were lost
yielding to mystery
allowing the shadows their altered forms.

Around a north bend she stopped us
where we caught her freeze frame
a doe in mist
her coat glowing golden in floodlight.

We thought the night deceived us.

Surely this was no deer
whose attachment is to air:
fluid grace of wind on open meadows
ethereal weft through a warp of trees.

But she was unmistakable on legs of soft
    stone
a stillness so cunning. Where the light
fell into her eyes we followed
down the cavern of her gaze.

And myths drained away in darkness
    where she held us.

We listened for the pulse of the wind to
    quicken
some breath of innocence to free us.
But the night hung limp as shrouds
all wild things struck gentle.

— Judy von der Nuell

Sentiment is the poetry of the imagination. — Lamartine

WHEN I GROW UP

I want to live in an apple orchard
When I grow up.
My mom says that it's possible
If I don't goof up.
So I'm working on a plan
For my club house to expand.
It would change quite a lot,
With an elevator for Spot.
So he wouldn't sit and cry
When he wanted to come up.

It'll be great in an apple orchard
When I grow up.
I told my dad and he thinks so,
Cause he said, "yup".
Oh, I'll be big and tall.
I'll be careful not to fall,
And I'll serve my own meals.
Yeah, a pig roast on wheels.
I'll find the biggest apple
To fill the pigs mouth up.

— Mary Jo Van Lanen

Eating Watermelon in Wisconsin

Oh, the slurping sound of watermelon
as the juice dribbled down our chins
and the sweet sweet slush filled our
    bellies
til we could eat no more.
To lie back and watch the stars,
talking of the apples we had thrown at cars
and the dirt fights we had behind the barn
made us want to spend at least a few more
    years
eating watermelon in Wisconsin.

     — Gregory Vidas

Harvesting Apples I
(Blitzenreute, Oberschwaben)

A few last falling leaves
settled like yellow dust
on the red and green apples
lying moist and voluptuous
at my feet.

The sun was leaving me
and the delicious apples
and the fallen leaves
on the west grass --
in the coming fog.

     — Gregory Vidas

MORNING MISTS

Most mornings
A stillness reigns over the northern peninsula,
A sleepy silence attended by wispy fog
Slumbering in our garden pocket,
Drowsing in the orchard.

Nudged by the warm face of the sun
And the fresh breath of the bay,
The morning mists of Door
Arise
Like the rest of us
For the day's short stay.

     — Gary Jones

MIDDLE MAY

I strolled through the wild strawberry blooms
In the demi-shade of the burgeoning apple trees,
A spray of wild asparagus in one hand,
A branch of wild plum blossoms in the other:
Nature's consolation
For the cruel prank
That was Door County's winter.

     — Gary Jones

SYSTER MARTHA

Syster Martha and I carried
4 shopping bags of
FOR GET ME NOTS
3 miles from town onto the point
I said one plant is enough.
"No, Yimmy--!" she said
and determined
that now, 35 years
later the road is edged with
Blue Lace in June.

     — J.K. Woitesek

Humiliation

It was Celine, that damned woman,
wanted to go bowling, wanted
to take a trip to Door County.
Warm, Indian summer night,
moon as big as a Beefsteak tomato.
And the beers, dozens of Miller High Lifes,
rolling around in my belly.
We waited for an open lane and she said
she was going to take a whiz . . . 45 minutes
before I went looking for her and we still
hadn't bowled. All the time she was
    sleeping
it off in the Ford pick-up.
Me, hollering into the lady's can, "Celine,
Celine honey where are you?" Finally,
fearing she's passed out and drowned,
I decided to take a peek.
Man oh man, what a riot that was.
Reminded me of gathering eggs
from pa's meanest hens.
As far as I'm concerned
women are plain stupid
and ornery to boot. $77.50 for disorderly
conduct that would have gone for a pair
of new Redwings and a couple hours of
    Sheepshead.
Worst of all that damned Celine,
laughing like a crow all 150 miles back
    home.

-Maggie Perry

The Arrowhead

Bright sun and wind conspire
to bring to light a gift:
this dark shape born of fire
and sure hands. Lost in the drift
of time and sand that silent swept
to hide for ages this keen dart.

O brave I know well you wept
to lose this prime piece of your art.
Rest now in your centuried mound
for what was lost so long is found.
— J.K. Woitesek

The boy is indeed the true apple-eater, and is not to be questioned how he came by the fruit with which his pockets are filled. It belongs to him, and he may steal it if it can not be had in any other way. His own juicy flesh craves the juicy flesh of the apple. Sap draws sap. His fruit-eating has little reference to the state of his appetite. Whether he be full of meat or empty of meat he wants the apple just the same. Before meal or after meal it never comes amiss. The farm-boy munches apples all day long. He has nests of them in the hay-mow, mellowing, to which he makes frequent visits.

The apple is indeed the fruit of youth. As we grow old we crave apples less. It is an ominous sign. When you are ashamed to be seen eating them on the street; when you can carry them in your pocket and your hand not constantly find its way to them; when your neighbor has apples and you have none, and you make no nocturnal visits to his orchard; when your lunch-basket is without them and you can pass a winter's night by the fire-side with no thought of the fruit at your elbow, them be assured you are no longer a boy, either in heart or years.
— John Burroughs

illustration: Greg Steffen

*The longer I live the more my mind
dwells upon the beauty and the wonder
of the world. I hardly know which feeling
leads, wonderment or admiration.*
— *John Burroughs*

illustration: Mary Ellen Sisulak

My Pastoral

by M.E. Sisulak

A rolling glacial terrain dotted with second-growth trees and shrubs, bordered by old stone walls, picked from the field by Scandinavian settlers only a generation gone. Trees cut by sweat and muscle, hauled by horses, the stumps pulled by horse or man-power, the rough rocky ground cut for the first time by plough, tilled and planted. Broken orchards and over grown field. Apple and cherry trees, potatoes, field crops, only used for a few generations.

As a newcomer to Door County, country life and agriculture, I don't see condominiums or golf courses, I see **goats**.

Goats are on the upswing in this country. Small farmers are finding them ideally suited to marginal lands such as Door County. Myths about goats abound, making the true nature of the animal unknown. Goats are aggressive, compared to cows or sheep; intelligent and quite affectionate. They do not eat garbage or tin cans, as commonly thought, but they do like to "nibble" metal sur-

205

faces, clothes and hair. Goats eat only vegetation and are browsers, not grazers. They have only lower teeth which grind against a hard top palate. They enjoy young maple saplings, pines, ferns and an occasional mushroom, as well as many rough weed type plants. To the dismay of orchardists, goats love young apple trees and create havoc in the garden or flower bed.

Goats are commonly believed to be somewhat smelly. This is another unfortunate myth. While this may be true when they are not kept in clean areas, female goats, or "does," do not have anything but an unobtrusive animal odor. The "buck" or male goat, has sweat glands on the head near the horns, which attract the doe during mating season. The odor of the buck is rather permeating, much like strong mutton. The mating season of the goat begins as soon as the days begin to get shorter in the fall, and the doe gives birth in the spring after 150 days of gestation.

Young goats, or "kids", are the most delightful, playful creatures. Their antics consist of entertaining acro-batics; bounding, rearing and jumping, with high twists. **Disarray** seems to best describe the nature of the goat. It seems to "please" all goats for grain buckets to spill, or boards to clatter. One of the most phenomenal acts of goat behavior is to see two goats rear up on their hind legs, and with their heads tipped down, butt each other, crashing down onto their front legs.

Many goats have their horns removed at a young age. Unlike sheep, goats cannot be bred successfully **sans** horns. Horns can be quite dangerous to a herder as well as other goats. Unfortunately, de-horning makes the goat less able to ward off predators.

One of the greatest pleasures of goats, and the most widespread reason for raising them, is the delicious goat's milk, which they produce after kidding. A good milk goat will give up to a gallon of milk a day and average about 2 quarts for

illustration: Mary Ellen Sisulak

used for food production. In our country, as myths about goats diminish, the demand for goat's milk will increase, and Door County's second-growth woods and overgrown fields are an ideal place for goat husbandry.

approximately ten months. Goat's milk is similar to cow's milk in fat, water, protein, etc., but is higher in trace minerals and is more easily digested. It is often prescribed by doctors for people with digestive problems or allergies to cow's milk. Fresh goat's milk is mild, with only a slight difference in taste from cow's milk. To avoid a gamey flavor, goats should be milked in a clean area, away from the buck, and the milk should be cooled immediately. Some of the best cheeses are made from goat's milk, as well as yogurt, butter and ice cream.

There are many breeds of goats including lovely white Saanens, Nubians, with floppy ears, and Toggenburgs, with long ridge hair on the spine and white facial markings. One feature of the goat which seems to intrigue the novice most are "wattles". Wattles are two small floppy bags of skin which hang on either side of the neck. Some goats have them and some do not. No one has ever told me what purpose they serve, if any.

Often overlooked by large agriculturists, goat dairies of large size are becoming more common in the United States, especially on the west coast. Goat's milk and cheese are common fare in many countries, because marginal lands must be

The Fragrances of Autumn

by Lon Emerick

ANYONE who has ever watched a trained bird dog tracing the erratic path of a ruffed grouse in a stand of aspen on a moist October morning realizes that humans are denied a whole world of sensations — what a myriad of fragrances we miss with our paltry sense of smell! When compared to canine species with 100 times the olfactory power humans possess, we are practically smell-blind. Ironically, our inferior noses are further assailed by polluted air and jaded by the efforts of the cosmetic industry to eliminate or mask all natural odors with sprays, perfumes and deodorants.

Yet we can enlarge our awareness, we can train our olfactory system to tune in to the nuances of nature's rich smells. One of the best ways I have found to accomplish this is to visit an autumn forest before dawn; by temporarily eliminating vision, I can concentrate on the many fragrances of fall. The most compelling odor, certainly the most ubiquitous here in the north country, is the smell of newly-fallen leaves.

The smell of freshly-fallen leaves was especially pervasive the other morning when I woke before daylight and hiked into the woods near my home. It rose like a soothing balm all about me as I picked my way slowly through the darkened forest to an oak-covered ridge where I would keep a silent vigil. The path was moist and soft underfoot, silencing my footfalls, and I could detect the furtive rustling of small nighttime creatures. The silence was punctuated intermittently by the noisy descent of ripe acorns as they carromed off branches before finally hitting the forest floor with a solid thump. Sitting down under a giant oak tree, I leaned back and deeply drew in the heady fragrance of fallen leaves.

For me, this musty herbal odor of downed leaves is the very essence of autumn. The smell is particularly rich and persistent in the moist dawn air and as I sat sniffing, my mind was flooded with memories of other falls, of hunting and hiking on frosty mornings, of harvesting hazel nuts and apples, of gathering and splitting the winter's supply of firewood. I searched for the right words to describe this unique smell of fall. Pungent? Yes, in part, though that term doesn't quite fit the primal, organic essence of moist new humus. Aromatic? The forest floor is certainly aromatic in autumn, especially during a soft rain when the aroma of leafy decay is heavy in the air. I finally settled on ambrosial — to me the fragrance is altogether a divine sensation and I begin to long for it in late summer. In early September I detect its first nuances in groves of young aspen; the odor at that point is elusive and I must search out damp areas to find the heady fragrance. Then by the middle of October, the northern woods are an olfactory paradise.

Now the first gray light of dawn filtered down through the trees on the ridge where I sat. How sweet it is to listen and watch the forest come alive at daybreak! No other time is quite so magical as the birth of a new day; the

photo: Bryon Smith

moments then are fresh, vital and not yet used by others. Closing my eyes, I listened intently: migrating birds, probably white-throated sparrows, rustled among the leaves; a gray squirrel scolded from the top of a nearby oak; acorns clattered down and thudded on an old burnt stump behind me. The ridge runs east and west and from where I sat facing south I could see down the steep slope; far below in the narrow valley a thick shroud of fog hugged the tops of a dense copse of quaking aspen. Turning slightly to scan the ridge, I was startled to see a four-point white-tail buck, sleek now in his gray-brown winter coat, feeding on the mast; the dawn was so quiet that I could hear the crunching of acorns. The deer ignored the intermittent noise of falling nuts but was instantly alert when I changed position to obtain a better view and scraped my sleeve on the rough bark of the red oak tree. He froze for a moment and then vanished in the underbrush as only a cautious whitetail deer can.

It was time for me, too, to leave the ridge but I prolonged my early morning sojourn by taking the longer, more scenic route home. Autumn is a season for wandering, for floating along like leaves in the air. Under the oaks I inspected the place where the deer had pawed among the leaves for the acorns. In fall, whitetail deer prepare for the long winter and uncertain food supply by building up a thick layer of fat; mast is a prime source of such nourishment. Descending the steep slope I shuffled through the carpet of maple and birch leaves to raise the delightful odor. In a low spot near the edge of the aspen thicket, I bent down and charged my senses deeply. Looking closely, I noticed that small beads of water, condensed from the morning fog, shimmered like spots of mercury on the undersides of downed and blackened aspen leaves, while those lying face-up were slick and brilliant yellow with moisture. The lowly aspen or "popple" has the most extensive range and is the most prolific of any tree in the north. In fall it is one of my favorites — it's here in groves of young popple trees that the tang and ferment of fallen leaves is strongest.

photo: Bryon Smith

Plucking a small aspen twig, I moved up the valley to an open field which once served as a pasture for a long-forgotten dairy farmer. Row upon row of goldenrod, now a uniform light gray, guard the edge of the field; a score of milkweeds, their fluffy open pods rotating gently in the morning breeze, line an ancient farm lane. I sniffed each deeply but could detect no odor. Nearby I picked one frost-blackened aster and crushed its brittle petals in my palm; when I bent closely its delicate perfume could still be discerned. But it was the fragrance of aspen leaves which lingered in my memory as I hurried home and prepared for my morning classes; the small aspen twig rode in my coat lapel all day and reminded me of the dawn vigil on the oak ridge.

There are, of course, many other fragrances associated with autumn. In early fall I seek out the farming regions near town to soak in the aroma of the moist dark earth lying open in new furrows. Often I stop and chat with one particular old farmer, a gentleman of Finnish heritage with a thick melodious accent. We talk about the rich fecund smell of newly plowed land and I note with some envy his serene expression as he gazes over his fields. During our autumn conversations, the farmer often stoops and picks up a handful of soil; as he sifts it through his fingers, his touch is affectionate, almost reverent. I try to time my visit to coincide with the onion harvest, for after the mechanical picker has completed its raucous circuit, I am often invited to glean a portion of the fields. On a warm afternoon in late September there is nothing more odoriferous than a newly harvested onion field.

Falls also mean the delicious fruity fragrance of ripe apples; whenever I smell them I recall vividly the cooling shed at an orchard my parents visited frequently in the autumns of my youth. Here were stored dozens of peck and bushel baskets of Jonathons and Winesaps ready for sale or shipping. It was dark in the shed — only a single large light bulb illuminated the spacious room — but despite the gloom and cold I would sit quietly watching the orchard workers sorting and assembling the apples. My patience was often rewarded with a cold firm Jonathon; savoring the tart juicy fruit, I inhaled the pleasant aroma of hundreds of apples.

Both taste and smell are chemical senses and, in fact, are closely related; in the absence of smell, food is bland

and tasteless. A tankard of cider fresh from the press is a treat not only for the tastebuds but also has a delightful aroma. Although I like cider at room temperature — when it is chilled the savory nuances are dulled — my favorite preparation is spiced and mulled. Take a large container of about nine cups and to the cider add a handful of brown sugar, a pinch of cloves and one or two sticks of cinnamon. Heat, but do not boil, over a low flame, stirring occasionally. The result is a delicious, spicy-smelling, very tasty warming drink. On all my fall excursions to collect winter fire-wood I carry a thermos of hot cider and enjoy the treat while resting from sawing and chopping.

Far from being a chore, gathering firewood in the fall is an annual labor of love, and one I prefer to do with simple hand tools. I could cut more wood, and do it faster, with a chain saw; neighbors and friends have smiled at my efforts and offered to lend their power tools. I resist the temptation, however, because I believe we have over the years devalued human labor in favor of energy consuming machines; in my judgment, we are out of touch with ways of working and values honed over centuries of living. We even have computers to think for us. It is incredibly satisfying for someone who spends his days in a sedentary profession, who deals hourly with imponderables and probabilities, to use his muscles for a direct simple task. I like the solid sound and feel when a log splits correctly with a single blow; it is fulfilling to see the woodpile grow and know it is a product of my own labor; most of all I admire the sharp smell of resin from the fresh cuts and the growing pile of sawdust.

The pines, particularly jackpine, have an aromatic resin which fills my senses at each pull of the saw. Maple and birch split cleanly and exude a subtle fragrance which reminds me of sunshine and warm summer rain. My favorite, though only fair as fire-place fuel, is balsam poplar which I prefer by its alias, Balm-of-Gilead. The young leaves and large buds of the Balm-of-Gilead are saturated with a fragrant sticky wax which is alleged to have healing properties; honey bees use it in sealing their hives. One fall while backpacking on a long and arduous trail, I made a small sachet of buds taken from a Balm-of-Gilead

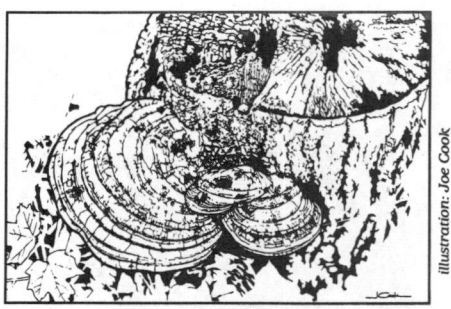

illustration: Joe Cook

and kept its soothing smell near my pillow each night. The aroma released when it is sawed and chopped is the same as the herbal essence of downed leaves. There is even a hint of that leafy door when the split logs burn in the fireplace.

An open fire is a delight to all the senses: the crackling and soft guttering; the dancing red and orange flames; the glowing warmth it spreads; and the bouquet of smells which are released as the wood ignites. Sunshine accumulated for years in the wood fibers is released in an open fire. Despite all our technological sophistication and several genera-tions of urban living, we are still drawn to an open hearth. In order to concen-trate on the unique smell of wood smoke, I take long walks on autumn evenings and thus enjoy my neigh-bors wood-gathering labors as well as my own.

THE PENINSULA PLAYERS
at The Theatre in a Garden

AMERICA'S OLDEST PROFESSIONAL
RESIDENT SUMMER THEATRE

Tues. thru Sat. 8:30 p.m.   Sun. 7:30 p.m.
Fish Creek, Wisconsin 54212   414-868-3287

Fall is also the time of the hunting season and the smells of preparation have worn deep grooves in my memory: the odor of warm bear grease being applied to leather boots; red and black buffalo plaid wood clothing smelling of the cedar chest and moth balls; the sharp acrid aroma of Hoppe's Number Nine nitro solvent as the guns are cleaned and placed back in the rack; bacon frying and coffee perking in the dim frosty mornings as the hunters hurry to prepare for opening day; the fragrance of soups and stews drifting out of the cabin as tired hunters return from the snowy woods; the pervasive odor of my grandfather's black briar pipe. He smoked his own blend of two common brands of tobacco. Once years later while waiting for a flight in a large air terminal, that same unique smell drifted to where I sat reading and in an instant I was mentally transported back to the Old Man's simple log cabin.

Odors evoke ancient memories and stir long-forgotten images because the olfactory is perhaps the oldest of our five senses. Tiny receptors located in the nose report their messages to the olfactory lobe in the most primitive portion of the

brain, the hippocampus; the latter area is responsible for the storage of memories, particularly associated with emotional satisfaction. Merchants know that a pleasant smell, even though it may be consciously detected, will bias a person's judgment. Sales of lingerie are facilitated by subtle perfume, and used cars are purchased more swiftly when the interiors are sprayed with "new car" smell.

Similarly the natural odors of each season, because they are so closely associated with our heritage and with centuries of primitive existence, evoke powerful responses in us. The fragrances of autumn, particularly those of downed leaves, may produce restlessness, melancholy, even exhiliration. The essence affects me in three interrelated ways. First, it means **fulfillment**, an outward and visible signal that the ever-repeating, never-ending cycle of natural events which commenced with the first blush of green in spring is moving inexorably forward according to ancient natural rhythms. In the second place, the smell of fresh decaying leaves offers a **promise** of a new season, it conveys to all creatures

illustration: Greg Steffen

the eternal vow that the earth shall rise again, that the links between the seasons are yet secure. It is an ending and a new beginning. Finally, the fragrances of autumn teach me again the lesson that "to everything there is a season, and a time to every purpose under heaven", and gives me a **reminder** that I, too, am an integral part of the natural order. A fall morning is a good time to hold communion with nature and to offer a personal tithing to the passing of the seasons.

When I was younger I sought some method of preserving the smell of fall so that I might experience it in all seasons. I tried to capture the herbal essence in candles and incense but both ventures failed. Now that I am older and have put away such childish thoughts, I am glad that I failed for I might have surfeited my sense of smell and lost the special delight that each new autumn brings. The fragrance remains poised in my soul, ready to remind me of an oak ridge at dawn, a misty aspen thicket and a quilt of scarlet and gold thrown carelessly upon the forest floor. The sad-sweet woodland perfume! It wafts upward even now in my imagination, laden with memories and evoking that strange mixture of nostalgia and joy which is the very essence of autumn.

Excerpt from the unpublished book "The Superior Peninsula"

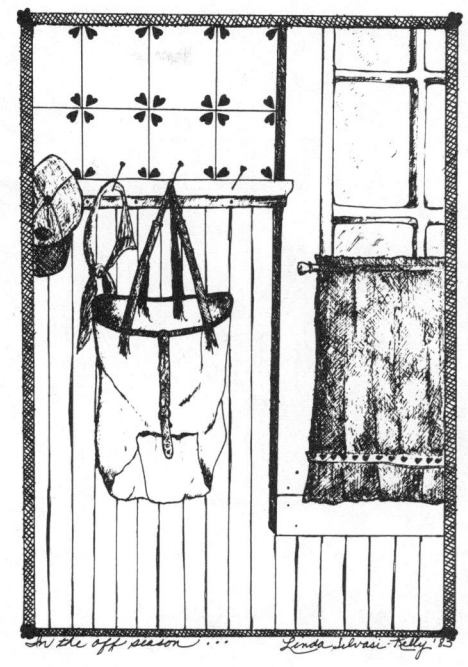

In the off season... Linda Silvası-Kelly '83

Ingwersen Studio/Gallery
Sister Bay

Northern Spy
Northeast and Great Lakes regions. Nov. through May ...

... good for snacks, fruit cups, salads, baking, all-purpose cooking.

217

Door County: The Winter Playground of the Midwest

by Mike Nelson

ANY vacationers make a great escape to the Door Peninsula in the summer, autumn, and spring seasons to engage in fishing, camping, hiking, hunting and swimming.

During the winter season just as many vacationers escape to Door County. By no means does the county hibernate. It remains quite alive, living up to its nickname of the "Cape Cod of the Midwest" as it becomes the winter playground of the Midwest.

In the winter season most of the tourist attractions are closed, waiting to reopen in the spring. The sports of Door County in the winter are centered around the ice fishing, cross-country skiing and downhill skiing.

Ice Fishing - Winter used to be the time when fishermen would store the fishing rod until spring. Today, that has changed, the fishing rod isn't stored, instead it's employed for ice fishing. Ice fishing has mushroomed into a popular winter sport. Many fishermen (men, women, and kids) have discovered that winter ice fishing is a great way to escape from cabin fever. Ice shanties of every shape and description lace the shores of Door County.

The ice fishermen can catch rainbow and brown trout, walleye and perch in Green Bay and Lake Michigan. Northerns and pan fish are found in Door County's inland lakes of Clark's, Kangaroo and Europe. Popular locations for ice fishing are found off the shores of Little Sturgeon waters of Sand Bay, Rileys Bay, Sherwood Point in Southern Door County, and along the shores of Horseshoe Bay, Egg Harbor, Fish Creek, Ephraim and Sister Bay in Northern Door.

Skiing — The sport of skiing can be enjoyed throughout the county. Door County abounds with over 50 miles of ski trails. The Peninsula State Park is located in Northern Door County between Fish Creek and Ephraim, and features 12 miles of cross-country trails. All the trails, which are named, journey throughout the parks territory and along its craggy shoreline. In winter a portion of the Tennison Bay camping ground is open for winter camping. The park also provides an indoor shelter, pit toilets and a water supply. A camping fee is charged and all vehicles are required to have a park admission sticker. The park also features marked snowmobile trails.

The Newport State Park is found 4

miles northeast of Ellison Bay on Newport Road. The park features 20 miles of cross-country skiing trails, which are nestled in the park's wilderness region. These trails overlook the beautiful waters of Lake Michigan in Rowleys Bay, Europe Bay and Newport Bay. In the winter the park maintains picnic grills, firewood, and water. Newport state park offers 13 backpack camping sites for winter camping. Park admission stickers are required for all vehicles.

The Whitefish Dunes state park is located near Clark's Lake. The park has 12 miles of cross-country skiing trails which travel throughout the park's wooded region. Snowmobiling is prohibited.

Potawatomi state park is found in Door County's southern region. The park is located 2½ miles west of Sturgeon Bay. It offers 1,100 acres of cross-country ski trails that travel throughout the park's wooded area. The park has snowmobile trails and also features downhill skiing. The Potawatomi Ski Hill, the only downhill ski

slope in the county, is operated by a local group of ski enthusiasts. The ski hill features a chair lift and is open every weekend afternoon and at other times during the week when there is snow.

Cross-country skiing is also featured in other areas of the county.

A great escape during the wintertime in Door County is an excellent adventure for the entire family to enjoy.

As a writer, I have only one desire - to fill you with fire, to pour into you the distilled essence of the sun itself. I want every thought, every word, every act of mine to make you feel that you are receiving into your body, into your mind, into your soul, the sacred spirit that changes clay into men and men into gods.
— Thomas Dreier

When men are rightly occupied, their amusement grows out of their work, as the color petals out of a fruitful flower; when they are faithfully helpful and compassionate, all their emotions are steady, deep, perpetual and vivifying to the soul as is the natural pulse to the body. *— John Ruskin*

Gallery Guide

Presented here is a brief review and updating of the gallery guide listing from the first issue of the Almanak. Every year new galleries appear and old ones disappear so we recommend the use of the Peninsula Arts Association's listing of current galleries issued each year for a more detailed and up to date guide.

Sturgeon Bay

MILLER ART CENTER: Door County Library. Houses a permanent collection by regional artists. Changing exhibits coordinated by curator R. Lyons are featured in the main gallery.

GERHARD G.F. MILLER GALLERY: Bay Shore Drive. Egg tempera, watercolors and pencil drawings done in a traditional style.

PUDGE AND MARY DEGRAFF: 5th & Oregon St. Handcarved and painted wooden figures and wall hanging.

WATERMARK GALLERY: 215 N. Third Ave. Photographs by Wayne and Cliff Harmann. Original artwork in a variety of media by many well known Wisconsin artists.

GOLD & SILVER CREATIONS: 742 Jefferson Street. Custom-made contemporary jewelry by Greg & Samara Christian.

Egg Harbor

HELEN STANDARD STUDIO: Hwy. 42. Paintings and pottery, featuring portraits.

DOOR COUNTY SCENES: County G. Donna Remillard. Oils, watercolors, drawings - traditional.

DICK DAWE: Lost Lake Road. Watercolors of Door County and other subject matter - traditional.

PORTE GALLERY: Memorial Drive. Paintings and serigraph prints by Joe Cook.

ROGER STARK: Hwy. 42. Traditional oil painting, reproductions available.

CIRCLE ARTS: Hwy. 42. Cooperative gallery featuring a variety of artists in various media.

Juddville

PANGAEA GALLERY: Juddville Road. Betty and Lionel Wathall. Contemporary and traditional oils, watercolors, prints.

BLUEMLE-VON KOFFLER STUDIO: Hwy. 42. Contemporary hot glass and stained glass.

Fish Creek

PIEPER AND McCREADY POTTERY: Peninsula Players Road. Functional stoneware and porcelain.

EDGEWOOD ORCHARD GALLERIES: Peninsula Players Road. Artwork in various media by many contemporary artists, including paintings by Pam Berns and silverpoint drawings by Flora Langlois.

G. DEFORE: Hwy. 42. Decorative clock cases and movements made by George DeFore.

EMMETT JOHN STUDIO-GALLERY: Founder's Square. Featuring oil and pastel portraits.

FOUNDER'S SQUARE GALLERY: Founder's Square. Represents a variety of artistry in various media.

CASTLES IN THE SKY GALLERY: Proud Mary Shops. Serigraph prints by Greg Steffan.

SPIELMAN'S WOOD WORKS: Hwy. 42. Hand crafted wooden wares and furniture.

POTTER'S WHEEL: Hwy. 42. Stoneware and porcelain by Abe Cohn and other fine craftsmen.

UTZINGER STUDIO-GALLERY: Gibraltar Road. Oil and pastel paintings - landscape, still life and portraits.

MAPLE GROVE GALLERY: County F & Maple Grove Road. Weavings by Gloria Hardiman and functional pottery by George Hardiman.

WEATHERGATE GALLERY: Maple Grove Road. Weavings, paintings and crafts by Doris Peterson.

Ephraim

GRESKO & CO.: Hwy. 42. Silk-screened fabrics by Carol Gresko.

ARNOLD ALANIZ: Hwy. 42. Watercolor and lithograph landscapes.

HANSEATIC ART GALLERY: County Q. Watercolors, oils and acrylics by Karsten and Ellen Sprogoe Topelmann.

STATHEM ENAMELS: County Q. Copper enamel bowls, plaques and jewelry.

J.J. O'CONNOR GALLERY: County Q. Oil and acrylic painting, pen & ink drawings.

CEDAR RIDGE GALLERY: Cedar & Moravia Streets. Watercolors and oils by M.W. Ranly.

C.L. PETERSON: 73 Moravia Street. Watercolors, oils and pen & ink drawings. Traditional land and seascapes, sailing ships. Reproductions available.

ROBERT L. PENCE GALLERY: Hwy. 42. Oil paintings of rural scenes. Reproductions available.

HARDY GALLERY: Anderson Dock. Summer long exhibit of Door County artists along with changing feature shows.

BLUE DOLPHIN: Hwy. 42. Features watercolors by Fawn Shillinglaw, rosemaling by Ruth Wolfgram and photography by Bruce Mielke.

VILLAGE CAMERA: Hwy. 42. Photography by Gerry Miller. Watercolors by Ken Bean.

INTERFIBERS: Hwy. 42. Weaving and hand crafted furniture by Wendy and David Hatch.

SPUD'S WOOD TURNINGS: Hwy. 42. Hand turned lamps, bowls and vases.

THE PAINT BOX GALLERY: At the Red Barns. Original graphics, paintings, pottery and glass by various artists. Woodcuts by R. Lyons.

THE ART MARKET: Town Line Road. Watercolors, oils, pottery by various artists from the Green Bay area.

WINDMILL GALLERY: Town Line Road. Contemporary oil paintings by Pat Bower.

Sister Bay

JACK ANDERSON GALLERY: Hwy. 42. Watercolors by Jack Anderson, Phil Austin and Bridget Austin. Oils by J. Ingwersen and William Pribble.

McNAMARA STUDIO-GALLERY: Fieldcrest Road. Impressionistic oil and pastel painting.

LIBERTY SCHOOL HOUSE GALLERY: Hwy. 57. Photographs and etched glass by Annie Peil.

INGWERSEN STUDIO-GALLERY: Old Stage Road. Landscapes, still-lifes and portraits in oil and pastel by James Ingwersen.

LOUIS SMOLAK SCULPTURE: Old Stage Road. Bronze, wood and stone sculpture. By appointment only.

EVERGREEN FARM GALLERY: Hwy. 57. Watercolors and silverpoint drawings by James Range.

BELLAIRE GALLERY ANTIQUES: Hwy. 42. Fine antiques and original artworks.

TIMBERDOODLE WILDLIFE GALLERY: Country Walk Mall. Paintings and limited edition reproductions, wood carvings.

EIGHT OF PENTACLES: Walkway Mall. Stained glass by Gary Chaudoir. Also a variety of work by regional artists.

MILL ROAD GALLERY: Mill Road. Wildlife paintings by Tom Seagard. Landscapes by Brigitte Kozma Seagard.

PIONEER GALLERY: Hwy. 42. Watercolors and oils by Joan Champeau.

SILVERCROFT STUDIO: 1848 County ZZ. Silver jewelry by Sylvia Youell.

GRANARY STUDIO-GALLERY: County ZZ. Watercolors by Carol Krumenacher, G. Carpenter and G. Verburgt.

HARTMAN GALLERY: Sumac off County ZZ. Drawings by Ralph Hartman and craftworks.

Ellison Bay

CLAY BAY POTTERY: Hwy. 42. Stoneware and porcelain pottery by David and Jeanne Aurelius. Leatherwork by Mary Ellen Sisulak.

COLLECTOR'S CORNER: Hwy. 42. Paintings and original graphics by international artists.

ELLISON BAY POTTERY: 12156 Garrett Bay Road. Pottery by Tom Dietrich. Paintings by Tom and Margaret Dietrich.

TRIA GALLERY: Hwy. 42. Ruth and Phillip Philipon. Contemporary paintings, graphics sculpture.

Gills Rock

GILLS ROCK STONEWARE: Pottery by Larry Thorson.

Baileys Harbor

DEWITT JEWELRY: 9000 W. Meadow Lane. Antique and contemporary jewelry by Amanda DeWitt.

THE RED GERANIUM: Hwy. 57. Pottery, paintings and jewelry.

Jacksonport

MEUNIER GALLERY: Hwy. 57. Paintings and portraits by Jenny Meunier. Recorded original music of Daniel Meunier.

Valmy

WHITEFISH BAY FARM GALLERY: Paintings, photography and graphics by midwestern artists. Weavings by Ernie and Grace Waidelich.

Be glad of life because it gives you the chance to love and to work and to play and to look up at the stars.

— Henry Van Dyke

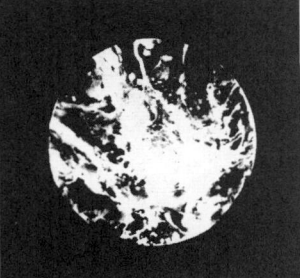

The perfect historian is he in whose work the character and spirit of an age is exhibited in miniature. He relates no fact, he attributes no expression to his characters, which is not authenticated by sufficient testimony. By judicious selection, rejection and arrangement, he gives to truth those attractions which have been usurped by fiction. In his narrative a due subordination is observed: some transactions are prominent; others retire. But the scale on which he represents them is increased or diminished not according to the dignity of the persons concerned in them, but according to the degree in which they elucidate the condition of society and the nature of man. He shows us the court, the camp and the senate. But he shows us also the nation. He considers no anecdote, no peculiarity of manner, no familiar saying, as too significant for his notice which is not too insignificant to illustrate the operation of laws, or religion, and of education, and to mark the progress of the human mind. Men will not merely be described, but will be made intimately known to us. — *Macaulay*